FOR THE REVISED EXAM

Fast Track

to
C.A.E.

Coursebook

Alan Stanton Susan Morris

Map of the book

GRAMMAR NOTES *pages 197–213*   **CHECKLIST FOR WRITING** *page 214*

Exam Overview

The Certificate in Advanced English (CAE) is an advanced language qualification for students who want to use English in a work or study environment.

There are five papers in all, which test different aspects of your English. Each paper contributes 40 marks to an overall total of 200. You have to write your answers on special answer sheets.

In order to pass the exam you need to achieve a grade A, B or C. Grades D and E are fail grades.

Paper 1 Reading
(1 hour 15 minutes)

The Reading Paper contains four texts (about 3,000 words in total) and 45—50 questions. The texts may be taken from magazines, newspapers, non-literary books, brochures or leaflets. They can be descriptive, narrative, imaginative or persuasive, give information, an opinion, advice or instructions.

The tasks

Parts 1 and 4: Multiple matching

There are two multiple matching texts per paper, usually one longer 2-page text and one shorter 1-page text. You have to match 12—22 statements or questions (prompts) with items (options) from the text. This task may involve:
* matching people to statements. (see Unit 1, page 10)
* matching sections to statements. (see Unit 2, page 22; Unit 4, page 46)

▶▶ Multiple matching tests your ability to read a text quickly for the main ideas. It also tests your ability to identify specific words, phrases and items of information.

Part 2: Gapped text

There is one gapped text in the exam, which may have six or seven paragraphs extracted. You have to decide where these paragraphs fit. There is always one extra paragraph that doesn't fit anywhere. (see Unit 12, page 162)

▶▶ To do this task you need to understand the structure and progression of a text. This could involve identifying a sequence of events or the development of an argument. Your ability to recognise linking devices such as reference words will be tested.

Part 3: Multiple choice questions

There is one multiple choice text with about five to seven questions. Each question has four possible answers (A, B, C or D), from which you must choose one. The questions will follow the order of the text. (see Unit 3, page 36)

▶▶ To complete this task successfully you have to study parts of the text closely. Your ability to understand register, attitude and style, and to deduce meaning from context will be tested.

Paper 2 Writing
(2 hours)

The Writing Paper has two Parts. **Part 1** is a compulsory writing task. This question will have up to 400 words of input for you to select from and use in your answer. There may be several input texts such as realistic letters, advertisements, questionnaires and leaflets, and some texts may have handwritten annotations. There could also be a visual element, e.g. an illustration.

In **Part 2** there are four tasks from which you choose one. The tasks are about four to six lines each. There will usually be one work-related question.

Parts 1 and 2 are given equal marks. For each writing task you have to write about 250 words.

The tasks

The type of tasks you may be asked to write include:
* newspaper/magazine articles (see Unit 4, page 54)
* formal and informal letters (see Unit 3, page 42; Unit 6, page 87)
* personal notes and messages (see Unit 13, page 178)

- reports (see Unit 8, page 110)
- reviews (see Unit 5, page 68)
- leaflets and information sheets (see Unit 13, page 178)
- tourist brochures (see Unit 11, page 152)

▶▶ In Part 1 your ability to respond to text input will be tested, as well as your ability to select from and summarise the input.
In both Parts 1 and 2 you will be expected to:
- identify the target reader and choose an appropriate register and style.
- choose the correct layout and conventions (for letters, reports etc.).
- use a wide range of structures and vocabulary.
- use accurate spelling and punctuation.
- use linking words and demonstrate good text organisation.

Paper 3 English in Use
(1 hour 30 minutes)

There are six Parts in the English in Use Paper and 80 questions in total. Each task is based on a short text. The texts may be newspaper/magazine articles, letters, leaflets, advertisements and extracts from non-literary books. Each Part begins with one or more examples.

The tasks

Part 1: Multiple choice cloze

This is a text with 15 single-word gaps. For each gap there are four multiple choice options. (see Unit 9, page 117)

▶▶ This task tests your knowledge of vocabulary. You need to understand word partnerships such as collocation and fixed expressions. It may also test your knowledge of linking words.

Part 2: Structural cloze

This text is an open cloze with 15 gaps. Only structural words are omitted. Each gap must be completed with one word. (see Unit 5, page 64)

▶▶ This task tests your understanding of the way sentences are formed in English. You will need to understand context and grammatical patterns.

Part 3: Error correction

This is a short text with 16 numbered lines. Some of the lines are correct, but most have one mistake. The task is **either** to identify
- additional wrong words. The extra words are grammatical. (see Unit 11, page 143)
or to correct
- spelling and punctuation errors. (see Unit 7, page 92)

▶▶ These tasks test your understanding of underlying grammar, and your knowledge of spelling and punctuation.

Part 4: Word formation

This consists of two short texts with 15 gaps in total plus prompt words for each gap. The task requires you to form the correct word from the prompt word. This may require adding suffixes and prefixes, using negatives and plurals or making an internal change to the word given. (see Unit 5, page 66)

▶▶ This task tests your word-building skills and your ability to identify the part of speech required from the context.

Part 5: Register cloze

In this task there are two short texts. Each text contains the same information, but is written in a different register. The first text is complete, and the second has 13 gaps. The second text has a different target reader. You have to complete this text using the information, but not the words, from the first text. (see Unit 7, page 98)

▶▶ The register cloze tests your knowledge and application of style and register. It tests your ability to re-express words and phrases in a different way.

Part 6: Discourse cloze

This text has six phrases or sentences missing. You have to complete the text by choosing the correct phrases or sentences from ten options. (see Unit 9, page 122)

▶▶ This task tests your knowledge of the grammatical and lexical links within a text.

Paper 4 Listening

(approximately 45 minutes)

There are four parts and 30—40 questions in total. In Parts 1, 3 and 4 you will hear each recording twice. In Part 2 you will hear it once only.

The tasks

Part 1: You will hear a monologue of about two minutes. It could be a radio broadcast, speech, telephone message, talk, lecture, etc. You will have to complete sentences, take notes or fill in a table or grid. Your completed answer will form a summary of what you have heard on the recording. (see Unit 4, page 49)

Part 2: You will hear a monologue (or possibly two speakers) of about two minutes once only. The text types are similar to those in Part 1. You will have to take notes or fill in a form. (see Unit 9, page 124)

▶▶ Parts 1 and 2 test your understanding of and application of specific information in the monologue.

Part 3: You will hear a conversation of about four minutes. The text types are similar to those in Part 1 plus interviews and meetings. You will either:
- complete sentences or write short notes (see Unit 8, page 106)

or
- answer multiple choice questions. (see Unit 4, page 52)

▶▶ In Part 3 you will be tested on the attitude and opinion of the speaker, as well as your understanding of directly stated information.

Part 4: You will hear five short extracts of about thirty seconds each. The task is **either**:
- two multiple matching tasks, matching ideas, opinions and information with the speakers (see Unit 2, page 26)

or
- a three-option multiple choice task. (see Unit 13, page 178)

▶▶ Part 4 tests your understanding of the context, speaker identity, opinion, topic or language function.

Paper 5 Speaking

(approximately 15 minutes)

There will be two students and two examiners. One examiner concentrates on assessing your performance and the other will ask you questions and give you instructions. The Speaking Test is divided into four parts.

▶▶ General skills tested by the Speaking paper include your ability to:
- speak fluently and accurately.
- use a wide range of structures and vocabulary.
- produce correct pronunciation of individual sounds, stress and intonation.
- achieve the task which has been set.
- respond to and interact with your partner.

The tasks

Part 1: The examiner will ask you some general questions about yourself, your interests and hobbies. (see Unit 1, page 16)

▶▶ Part 1 tests your ability to introduce yourself and your use of social and interactional language.

Part 2: You and your partner will each be given a different photograph, diagram or cartoon. You have to take it in turns to talk about your picture for about one minute. You will need to talk about the themes and ideas suggested by the pictures, as well as their content. (see Unit 4, page 53)

▶▶ Part 2 tests your ability to describe and comment, to speak at length and to ask and answer questions.

Part 3: Both you and your partner talk together without interruption by the examiner. Visual material is used in a problem-solving or decision-making task. (see Unit 3, page 40)

▶▶ Your ability to negotiate, collaborate and take turns with your partner is tested.

Part 4: The examiner develops the subject introduced in Part 3. You will be asked to report any decisions or conclusions you have reached, followed by more general questions related to the topic. (see Unit 13, page 173)

▶▶ This focuses on your ability to summarise and report back conclusions, as well as your skill in developing a discussion.

Making an impression

SPEAKING 1

1 In pairs, discuss your first impressions of the people in the photographs. Answer these questions.

1 What kind of job do you think each person does?

2 What do you think they're like? Choose from these words and phrases.

outgoing / self-confident / approachable / sociable / shy / dull and boring / conceited / aggressive / chatty / reserved / easy-going / easy to get on with / good company / a bore / a bully

2 Compare your impressions with other students. Discuss which of these factors influenced you most.

- physical appearance
- clothes
- facial expression
- body language

Language Bank

Speculating

He/She could (well) be a sales executive.

I'd guess he/she works in an office/in finance/as a ...

He/She looks rather/a bit aggressive/dull (to me).

He/She looks like a pretty/very outgoing person.

I'd say he's/she's probably quite a self-confident person/a bit of a bore.

I'd say he/she wasn't (particularly) approachable.

Giving reasons

He's/She's quite/very good-looking/attractive/ well-dressed/well-groomed/casually dressed/scruffy.

He's/She's got a rather bad-tempered/self-satisfied expression on his/her face.

He/She looks quite relaxed/tense.

LISTENING 1

1 📼 You are going to hear four people, Aengus, Margaret, Joe and Barbara, describing how they assess and form impressions of people. Listen to the recording once and note down the main factor(s) that influence each speaker when they first meet someone. Then compare your notes with a partner. Did anything surprise you?

2 The following expressions appeared in the recording. Check that you understand what they mean, using a dictionary if necessary. Which word(s) is/are colloquial?

1 if you *rabbit on* about nothing all the time ...
2 it can *lead you up the wrong path* ...
3 to *fit in with* people
4 some people are ... *stand-offish* and that makes you *back off* a little ...
5 it was a different *climate* back then ... (figurative)
6 you do *tend to* judge them ...

3 📼 Read the descriptions and listen to the recording again. Decide which speaker they apply to. There are two for each speaker.

Which speaker

A is affected by people's personality type?

B finds it difficult to resist judging people immediately?

C places an emphasis on what people say, not how they say it?

D has learnt to mistrust first impressions?

E has had to change the way he/she speaks?

F thinks some people adapt to different situations more easily than others?

G mentions his/her personal dress code?

H has modified a previously-held opinion as he/she got older?

Speaker 1 Aengus ....

Speaker 2 Margaret ....

Speaker 3 Joe ....

Speaker 4 Barbara ....

4 Here are some tips on how to approach listening tasks in the CAE exam. Which tips apply to the task you have just done?

- The questions summarise and paraphrase what the speakers say, so listen for different ways of saying the same thing.
- Getting the answers right can depend on hearing a few key words.
- Information is often repeated or recycled.
- Paying attention to the speaker's tone of voice and stress patterns can help to identify his/her attitude to the subject.

VOCABULARY

Connotation

1 Many words have positive or negative associations — connotations — in addition to their basic meaning. For example, the adjectives *slim* and *thin* have more or less the same meaning. But to call someone *slim* is a compliment. To call them *thin* or even worse, *skinny,* is not!

Look at these sets of words. Which ones have positive, neutral or negative connotations?

1 self-confident / arrogant
2 aggressive / assertive
3 friendly / familiar
4 trusting / gullible
5 mean / tight-fisted / thrifty
6 fussy / meticulous / careful

2 Complete these sentences with an appropriate word from Exercise 1.

1 You fall for his tricks every time! You're so .... !

2 Paul is absolutely .... in his attention to detail.

3 Don't let other people take advantage of you. Learn to stand up for yourself and be more .... !

4 My friend is very .... about his appearance — he wouldn't dream of wearing last year's fashions.

5 The MD is a .... old skinflint — he's cancelled the office party to save money.

READING

Exam File: Parts 1 and 4, Multiple matching

In Paper 1 of the CAE exam, there are two multiple matching texts. This task type tests your ability to read rapidly but with comprehension, using the techniques of **skimming** and **scanning**. Don't be put off by the large amount of text! You don't need to read or understand every word.

The exercises below show you how to approach a typical Part 1 multiple matching task.

1 Skim the article opposite very quickly and complete the summary below without looking back at the text. When you skim, read only:

- the headline/title and any sub-headings: these often summarise the main idea of the text.
- the first two or three paragraphs: these introduce the subject of the text.
- the first, second and last sentence of each paragraph: one of these is likely to be the topic sentence.
- the concluding paragraph: this gives a summary of the main ideas or a conclusion.

The article describes a course in assertiveness training being run at ... in ... . The aim of the training is to help pupils who ... . The course teaches them how to ... . One of the methods used is ... . According to the teacher who runs the course, the method is successful if pupils ... . She thinks that all schools should ..., but warns that ... .

2 Find these words and expressions in the article. Use the context to help you work out their meaning. Then check your answers by matching them with the appropriate definition A—H.

1 confront (a problem/person) *(headline/lines 3/54)*
2 give in *(line 4)*
3 wind someone up *(line 21)*
4 get someone down *(line 22)*
5 tough *(line 55)*
6 be armed *(line 79)*
7 rise to the bait *(line 110)*
8 beyond someone's scope *(line 127)*

A make someone feel unhappy, depressed
B difficult, hard
C try to deal with something that can't be avoided
D react in exactly the way someone expected you to
E outside someone's area of knowledge or expertise
F deliberately annoy or provoke someone
G admit you are defeated, submit
H be prepared

1 The multiple matching task asks you to match prompts with names of people. Scan the article to find the names listed A—D, and underline them.

2 Read the statements and match each one with the person to whom it applies (A, B, C or D). Use the names you have underlined to help you locate the relevant part of the text. Read that part carefully.

A Maria	
B Nadia	
C Anita	
D Anna Hordyk	
She has a problem with a younger member of her family.	**1** ....
She has recognised a problem with her own behaviour.	**2** ....
She chooses to try a difficult way out of her problem.	**3** ....
She indicates that some people's behaviour can't always be changed for the better.	**4** ....
She needs practice to get things right.	**5** ....
She finds it hard to deal with a brother's insults.	**6** ....
Her problem is different from that of other members of the group.	**7** ....
She feels resentful when she is forced to submit.	**8** ....
She emphasises the importance of combining theory and action.	**9** ....
She is aware of the limits of what she can do.	**10** ....

4 Read out the sentences that gave you the answers. Compare the way the ideas and information are expressed in the text and in the prompts above. For example:

Question 1: ... a younger member of her family
Text (para 2): Anita, 13, ... 11-year-old brother

Role-playing with attitude

Assertiveness training is helping shy and bullied pupils to confront their problems

Maria, a quiet 13-year-old, is dominated by her older cousin. When confronted with his bullying, she always gives in, but inside she is
5 seething with anger. In the centre of a circle of classmates at Connaught School in east London, she shares her troubles. "He is horrible and sexist - calls me a pathetic girl, an airhead, all
10 the names he can think of to make me feel bad. Sometimes I end up screaming that he is a barbarian. Whatever I say, he always seems to win."

15 The group nods. They are all volunteers at an assertiveness training course and Maria is not the only one with problems. Anita, also 13, is here because she cannot stop
20 arguing with her 11-year-old brother. "He winds me up, calls me fat. I shout back. It really gets me down," she says.

Most of the pupils admit they have
25 volunteered because they are shy and need to build their confidence. But not all of them. Nadia, 12, is there to control a hot temper. "I can get so angry and aggressive that my face
30 turns red. I needed to do something about it," she confesses.

Assertiveness training is growing in pockets around the country. At Connaught, an all-girls school, it
35 takes place after school for an hour and a half each week. Anna Hordyk, a teacher and trained counsellor, takes the sessions. The courses cover how to say no, how to express controlled
40 anger and how to use compliments assertively, using discussion and role-play. They last for eight weeks and, once the course is completed, pupils can join a weekly club. By the
45 time they reach the club, they have succeeded in improving their speaking skills and are able to express their feelings and identify their mistakes.

50 Maria elects to work through her problem with role-play, choosing Nadia to act as her 15-year-old cousin. She decides her strategy has to be to confront the boy — the
55 toughest course of action. They act out a real-life scene from the past, an episode where Maria wanted to use her cousin's computer and he refused. Nadia rants, "No, you cannot
60 use my computer, because you are a girl, an airhead, a stupid idiot that likes books." Maria's shoulders hunch and the pitch of her voice rises.

"Can't you listen to me?" she
65 pleads. She knows she has lost. It is left to the rest of the seventeen girls in the group to criticise her performance. Her body language was wrong, she should have put her
70 shoulders back instead of hunching them forwards, her voice whined, she needn't have defended herself, she should have maintained eye-contact, stuck to the point and repeated her
75 message, a trick known as 'the broken record tactic'.

Maria's main objective is to stop the verbal abuse. Third time lucky, armed with a better technique,
80 shoulders back, she bluntly states, "Yes, I am a girl and I am proud of it. You might have a problem with that, but I want you to treat me as an equal." The 'cousin' shouts, "Why?"
85 She squares up and replies, "Why not?" Nadia is silenced. The class applauds. Aware that in real life you do not get three tries to get it right, Maria is determined she will try to
90 use the technique on her cousin. "Speaking up felt good," she says.

Ms Hordyk insists that the success of role-playing depends on how well students understand the theory
95 and can put it to practical use. "The objective is to give them the self-confidence and self-respect to say what they want without putting themselves or the other person down.
100 It is about learning that being clear, direct and honest can actually achieve positive results." However, she stresses that it is not a solution to every confrontation or problem.
105 Perhaps the most important lesson is to realise that if you are confronted with a bully, or someone who is racist or sexist, you will not necessarily be able to change their behaviour.
110 Sometimes it is assertive not to rise to the bait but to walk away instead.

Ms Hordyk believes assertiveness training should be part of the curriculum for boys and girls, but
115 only if teachers have gone through a thorough training programme. "The role-playing can sometimes reveal serious problems that children are experiencing. If a child is upset while
120 witnessing another's role-play, you have to be aware that it has been a trigger for something. Theoretically, you have to be prepared for something serious that could be
125 uncovered inadvertently. If that occurred, a child would then need extensive counselling beyond a teacher's scope. It is an area where we have to tread very carefully."

airhead: stupid person *(slang)*

5 The article you have just read contains quite a number of phrasal verbs. These are very common in English, particularly in speech and less formal writing. They occur frequently in the reading texts in Paper 1 and may be tested in Paper 3, so it's important for you to consolidate and extend your knowledge in this area. Make a point of noting down the phrasal verbs you come across during your reading.

Look for phrasal verbs in the text on page 11 and match them with their neutral or more formal equivalents below.

1 finish by doing *(para 1)*
2 take action to deal with a problem *(para 7)*
3 say what you really mean *(para 7)*
4 humiliate *(para 8)*
5 complete *(para 9)*

6 Discuss these questions in groups.

1 Are assertiveness training courses available in your country? Who are they usually intended for? Do you think they are a good idea?
2 Is bullying a problem in schools in your country? What steps are taken to deal with it?

LANGUAGE STUDY 1

Modal verbs review (Notes pages 197—198)

Meaning: present and future

1 Modal verbs are used to express a wide range of communicative functions. They can be grouped into two main meaning areas:

A degrees of likelihood (certainty, probability, possibility), assumption and deduction.
B ability or opportunity, permission, obligation/duty, necessity.

Read the sets of examples and decide what each modal verb means. To help you, try replacing them with expressions like *be likely, maybe, probably, be able to, be allowed to, be necessary to, be obliged to.*

1 *can/can't*
   a. Being clear, direct and honest can actually achieve positive results.
   b. Role-playing can sometimes reveal serious problems.
   c. That can't be Tom, can it? He looks so different!

2 *could/couldn't*
   a. You have to be prepared for something that could happen.

b. Could I ask a question?
   c. I'm afraid I couldn't tell you where he's gone.

3 *may/might*
   a. May I interrupt for a moment?
   b. You may/might be right, I'm not sure.
   c. He obviously isn't coming so we may/might as well go home.

4 *should/ought to*
   a. Assertiveness training ought to/should be part of the curriculum.
   b. The course should help me gain confidence — I hope so!
   c. You oughtn't to/shouldn't tell lies.

5 *will/would*
   a. They'll be half way to New York by now.
   b. Will/Would you do something for me?

6 *must*
   a. This must be John now, I can hear his voice.
   b. I mustn't keep you talking any longer, I'm sure you must be very busy.

> ! *don't have to / must not*
>
> What's the difference in meaning?
> a. I don't have to go to work tomorrow, it's Saturday.
> b. You mustn't go to work, you're too ill.

Past time reference: *could, would*

2 The modal verbs *could* and *would* can refer to the past as well as the present and future without changing their form or adding a perfect infinitive. Match the examples with their meaning, then answer the question below.

1 past ability
2 past habit
3 past possibility
4 permission

a. By the age of five, I could read fluently.
b. As a teenager, I could borrow my father's car whenever I wanted.
c. We would often spend holidays in the country when we were children.
d. Holidays could get very boring for us children.
e. Could you see what was happening from where you were standing?

In which sentences can the modal be replaced by
- used to?
- was/were able to?
- was/were allowed to?

3

1 These sentences all refer to past ability. Can you explain why they are wrong? (Check the Notes on page 197 if you're not sure.)

1 I missed the last train last night, but I could get a lift home with a friend.

2 Peter could borrow his father's car last Saturday to take his girlfriend out.

3 Yesterday I could finish my homework by eight o'clock.

2 Re-express the sentences, using an appropriate verb from the list.

was able to / managed to / succeeded in -ing / was allowed to

4 Write sentences describing:

- a skill or ability you had mastered by the age of 5/10/15.
- two things you achieved with difficulty and are proud of in the field of sports, studies, work.
- three things you were allowed to do as a child.
- three things you weren't permitted to do.

Compare your sentences with a partner.

Modals + perfect infinitive

5 Modal verbs can be used with the perfect infinitive to comment on past actions, speculate about past possibilities, make assumptions or deductions.

1 Read this dialogue. What do you think the problem is?

A: They might have forgotten about it.
B: I wouldn't have thought so. I only spoke to them two days ago.
A: Something could have come up.
B: But surely they would have phoned? They must have got lost. Perhaps I should have sent them a map.
A: They can't have got lost, they've been here before.
B: There may have been an accident.
A: Anything can have happened. Oh, well. I needn't have made so much food after all!

2 Listen to the recording. Notice how the auxiliary verb *have* is usually unstressed, and quite hard to hear. Practise the dialogue in pairs.

> **!** *needn't have done / didn't need to*
>
> Who didn't hurry? Who hurried unnecessarily?
> a. Jane needn't have hurried. The bus was late.
> b. Sam didn't need to hurry after all. He was informed the meeting would start late.

6 Read this letter to the Advice Column of a magazine. In groups, discuss how you would reply.

" Recently I invited a friend to lunch in a nice restaurant. She was served quite quickly and I was told that my order would also be served 'in a moment'. I told my friend not to wait for me as her food would go cold. Just as she was finishing her meal, my order arrived. It was cold. The waitress must have forgotten to pick it up when it was hot. I didn't complain about the poor service, but I decided not to leave a tip, although I am normally a very generous tipper. My friend, however, insisted on leaving a tip herself, as she said the service she received was fine. I told her I thought she was wrong to do this. For one thing, she was my guest. Secondly, the service was not good, because both meals should have been served at the same time. What's your opinion? Who was right? **"**

Sally, 20, student

7 In pairs or groups, discuss the strategies you employ when you have problems in restaurants, shops or with public officials or with colleagues or family. Describe an occasion when:

1 you were assertive and you feel you achieved what you wanted.

2 you should have been more assertive.

The rest of the group should comment on what you did.

13

LISTENING 2

Exam File: Part 1, Sentence completion

In Part 1 of the Listening Paper you may be asked to complete sentences using up to three words; sometimes you have to write down numbers. Your completed answer will form a summary of what you have heard in the recording. Here are some tips.

- Always read the incomplete sentences first to get a general idea of the topic, and try to predict the missing words.
- The incomplete sentences are often a paraphrase of what you hear in the recording, so listen for different ways of saying the same thing.
- Make sure that the word or phrase you write fits grammatically.

1 Look at this list of jobs. In which jobs do you think appearance matters most/least?

bricklayer / telephone sales personnel / air steward(ess) / mechanic / hotel receptionist / factory worker / model / lawyer / sales assistant in a shop

2 Read these statements and check that you understand the words in italics. Say if you agree or disagree with the statements.

1 Attractive people have *an inbuilt advantage* over others when it comes to getting a job.
2 Men have better chances of *getting promoted* than women.
3 *Discrimination* against people on the basis of physical characteristics should be prohibited by law.
4 *Tougher legislation* should be introduced to protect people against *unfair dismissal*.

3 You will hear part of a radio programme about the relationship between appearance and employment opportunities.

1 Read the task and think about:
- the type of information needed for each gap.
- the phrase you will hear in the recording. For example, the first sentence paraphrases this information in the recording:

'A study they conducted, based on xxx people, showed that ... '

2 Now listen and write your answers. You will hear the recording twice.

Does the way you look affect your career chances?

To find the answer, Jeff Biddle and Daniel Hamermesh of the University of Texas surveyed (1) .... people.
They discovered that good-looking people were paid around (2) .... more.
Biddle and Hamermesh then spent 15 years following the careers of a selected group of (3) ....
They found that the better-looking ones had better chances of (4) .... than the others.
They also found that more was expected of the better-looking ones by their (5) ....
However, a reaction is now occurring against this kind of (6) .... in the work place.
The courts are awarding compensation in cases of unfair (7) ....
In Santa Cruz, discrimination on the basis of a person's (8) .... is now forbidden.
The only criterion for employment is whether a person is able to (9) ....

4 Discuss this question.

What things can you do to make the best possible impression at a job interview? Make a list of *dos* and *don'ts*.

ENGLISH IN USE

Fixed expressions

1 Some words occur together so regularly that they have the status of fixed expressions. This means that when you see one word you can accurately predict what comes next. Can you fill in the missing word in these pairs?

1 Don't invite Peter to the party, he's so *dull and* ....

2 Mrs Smith's house is always *neat and* ....

3 The crew of the stricken yacht have been rescued and are now back home *safe and* ....

4 Free *board and* .... will be provided to volunteers.

5 It's £25 per night for *bed and* ....

6 I don't like *country and* .... music.

Adjective/noun collocations

2 Cross out the adjective that does **not** collocate with the noun in these examples.

1 Never judge people on initial/preliminary/first impressions.

2 Aengus has got pale/fair/blonde hair.

3 Mary's complexion is quite pale/fair/blonde.

4 Our school is a very good-looking/attractive/beautiful building.

5 Nadia has to learn to control a bad/hot/boiling temper.

6 Being assertive can achieve positive/self-confident/successful results.

Verb/noun collocations

1 Cross out the noun which does **not** collocate with the verb.

1 to make   a mistake/an error/a fault

2 to award   compensation/a fee/a prize

3 to achieve   success/a prize/an ambition

2 Cross out the verb which does **not** collocate with the noun.

1 to draw/pull/attract   attention to

2 to win/produce/achieve   a result

3 to set/put/turn   to use

4 Complete the following sentences by choosing A, B, C or D. You have come across all these expressions in this unit.

1 I think that is the most appropriate .... of action to follow.
  A path   **B** course   **C** method   **D** way

2 If you want to win an argument, it's important to stick to the .... .
  A point   **B** aim   **C** purpose   **D** reason

3 Jack .... me some very good advice about the interview.
  A told   **B** made   **C** placed   **D** gave

4 In this job, you meet a large .... of people.
  A group   **B** deal   **C** amount   **D** number

5 With this method, we will .... good results.
  A take   **B** win   **C** achieve   **D** receive

6 I can't advise you on this matter — it's .... my scope.
  A beyond   **B** above   **C** off   **D** past

7 It is forbidden to dismiss an employee on the .... of personal appearance.
  A basis   **B** foundation   **C** ground
  D evidence

8 We were asked to test the product and give it a mark on a .... from one to five.
  A scale   **B** range   **C** rank   **D** grade

9 You should avoid .... people on first impressions.
  A estimating   **B** assessing   **C** judging
  D regarding

LANGUAGE STUDY 2

Tense review: Present perfect simple/continuous (Notes page 198)

1 Read these examples. Underline any time adverbials. When do we use the present perfect tense? When do we use the past simple tense?

1 a. I've lived in the same town all my life.
  b. I lived in the same town all my childhood.

2 a. I've always loved reading.
  b. I loved reading when I was younger, but I don't have time now.

3 a. This is the first time I've ever been abroad.
  b. The first time I ever went abroad was last year.

4 a. I've just finished my exams, so I can relax.
  b. I finished my exams two days ago, so I'm relaxing now.

5 a. I've worked for Bafta Corporation for three years, ever since I left school.
  b. I worked for Bafta Corporation for three years after I left school.

2 Read these pairs of examples. What is the difference between the present perfect simple and continuous tenses?

1 a. I've been studying English for ten years.
  b. I've studied English for ten years.

2 a. I've been waiting ages for this moment.
  b. I've waited ages for this moment.

3 a. I've been reading a good book this week.
  b. I've read a good book this week.

4 a. I've been painting the kitchen today.
  b. I've painted the kitchen today.

3 Can you explain why these sentences are wrong?

1 We've been knowing each other since we were children.

2 I've always been believing that learning a language is important.

3 This ring has been belonging to my family for generations.

4 I haven't been seeing you for ages.

4 Underline the most appropriate tense(s) in these sentences.

1 I understand you *stayed/have stayed/have been staying* here since June.

2 Peter *received/has received/has been receiving* the most wonderful job offer, and he's going to take it.

3 So you're a teacher. How long *did you teach/have you taught/have you been teaching*?

4 I *had/have had/have been having* short hair as a child.

5 How nice to see you again. What *did you do/have you done/have you been doing* since we last met?

6 I *wrote/have written/have been writing* to him two weeks ago, but *didn't receive/haven't received/haven't been receiving* an answer yet.

5 Correct these sentences, which contain typical errors made by learners of English.

1 I have passed all my exams a year ago.

2 I have received your letter yesterday.

3 It's the first time I visit this museum.

4 I have heard that you live in England for a year now.

5 I work in this company since two years ago.

6 It is only one month that I study this subject.

7 It's been a long time since we don't see each other.

8 It's three years since I knew Veronique.

SPEAKING 2

Exam File: Part 1, Social language

In Part 1 of the Speaking Test, the interlocutor asks the candidates to say something about each other, or to ask each other questions if they don't know each other. This part lasts about three minutes. It's your first chance to make a good impression. Here are some tips.

• Show interest in your partner by looking at him/her, nodding and encouraging him/her to say more.

• In this part of the interview, you are not expected to produce difficult and complicated language, but you should speak fluently and without hesitation.

1 Make a list of questions that you can ask your partner to help you find out some information about him/her. Choose from these topic areas.

- Home town
- Hobbies/Interests
- Education/Employment
- Family
- Future plans

Be ready to answer similar questions about yourself.

2 In groups of three, role play the first part of the Speaking Test. Students A and B should be the candidates. Student C should be the interlocutor and time the candidates, allowing them one minute each to ask each other questions, and one minute to say something about their partner. Try to use expressions from the Language Bank to respond to each other.

3 When you have finished, Student C should evaluate the performance of the two 'candidates', using these evaluation criteria:

- general impression
- fluency and pronunciation
- accuracy
- interactive communication

Language Bank

Reacting to what someone says

I see.

Oh, really? / Oh, did you/have you?

That's interesting.

That must be interesting/challenging ...

Encouraging someone to say more

So how long have you ...?

When/Why did you ...?

Are you planning to ...?

Do you think you will ...?

Evaluating

You should have said '...', not '...'

You should have looked at your partner when he/she was speaking.

WRITING

Exam File: Part 2, Formal letter

In the Writing Paper you have to answer two questions, writing about 250 words for each. All the writing activities in the exam reflect the types of writing you do in real life. The questions specify the reason for writing and the target audience. To be successful, you need to:

• read the questions carefully, and do exactly what they ask for.

• avoid reproducing the input material in your answers.

• use a format, style and register that are appropriate to the type of writing you have been asked to produce, and to the target audience.

Your answers will be marked on the basis of how well you carried out the required task, and on the appropriacy and accuracy of your language.

1 You may be asked to produce any of the following types of writing in the exam. Which of these text types do you write a) in your own language b) in English? How often?

- personal notes and messages
- informal letters
- formal letters
- leaflets
- articles (e.g. for a club newsletter/school magazine)
- reports
- reviews of books and films

2 For each type of writing, decide:

1 who is probably going to read it: family/friends/fellow-students/colleagues/boss/the public ...?

2 what is the likely purpose: to inform/to entertain/to persuade/to keep in touch ...?

3 what register is most appropriate: formal/semi-formal/colloquial?

4 what is the most appropriate tone to adopt: factual/humorous/ironic/sensational ...?

5 what special features regarding lay-out and organisation it has? For example:

informal letter: own address top right, date directly below, salutation on the left (Dear ...,)

article: headline, sub-headings, clear paragraphing

3 Which type of writing do you think is most/least difficult? Why?

2 You are going to read some examples where people have written about themselves.

 For each piece of writing, identify:

- the text type   • the target reader
- the purpose for writing

2 Now answer the questions below each text. Think about the effectiveness of:

- content   • register and tone   • organisation

in relation to the target reader and the purpose for writing.

Text 1

WANT THINGS TO CHANGE IN COLLEGE?

then vote for
Shirley Grainger
as student representative!

I'm a third year student in Media Studies and I've been involved in student action in the college since I arrived here. In my first year, I worked on the student newspaper and started the campaign to improve facilities and opening times in the canteen. Now I want to represent the student body in the management decisions made by the college. As you can see I have the experience and commitment that will make me successful. In order to be sure to represent the feelings of students, the representative needs to LISTEN. I will make sure this happens by being available at a regular time each week in the student common room.
Channel your views and opinions through me. You can be sure I'll push the point of view of all students as hard as I can.

A vote for me won't be wasted.

You see this on a notice-board at college. Why would or wouldn't you vote for Shirley?

- Does her statement give you enough information to help you make up your mind?
- How would you describe the tone? How do you react to it?

Text 2

> ### FLAT-SHARER REQUIRED.
>
> *NEED SOMEWHERE TO LIVE?*
> *I'M A 20-YEAR-OLD TOLERANT NON-SMOKER, AND I*
> *DON'T DRINK EITHER.*
> *MY LAST FLATMATE HAS JUST LEFT, SO I NEED A*
> *REPLACEMENT.*
> *YOUR OWN ROOM IN FLAT NEAR BUS STATION.*
> *SHARE ALL EXPENSES AND CHORES.*
> *CONTACT CHARLOTTE – FIND ME IN THE COFFEE BAR.*

You see this card in a shop window. Why would or wouldn't you like to live in this flat?

- Is there anything about the advertisement that puts you off?
- Does it contain any irrelevant information?
- Does the information follow a clear, logical sequence?

Text 3

Dear Anna

I got your name from the penfriend agency. It's my chance to tell you all about myself. There's not much to tell. I come from an ordinary family. I have a mother, father, brother — his name's Freddy, he's fourteen and a pain.

I go to school. That's really boring. My town is very dull. There's nothing to do. Everything gets very quiet when the shops close. I've got a bike and I ride to school every day. It's dangerous because everyone drives so fast round here. Freddy got knocked off his bike last year and had to go to hospital.

I've got some hobbies. I'll tell you about them next time.

Write to me soon.

Love from Kirsty

You have received this letter from someone you don't know. If you were Anna, would you write back? Why/why not? Does the letter show a good variety of sentence patterns?

Text 4

26 Onslow Road
Oxford
OX2 3BZ

Mr John Franks
Project Manager
Archaeological Digs
20 Reed Avenue
London W1A 7CC   17 May 20-

Dear Mr Franks

I have seen your advertisement in today's edition of
'The Oxford Mail' asking for enthusiastic volunteers
to work on the archaeological dig due to take place
at Helstone quarries between 30 June and 31 August.

As a student about to finish my second year studying
history at Farringdon University, I have had the
opportunity to attend a number of courses on
archaeological techniques. I also gained practical
experience last summer on a two-week dig excavating
an Iron Age settlement in Oxfordshire.

I would be available for the whole period required,
and would be able to work on the basis that board and
lodging will be provided but that there will be no
payment.

I should very much enjoy the opportunity to work on
the project and hope that you will be able to offer
me a place on the team. I look forward to receiving
further details in due course.

Yours sincerely

Howard Carter

Howard Carter

Would you consider accepting Howard on the project?

• Can you think of any information that he might have included, such as references?
• Is the register appropriate?
• Is the letter well laid out?

3 Read this writing task and follow the **Steps to Writing** below.

You have seen the following advertisement in a student magazine.

The **Lonsdale Trust** offer grants to young people to study abroad for up to six months.
Age limit 16—30.
The grant covers all expenses and provides some pocket money.
You must study or research a subject that you have already developed an interest in, and submit a 5,000 word report to the Trust at the end of the study period.

Apply by letter (no application forms) to:
The Secretary, The Lonsdale Trust,
153 Hatton Terrace, Bath BA1 9QF

Write your **letter** of application, giving full details of your education and interests, including the subject you wish to pursue, and explaining why you would be a suitable recipient of the grant.

Write approximately 250 words. You do not need to include addresses.

Step 1 Task interpretation
Identify what the task requires. What text type do you have to produce? Who will read it? What is your purpose in writing? What will be the most appropriate register and tone? How will you begin and end it?

Step 2 Generating ideas
What information do you need to include? Make a list of essential points in note form. Include any relevant experience you may have to support your application.

Step 3 Layout and organisation
Organise your ideas into paragraphs. How many paragraphs will you need to write in your letter? Note down any useful vocabulary.

Step 4 Write
1 When you write, try to include a range of vocabulary and structures for interest and variety. How many ways can you think of to combine these sentences?

1 I am responding to your advertisement in *Away from Home*. It offers grants to young people to study abroad.

2 I am a modern languages student. I am studying at Hull University. I am in my final year.

3 I am doing a thesis. My thesis is on Cervantes. I would welcome the opportunity to do further research in Spain.

2 Now write your letter. Leave a line between paragraphs for readability. Remember, you only have 250 words.

▶ Language Study 2 (page 16)

Step 5 Evaluate and edit
When you have finished, re-read and evaluate your work, using the Writing checklist on page 00. Make any necessary corrections.

Going too far

SPEAKING

1 Work in pairs. Choose two photographs each and take it in turns to talk about them. Answer these questions.

1 What is happening in each photograph?
2 Which activities seem to you the most dangerous? Think about what could go wrong.
3 What precautions can be taken to prevent accidents?
4 How do you think the people in the photographs feel before, during and after these activities? Choose from these words and phrases.

petrified / scared stiff / sick with fear / panic-stricken / frightened to death / exhilarated / thrilled / on top of the world / relieved

2 Do you agree with what your partner said? Say how **you** would feel if you were doing one of these activities.

3 Now discuss these questions.

1 What kind of person do you think takes risks like this, and why?

2 Do you admire risk takers, or do you think they're mad and irresponsible?

Language Bank

Describing a picture

The/Each photograph shows/is of a person/people doing something dangerous/taking a risk with their lives.

In one photograph there's something that looks like a ... . I think it's a thing for ...

Speculating

It looks as if/though they're enjoying themselves.

They must feel quite exhilarated/extremely relieved.

I imagine/suppose they're the sort of people who ...

Expressing opinions

Personally, I think .../ In my opinion/view ...

As far as I'm concerned, .../ To be honest, ...

LISTENING 1

Part 1, Sentence completion

1 You will hear a scientific explanation of why some people crave risk and are prepared to take their lives in their hands, while others get enough excitement from reading a thriller. Before you listen, read through the sentences below and check you understand all the words. Try to predict the missing words.

2 Now listen and complete the sentences using a few words. Make sure that the word or phrase you write fits the sentence grammatically. You will hear the recording twice.

3 Discuss this question.

What do you think of the explanation given by the psychologists? Did anything surprise you?

4 Find out which of these leisure activities your partner enjoys or would enjoy doing.

driving a fast car / parachuting / watching films / reading thrillers / going to concerts / scuba-diving / mountain-climbing / skiing / bird-watching / cooking

Would you describe your partner as an introvert or an extrovert?

Do risk seekers have a different brain chemistry?

To find out what happens in people's bodies when they take risks, psychologists studied trainee parachutists.

The results revealed that levels of adrenaline increased as much as (1) .... during the jump.

Noradrenaline levels increased by (2) ....

Adrenaline helps prepare the body to defend itself by producing energy (3) ....

Noradrenaline has the effect of making people (4) ....

People react to stimuli differently, depending on the way the brain (5) ....

The brain wave patterns in introverts are (6) ....

This means that their response to stimuli is (7) ....

Surprisingly, the nervous system of extroverts is (8) ....

So extroverts have to do risky things to give them enough (9) ....

It seems that people choose an exciting or relaxing environment according to how much stimulation their brain needs.

READING

1

1 Skim each text on pages 23—24 quickly to find out who it's about, and what happened to them. What is the link between the texts?

2 Which of these words best sums up the character of each person?

a loner / a daredevil / an extrovert
courageous / restless / unconventional / obsessive / wild / gregarious / exuberant

2

1 Read the multiple matching questions below and highlight key words which will help you decide what kind of information you need to look for. For example, in question 1, the key words are 'constant variety.' Look for references to different activities in the text.

2 Answer the questions by matching them with the person (A, B, C or D) to whom they apply. Follow the advice in the Exam File. (Note that in the exam there will be a minimum of 12 questions to match.)

Who		
needed constant variety in life?	1	
practised a sport where one mistake could be fatal?	2	
put his relationship with another person at risk because of his hobby?	3	
failed to settle down when friends did?	4	**A** Tommy
did not act on advice from a close relative?	5	**B** Dave
had successfully accomplished similar exploits before the one that killed him?	6	**C** Sarah
had a reputation for fearlessness at university?	7	**D** Darren
benefited psychologically from getting into trouble with the law?	8	
ran the risk of being banned from membership of an organisation?	9	
died in a road accident?	10	

The Adventurer

It was pitch dark at 3am and Tommy Leigh-Pemberton's battered white Zimbabwean-registered Rover was probably the only car on the road. He had done the journey hundreds of times before and was driving fast along the road leading to the suburbs of Harare when, at the approach to the President's palace, his car smashed into the steel barriers lowered each night outside the palace, killing him instantly.

Friends were saddened but not surprised by his death. A latter-day buccaneer, full of charm and exuberance, Tommy was a restless adventurer. At university, he had been a member of the Dangerous Sports Club and had sledged down the Alps on a table top. He had ridden from London to Singapore on a tricycle. He was a man who always lived close to the edge. No stunt was too dangerous, no challenge too awesome.

His background seemed unremarkable: a large, comfortable family home, a place at Eton and a calm, assured future. Things began to change when he reached Oxford University. Members of the Dangerous Sports Club were 'wild but good fun. They lived like maniacs, as if there were no tomorrow.' Leigh-Pemberton earned a reputation for physical courage and a healthy disrespect for authority. He was one of the first to perform a bunjee jump off Clifton Suspension Bridge, organised for 6am to escape the attention of the police.

By their late twenties, most of his contemporaries had given up their wild activities and knuckled down to doing respectable jobs in banking. Tommy Leigh-Pemberton tried to follow suit but could never settle into a nine-to-five job. After two years of stockbroking, he threw in the conventional life forever.

How and why the accident happened is a mystery. Leigh-Pemberton had been living in Zimbabwe for almost 18 months and would have known about the security barriers. His death is particularly tragic because it seemed that, after years of drifting from one crazy expedition to the next, he had finally found the ideal life in Zimbabwe. He had been organising tours which included hot-air ballooning, ultralight plane rides and high-risk bush trips.

Now the wreckage of his car sits in the graveyard of the vehicle inspection depot in Harare, glass from the shattered windscreen glittering in the sun.

buccaneer: pirate

Eton: a famous public (fee-paying) school for boys.

The Computer Buff

When Dave, a 29-year-old computer consultant, ignored his beautiful young wife Sarah and sat up tapping feverishly into a laptop until 4am, she realised that their marriage, less than two years old, was over. Dave was not a classic computer nut, a loner incapable of forming loving bonds. Far from it: he and Sarah were the perfect young middle-class couple, graduates, both earning well and living in a comfortable London flat.

Sarah and Dave were at university when they met, he a medical student, she reading music. Sarah chose to ignore his preoccupation with computers even when, after getting his medical degree, he dropped doctoring to pursue a computer-based career.

Sarah said, "When I met him, he was obviously mad about computers but only as a hobby. I ignored what my mother told me about avoiding men with hobbies. He seemed to be obsessed with getting better and better at doing whatever it was he did. Yet at the start, we were terribly romantic. Things went wrong within a year. I felt he was doing too much computing at home. He would stay up late every night typing away, sending messages to other computer buffs, who were just as obsessed as Dave was. Equipment kept arriving at our flat. I remember once a new computer coming and he was in ecstasies unpacking it."

Eventually, Dave was caught by a security guard stealing computer equipment from his office at six in the morning. He was convicted and received a one-year sentence.

"Being caught was an extraordinary shock to Dave," Sarah recalls. "They came and took all his computers away, but in the six months he was awaiting trial, a change came over him. I saw him become much more gregarious. At the time I thought the whole arrest and conviction were appalling. But the whole nightmare gave him the short, sharp shock he needed to separate him from computers. I think he appreciates that too."

short, sharp shock: this refers to a system of short but firm punishment for young criminals

The high-flyer

On May 20, Darren Newton walked into the London Hilton and took the elevator to the 27th floor. He stepped out onto the roof, moved to the edge and jumped. He wasn't ill or depressed and it was only the fact that he had a parachute on his back that made anyone take any notice at all. Darren was a BASE jumper, a man who parachuted not from aeroplanes but from fixed objects. BASE stands for Building, Antennae, Span and Earthbound object, and in order to join the ranks of this unofficial organisation you must jump from one of each.

When parachutists jump from a plane, their height above the ground allows them to adjust their position and correct mistakes. In BASE jumping, once a mistake is made, there is no time to pull a reserve chute and no air to adjust position. The British Parachute Association believes this makes the activity too dangerous and bans members who participate and are discovered.

Darren Newton was an experienced sky diver, with over 150 jumps. As soon as he leapt, Darren looked down and his feet tangled in the lines of his parachute. Darren fell 100 metres, landing in a canopy above the hotel's door. The London Hilton is a public place to die and so Darren's final tragic moments were raked over in public. Journalists employed the language usually brought out on these occasions: 'Daredevil' Darren Newton, the 25-year-old thrill seeker.

We can shake our heads at people doing dangerous things that officials and authority disapprove of, but we all take risks. We drive in cars and smoke cigarettes and run across the street without looking. Society deems these risks acceptable. It also accepts mountaineering, which sees more deaths in six months than there have ever been in BASE jumping. The American BASE jumper Rick Sylvester made the most famous BASE jump of all, off the top of Mount Asgard in Baffin Island, for the opening sequence of a James Bond movie. A BASE jump done for the entertainment of millions cannot be acceptable if what people do privately is not.

---

3 Find where these expressions are used in the texts on pages 23—24. Can you explain their meaning, using a synonym, a definition or examples?

The Adventurer
1 pitch dark *(line 1)*
2 live close to the edge *(line 30)*
3 knuckle down to *(line 57)*
4 follow suit *(line 60)*
5 throw sth in *(line 64)*
6 drift *(line 75)*

The Computer Buff
7 a computer nut *(line 5)*
8 be mad about *(line 14)*
9 in ecstasies *(line 24)*

The High-flyer
10 take any notice (of) *(line 12)*
11 join the ranks of *(line 20)*
12 rake over *(line 52)*

4 What verbs are used with these nouns in the texts?

1 .... a reputation for
2 .... a (prison) sentence
3 .... trial
4 .... risks

What other verbs collocate with the same nouns?

5 Discuss these statements in groups, and decide which you agree with. Then report your conclusions to the rest of the class. Be prepared to give reasons.

1 People should have complete freedom to take risks with their own lives.

2 Governments should ban dangerous sports such as mountaineering, boxing and horse racing.

LANGUAGE STUDY 1

Review of relative clauses (Notes page 199)

1 Underline the relative clauses in these examples from Listening 1, and circle the noun(s) referred to by the relative pronoun. Then answer the questions below. Refer to the Grammar Notes to check your answers.

a. Are (people) who chase after risks different from everyone else?
b. ... and that another hormone, which is called noradrenaline, had increased by 150%.
c. Extroverts become attracted to high risk activities that provide them with the excitement which they need.
d. The whole nightmare gave him the shock which he needed to separate him from computers.

In which example(s):

1 does the relative clause give additional, non-essential information that could be omitted without affecting the meaning of the sentence? What is this type of relative clause called?

2 does the relative clause add essential information about the preceding noun, distinguishing it from other nouns? What do we call this type of relative clause?

3 could an alternative relative pronoun be used?

4 can the relative pronoun be omitted altogether? Why?

5 can the relative pronoun be omitted only if the verb is also omitted?

2 Fill in the gaps in these sentences with an appropriate relative pronoun. If the pronoun can be omitted, put it in brackets ( ).

1 He was a latter-day buccaneer .... took many risks.

2 He's no longer the man .... I knew.

3 That's the van .... made the delivery.

4 It's a city .... I have visited many times.

3 Put commas round the relative clauses in these sentences where necessary.

1 People who have a slow-acting nervous system are attracted to high-risk activities.

2 Mount Asgard which is on Baffin Island was the scene of the most famous BASE jump of all.

3 He abandoned the medical course which he had never enjoyed.

4 Her mother whose advice Sarah did not take was against the marriage.

1 Sometimes the relative pronouns *which* and *who(m)* take a preposition. In informal language the preposition falls at the end of the clause. For example:

a. He removed the parachute from the bag *which* he had hidden it *in*.

In more formal language, the preposition goes before the relative pronoun.

b. He removed the parachute from the bag *in which* he had hidden it.

2 Underline the relative pronouns and related prepositions in these sentences, then answer the questions below.

a. The building in which I work is fifty storeys high.
b. The Neckar Valley, through which we'll be driving, is very beautiful.
c. The day on which they got married was Saturday.
d. The travel agent from whom I bought my holiday gave me free insurance.

1 In which of the above examples can you replace the relative pronoun with *when* or *where*?

2 Can you omit the relative pronoun in any of the examples?

5 Rewrite these sentences to include the information in brackets. The first one has been done as an example.

1 The hall (the concert was held there) was crowded.
   The hall in which/where the concert was held was crowded.

2 His evening classes (he went to them twice a week) were the most important thing in his life.

3 The year (he started university then) was 1905.

4 The hotel (my parents spent their honeymoon there) is going to be demolished.

5 The museum (the guide referred to it) is well worth a visit.

6 Martin Ford (you lent him your notes) has passed his exams with flying colours.

7 Jack Brown (we were talking about him yesterday) has just got married.

VOCABULARY

Phrasal verbs

1 Many phrasal verbs have a metaphorical meaning, which may be an extension of the literal one or relate to the meaning of the main word.

wind up *(literal)* if you wind up a mechanical device, you turn a knob round and round to make it operate; *(figurative)* if you wind up a person, you deliberately keep on saying things to annoy them.

rake (n.) a gardening tool

rake (v.) gather weeds or dead leaves together with a rake

rake over keep returning to and talking about sth unpleasant

Knowing this can help you to work out the meanings of phrasal verbs that you meet in reading texts, and to remember them.

2 Complete the sentences below with an appropriate verb from the list, in the correct form. Use the clues to help you.

chicken out of / root out / iron out / duck out of / throw in / trigger off

- If you call someone *chicken*, you mean they're too frightened to do something.
- If a plant *roots*, it successfully grows roots and establishes itself in a place.
- Card players *throw* their cards *in*to the middle of the table to indicate they're withdrawing from the game.
- To cause a gun to go off, you pull the *trigger*.
- When you *iron* clothes, you remove wrinkles and creases.
- If you *duck*, you dip your head under water quickly or lower it to avoid something.

1 The bunjee jump was organised for 2 p.m., but he .... at the last moment.

2 Situations of fear and tension .... an increase in adrenaline levels in the blood.

3 The leader of the expedition called a meeting to .... some last-minute problems.

4 The new management was determined to .... inefficiency in the company.

5 This isn't the right job for me. I'm going to .... and travel round the world.

6 Don't ask John to organise anything. He'll just try to .... his responsibilities.

LISTENING 2

Exam File: Part 4, Multiple matching

Part 4 of the Listening Paper consists of five short extracts of people talking on a related topic. The questions may consist of two multiple matching tasks. You have to match the extracts with two sets of up to five words or phrases from a choice of eight.

It's a good idea to study the questions before you listen, and think of words that you might expect to hear in each extract. Be careful! Some of the words may also apply to other extracts, so listen carefully for words that confirm the topic.

1 You will hear five extracts about people whose behaviour is very unusual. Look at options A—E in Exercise 2 below. Make a short list of words and phrases that you might expect to hear for each. For example:

gardener: *flowers, vegetables* ...

'politician': *election,* ...

What does the use of quotation marks for 'politician' suggest?

2 🖭 Listen and choose the word that best describes the person being talked about in each extract. Match the letter (A—E) with the number of the extract (1—5). Write the letter next to the number of the speaker. Note: In this exercise, there are only five options to choose from. Later exercises will have up to eight options, as in the exam.

A gardener	Speaker 1 ....
B 'politician'	Speaker 2 ....
C hunter	Speaker 3 ....
D inventor	Speaker 4 ....
E comedian	Speaker 5 ....

3 🖭 Now listen again and decide how the speaker knew about the person they describe. Match the letter with the extract.

Was it someone the speaker:

A had met socially?	Speaker 1 ....
B lived near?	Speaker 2 ....
C was related to?	Speaker 3 ....
D read about?	Speaker 4 ....
E heard of?	Speaker 5 ....

LANGUAGE STUDY 2

Tense review: Narrative tenses (Notes pages 199—200)

1 Read these extracts from the text *The Adventurer* on page 23, and highlight the verbs in the past simple, past continuous, past perfect and past perfect continuous tenses. Then complete the descriptions below with the correct tense.

a. He had done the journey hundreds of times before and was driving fast along the road leading to the suburbs of Harare when, at the approach to the President's palace, his car smashed into the steel barriers ...

b. Leigh-Pemberton had been living in Zimbabwe for almost 18 months ...

- We use the .... tense to recount the main events of a narrative in chronological sequence.

- We use the .... tense for interrupted acts or for background activities in narratives.

- We use the .... tense to refer to a past event that happened earlier than another past event, especially if there is no time expression to make the chronological sequence clear.

Note that the use of a continuous tense emphasises activity rather than completed achievement.

2 Look back at the text and find more examples of these tenses. Explain why they are used in each case.

2

1 📼 It's easy to confuse the use of past simple and past perfect in speech. Listen to the recording and underline the form of the verb you hear spoken.

1 I *sent*/I'*d sent* the parcel when I got your fax.

2 By their late twenties, his friends *settled down*/*had settled down* to respectable jobs.

3 He *read*/He'*d read* the documents before the meeting started.

4 Jack *lived*/*had lived* in Spain for many years before he returned to England.

5 We hardly *had*/We'*d* hardly *had* time to get over our surprise when there was more good news.

6 He *appeared*/He'*d appeared* in many films by the age of 25.

2 What's the difference between the use of the two tenses in the sentences above?

3

1 Put the verbs in this story into an appropriate past tense, simple or continuous tense.

I (1) .... (walk) briskly up the path to the cottage which I (2) .... (not visit) for two months. The grass (3) .... (grow) to a height of about twenty centimetres. Hardly surprising, since it (4) .... (rain) a lot, although that particular day (5) .... (be) dry and sunny. It was late afternoon and it (6) .... (get) colder. I (7) .... (put) my hand in my pocket, (8) .... (get) out the key and (9) .... (unlock) the door. Before leaving, I (10) .... (lock) every door and window. As I (11) .... (step) inside, I (12) .... (notice) that the air (13) .... (be) fresh. That (14) .... (cannot) be right. (15) .... (I imagine) things, or (16) .... (I hear) a creak from the top of the stairs?

2 The story is unfinished. In groups, work out an ending for the story. Start by making a list of questions to get you going. For example:

Who is the narrator?

Why hadn't he/she visited the cottage for two months?

4 Work in groups. Choose one of these newspaper headlines and imagine what happened. Think about how the situation had come about, how the people managed to survive, and what happened next. Prepare a short news article, using the key words supplied. Tell your story to the class.

Mountain rescue pair
survive 100m fall in avalanche

Key words: emergency call, dangerous conditions, try to rescue someone, climbing ropes

Alive – after four days in watery tomb

Key words: yacht, storm, SOS call, sink, a rescue team, the hull of a boat, air pocket

SIX CHILDREN BEAT THE JUNGLE

Key words: plane crash, survivors, trek, survival skills, a shelter

WRITING

Exam File: Part 1, Formal letter

Part 1 of the Writing Paper is a compulsory question. You have to produce a piece of writing in a specified format, in response to a practical reading input. This may consist of two or three texts totalling up to 400 words, e.g. a memo, a newspaper extract, a set of notes etc. Thus the task tests your ability to understand and process information as well as write.

Make sure you:

- read the instructions carefully and do exactly what they ask for. Highlight key words.

- plan before you start writing.

- include **all** the relevant information from the input.

- avoid using whole phrases from the input. Use your own words to show you have understood. This may require a change of register.

Read the writing task on page 29 carefully and follow the **Steps to Writing** below.

Step 1 Task interpretation

Identify what the task requires. Highlight the key points in the instructions. What text type do you have to produce? Who will read it? What is your purpose in writing? What will be the most appropriate register and tone? How will you begin and end it?

Step 2 Selecting and summarising

Read Lucy's letter and annotated newspaper article. You have to decide what information you need to include. Select only those points that are relevant to the set task, and leave out unimportant details.

Highlight the discrepancies between the newspaper article and the actual facts. Complete these notes.

Article	Reality
teenager	21 years old
first year student	final year student

Step 3 Layout and organisation

Think about the type of writing you have to produce. Your letter should have 3—5 paragraphs. Note down what you want to include in each paragraph.

Paragraph 1: Say who you are and why you are writing.

Paragraphs 2/3: Point out the inaccuracies in the article.

Concluding paragraph: Say what action you want to be taken. For example, ask for your letter to be published with an apology. Express the wish that they will do better in future.

▶ See page 19 for the layout of a formal letter.

Step 4 Write

1 Remember to use a range of vocabulary and structures for variety. Use linking words to connect your ideas.

1 How many ways can you think of to combine these sentences?

> *I would like to point out a number of inaccuracies in your recent article, 'Local Hero'. The article describes an incident. My friend Lucy Hebden was involved in the incident.*

2 What linking expressions can you use here?

> *.........., Lucy is not a first year student. ...., she is in her final year. ...., she left her friend's party at 11.30 p.m., not at 2.30 a.m.*

2 Write your letter. Leave a line between paragraphs to improve readability. Remember you only have about 250 words.

▶ Relative clauses (page 25); Narrative tenses (page 27)

▶ Language Bank (page 29)

Step 5 Evaluate and edit

When you have finished, re-read and evaluate your work carefully. Make any necessary corrections.

▶ Writing checklist (page 214)

A friend of yours, Lucy Hebden, was recently involved in an unpleasant incident late at night. A report of the incident has appeared in a local newspaper, but it contains a number of inaccuracies.

Read Lucy's letter, the newspaper report and Lucy's notes on the report. Then, using the information carefully, write a **letter** to the newspaper on Lucy's behalf, correcting the inaccuracies and pointing out how upset you and Lucy are about the quality of its reporting. You should use your own words as far as possible.

Write about 250 words. You do not need to include addresses.

Language Bank

Complaining/pointing out discrepancies
I am writing to complain about ...
I would like to point out that / *noun* ...
According to your article, ... whereas in fact ...
What actually happened was that ...
... as stated in your article.

Saying what you want doing
I would be grateful if you would ...
I very much hope that in future ...

Link words: listing points
First of all, ... Secondly, ... Furthermore
As well as *-ing*, ...

Local hero

LOCAL builder Tom Bradley became a hero last Saturday when he rescued teenager Lucy Hebden from a vicious attack.

I'm 21

final

Lucy, a first-year student at High Edge Community College, had been at a party for a friend's twenty-first birthday. It was 2.30 in the morning when she got into her car to drive home.

11.30p.m.

As she was driving along a narrow country road, she became aware of a car very close behind her, hooting its horn. Lucy accelerated in an attempt to draw away, but without success. She was rammed by the car and forced to swerve off the road.

Four boys got out of the car and Lucy was subjected to a torrent of verbal abuse. Luckily, help was at hand in the shape of local builder Tom Bradley, who was driving home from his parents' house.

not just that – see my letter

Reluctant hero Tom told this newspaper that he was aware that all was not well as he approached the scene. He pulled up and when the youths saw him they got straight back into their car and drove off.

Did he really?

Quick-thinking Tom had the foresight to write down the registration number of the boys' car, which helped the police in their search for the vehicle. This was later found abandoned on a nearby housing estate, but police are still trying to identify the youths. Luckily Tom was able to supply them with a full description. Well done, Tom!

I supplied the description!

Honestly, can you believe this report! I've made some comments on it for you to see where it's gone wrong. I can't believe the way the press has handled this. Here am I, the innocent victim, and yet I had to spend hours at the police station giving statements. Who is this Tom Bradley? I provided a description of the boys, not him. He just drove up, the boys got scared and then they drove off. He looked at my car, said "Do you think you can drive it?" and then drove off himself. He didn't talk to them or anything. And there was a lot more than verbal abuse. One of them pulled out a knife. I didn't know what was going to happen.

Of course it was scary. But I didn't need Tom Bradley. I was the one who reported everything to the police. Yet he gets his name in the paper! He's the hero!

ENGLISH IN USE 1

Exam File: Part 4, Word formation

Part 4 of Paper 3 requires you to complete gaps in two short texts by forming words from the base words given. This may mean forming a noun from a verb, an adjective from a noun etc. For example:

The price of *admission* to the concert is £12. ADMIT

To fill in the gap correctly, you have to decide:

- what part of speech is needed in the context.
- if the missing word should be positive or negative, singular or plural.
- whether you need to add a prefix or suffix.

Note: When you record a new word in your vocabulary notebook, note down its related forms as well. This will help you prepare for Paper 1 as well as Paper 3. Recognising and understanding prefixes and suffixes can often help you work out the meaning of unfamiliar words in a reading text.

1 Related words are formed from the same base or stem in the following ways in English:

- by adding a suffix to the end of a word, e.g.:
  agree (v.), agree**ment** (n.), agree**able** (adj.)
  understand (v.), understand**ing** (n., adj.)
- by adding a prefix to the front of a word, e.g.:
  agree (v.), **dis**agree (v.)
  understand (v.), **mis**understand (v.)
- through an internal change to the stem itself, e.g.:
  advi**s**e (v.), advi**c**e (n.)

What words can be formed from the following examples?

1 REALISE   What's the noun?
2 CONFIDENCE   What's the adjective?
3 CHOICE   What's the verb?
4 APPLAUSE   What's the verb?
5 SKILL   What's the adverb?
6 APPEAR   What's the opposite?

2 Complete these sentences with a word formed from the word in capitals.

1 His friends found Peter's strange .... hard to understand. BEHAVE
2 I'd .... you to make an appointment to see the doctor. ADVICE
3 A lot of what I learned on the course was of no .... use. PRACTICE
4 This setback could only .... my determination to succeed. STRONG
5 I don't believe that taking risks which put others in danger is .... ACCEPT
6 You behaved quite .... by leaving such a small child alone. RESPONSIBLE
7 His father .... of his wild exploits and threatened to cut him off. APPROVE
8 His writing is so poor, it's practically .... INTELLIGENT

PRONUNCIATION

Word stress

1 When we add a suffix, does it change the stress of a word? Read these sets of words and mark the stress on each word. Then listen to the recording to check.

Set 1
ATTRACT / ATTRACTIVE
BEHAVE / BEHAVIOUR
DISMISS / DISMISSAL

Set 2
LEGISLATE / LEGISLATION
DISCRIMINATE / DISCRIMINATION
CONTAMINATE / CONTAMINATION

Set 3
VOLUNTARY / VOLUNTEER
ENGINE / ENGINEER
LAUNDRY / LAUNDRETTE

Set 4
ATOM / ATOMIC
MAGNET / MAGNETIC
STRATEGY / STRATEGIC

Set 5
ORIGIN / ORIGINAL / ORIGINALITY
ADVERTISE / ADVERTISEMENT / ADVERTISER

2 When verbs and nouns have the same form, stress is often the only way to distinguish the word class. Read these pairs of sentences aloud with the correct stress on the word in italics. Then listen to the recording to check.

1 a. The researchers carried out a *survey* of several thousand people.
  b. We stood on the summit to *survey* the landscape.
2 a. The store is offering a 20% *discount* on discontinued lines.
  b. The financial markets are likely to *discount* the news of interest rate rises.
3 a. Please *permit* me to help you.
  b. You need a *permit* to park here.
4 a. May I *refill* your glass?
  b. He handed her his glass for a *refill*.
5 a. The *rebels* were arrested and imprisoned.
  b. Teenagers sometimes *rebel* against parental authority.

ENGLISH IN USE 2

1 Look at these sets of sentences. Three sentences in each set contain an extra, wrong word. Identify the extra words, and be ready to explain why they are wrong.

1 Articles (Notes page 200)

1 I'm studying the Economics at university.
2 John takes the train to work every day.
3 During our holiday we had a nice weather.
4 Relax and enjoy the nature in Scotland.

2 Prepositions

1 I'm not used to working with this machine.
2 Mary kindly paid for the bill.
3 Jack was lucky for to win first prize.
4 We reached to our destination at midnight.

3 Phrasal verbs

1 The travellers set off for at dawn.
2 Ted showed up his model of the 'Santa Maria'.
3 Sarah worked harder to make up for lost time.
4 The explorers' food had nearly run out of.

4 Auxiliary verbs

1 We had better leave at 6 a.m. on Saturday.
2 Our guests should have been arrived by now.
3 The robbers may have already be hidden the money.
4 I have been lived here for a long time.

5 Relative and personal pronouns (Notes page 199)

1 The police caught the prisoner who he escaped yesterday.
2 John who had been injured and was unable to continue playing.
3 He assured me the painting was genuine, which it couldn't be.
4 Mary told me a story which I didn't believe it at all.

6 Familiar and unfamiliar phrases

1 Problems with the engine caused lots delay.
2 The pupils went in in alphabetical order.
3 We better leave at 6 a.m. on Saturday.
4 They used to open fires for cooking.

2 Read the short text below straight through. Then read it again and underline the extra, wrong words. There is an extra word in every line.

1	Ultimately, the success of any presentation can only to be measured
2	from the audience's perspective. Although this is simply a common
3	sense, many of us who get so involved in our own subject, or our own
4	nervousness, that we forget to be think about the audience at all.
5	A few years ago I was scheduled to speak up at a telephone company
6	conference. The speaker who he preceded me on the programme
7	was reputed for to be one of the world's leading experts on the technology
8	of communication. He gave what was sounded like a tremendously
9	authoritative speech, most of which it was too technical for me to
10	understand. As it had turned out, most of those attending the conference
11	didn't understand it either. Even if an expert on the technology of
12	communication is not necessarily an expert at the communicating.

Getting to the top

SPEAKING 1

1

1 Work in pairs. Choose two photographs each and take turns to talk about them. Answer these questions.

1 What kind of success does each photograph represent: material, artistic ...?

2 What factors are most important to achieve these different types of success? For example:

- natural talent
- education and training
- hard work
- knowing the right people
- good luck
- drive and ambition

2 Do you agree or disagree with what your partner said? Say what kind of success you think is most important.

2 Look at this list. Which of the following would you like to do? Choose three and rank them in order of their attractiveness to you. Then compare your list with a partner and explain your choices.

- write a best-selling novel
- win an Olympic medal
- discover a cure for a disease which is now incurable
- be an entertainer who could make people laugh all around the world
- start a business which would employ thousands of people
- arrest a large number of dangerous criminals and put them behind bars
- invent a means of travelling to distant planets in a reasonable time

Language Bank

Expressing priorities

What I would most like to do is to write a best-seller.

I can't think of anything more satisfying than discovering a cure for ...

What's really important to me is to be able to help other people.

For me, the (next) most important thing would be to ...

Winning a medal wouldn't appeal to me much/at all.

LISTENING 1

Exam File: Part 4, Multiple matching

The task below is another example of a Part 4 question (extracts). Follow this procedure.

- Do the first task on the first listening and the second on the second listening.
- Before you listen, read the questions and think of words you could expect to hear in connection with each extract. Remember to listen for words that confirm the topic. Some words may be used metaphorically.
- For the second task, listen out for the speaker's tone of voice — is he/she happy/depressed, excited/bored, satisfied/frustrated? Understanding the speaker's attitude can help you make the right choice.

1 You will hear five extracts in which various people talk about opportunities taken and lost. Before you listen, look at these words and phrases, and check that you understand them. Which would you expect to hear in connection with options A—F below? Which expression(s) may have more than one meaning depending on the context?

making a mint	the outback
an auction	school
leading title	cattle station
producer	astronomical (adj.)
shares (n.)	bid (v.)

2 🔊 Listen and match each extract as you hear it with the option A—F that best describes the person. There is one statement that does not apply to any of the speakers.

Which speaker is

A a writer? Speaker **1** ....
B an art collector? Speaker **2** ....
C an economist? Speaker **3** ....
D a company director? Speaker **4** ....
E an astronomer? Speaker **5** ....
F a farmer?

3 🔊 Now listen again and decide which of these statements best sums up each situation. Match the summaries (A—F) with the speakers (1—5).

Which speaker

A is determined not to make the same mistake again? Speaker **1** ....
B has become very rich? Speaker **2** ....
C had his life changed for the better by a phone call? Speaker **3** ....
D got a job with a large company?
E has done well but thinks he could have done better? Speaker **4** ....
F missed a chance to make a lot of money? Speaker **5** ....

4 🔊 Listen to extracts 2, 3 and 5 again and answer these questions.

1 Who do you sympathise with most?
2 Would you have acted the same or differently in that situation?

LANGUAGE STUDY

Hypothesis (Notes pages 200—201)

Wish/If only

1 What we wish is always contrary to reality or fact. Read these examples of wishes. What are the facts?

a. I wish I hadn't hesitated.
   Fact: I hesitated.
b. If only he'd listened to his friend's advice.
   Fact: He didn't listen to his friend's advice.
c. I wish I'd studied harder at school.
d. I wish we had a bigger house.
e. If only I was/were rich!
f. Mark wishes he was/were at the beach.
g. I wish I could spend more time with my children.
h. I wish my neighbours would make less noise.
i. Ann wishes her husband would find a better job.
j. I wish I wasn't/weren't leaving tomorrow.
k. If only I didn't have to go to work on Monday.

2 Now answer these questions.

1 Which examples express a desire for something to be different:

   • in the past?   • now?   • in the future?

   What tense forms do we use to show hypothetical meaning?

2 What do you notice about the first person form of the verb *be* after *wish/if only*?

2 Which of these sentences are wrong? Why? Can you correct them?

1 I wish I would have my own flat.
2 I wish I had my own flat.
3 I wish you would have your own flat.
4 I wish you would buy your own flat and move out.
5 I wish you would give up smoking.
6 I wish I would give up smoking.

3 Re-express the ideas in these sentences using *I wish* and *If only*. Write one sentence for each situation.

1 I was really lazy at school. I regret that now.

2 I didn't see the Statue of Liberty when I was in New York. That was a pity.

3 I've got to go for an interview tomorrow. I'm not looking forward to it!

4 I'm very bad at Maths. It's a bit unfortunate, because I need it in my job.

5 Sally has a dentist's appointment next week. She doesn't really want to go!

6 I got married at 19. I realise now that I was too young!

7 I can't drive. That can be a real handicap.

8 My sister is always pestering me to help her with her homework, but I don't have the time.

Regret

1 Read these examples. What structures can follow the verb *regret*? Which happened first, the feeling of regret or the action?

a. He regretted *his decision* to set up his own business.
b. I'll always regret *not buying a place in Australia.*
c. Mary is beginning to regret *giving her honest opinion of the proposals.*
d. Many people regret *that they didn't study harder at school.*
e. He immediately regretted *what he had said.*

2 Now read these examples. When *regret* is followed by *to*-infinitive, which comes first, the feeling of regret or the action?

a. We regret *to inform* you that your application has been unsuccessful.
b. The company regrets *to announce* that the plant is to close next year.
c. I regret *to tell* you that we have just received some bad news.

Note that the verbs usually used in this pattern are verbs of saying. Would you expect to find this type of sentence more often in spoken or written English?

5 What would you say in the following situations, using *regret*?

1 You have to tell someone their 'winning' lottery ticket is a forgery.
2 You want to apologise for something you said.
3 You wish you had stayed longer in a town you liked.
4 You wish you hadn't given up your previous job.

6 Complete each of these sentences so they are true for you. Use a different structure each time.

1 I have never regretted ...
2 I'll always regret ...
3 One day I may regret ...

> **!** *regretfully / regrettably*
>
> What is the difference in meaning?
>
> a. *Regretfully*, he turned away from Maria's house and walked towards the station.
> b. *Regrettably*, our request for help was turned down.

Mixed conditional sentences

7 Read these examples and answer the questions below.

a. If you buy shares in a company, you become a shareholder with voting rights.
b. If you buy shares in that company, you will become very rich.
c. If you bought shares in that company, you would become very rich.
d. If you had bought shares in that company, you would have become very rich.

1 What tense forms are used in the *if*-clause and in the main (result) clause in each example?
2 Which example refers to something that:
 • is likely to happen?
 • is generally true?
 • is contrary to fact or unreal?
 • is unlikely to happen?

8 The tense/time combinations in the examples above are very common. But other combinations are also possible.

1 Read the examples and answer the questions.

a. If he had stayed in Australia, he might have bought his own farm.
b. He would be a rich man if he had bought shares in the company.
c. If I didn't have family responsibilities, I could have spent a year travelling round the world.
d. If he had gone to college, his job prospects would be better.
e. If I knew the answer, I would have told you last week.

1 What time is referred to in each clause in these examples?
2 What do you notice about the use of commas in the examples?

2 🖭 Try saying the sentences aloud as quickly as you can. Then listen to the recording and compare!

9 Read these sentences. Can you identify the two that are incorrect and correct them? What special meaning is expressed in sentence 2? Who might say this?

1 If you're late, I'll wait for you.
2 If you would come with me, I'll take you to the director's office.
3 If you had've been there, you would've seen us.
4 John would still be working there if the company had paid him a good salary.
5 You would be able to finish earlier if you would start earlier.
6 If the price'd been lower, I think I'd've bought it.
7 If you would like a free ticket, there are plenty available.
8 If I can do it, so can you.

10 Use your imagination to complete these sentences.

1 If my parents had emigrated to America when I was a child, ...
2 If I was/were good at physics, ...
3 If I had been born a hundred years ago, ...
4 I wouldn't be sitting here now if ...
5 I would be a millionaire if ...
6 I might have become a famous singer if ...

READING

Multiple choice questions test your detailed understanding of a text. There are usually 5—6 questions which follow the order of the text. All four options will be referred to in the text. Here is a suggested procedure.

- Skim the text quickly to find out what it's about.
- Read the stems (the words that introduce the options) before you read the text more carefully. Don't read the four options yet.
- As you read, note down answers to the questions or highlight those parts of the text which contain the answers. This will help you eliminate obviously incorrect options later.
- Read the options and choose the right answer, referring to the parts of the text you have highlighted.

1

1 Read the title of the article opposite and the first paragraph. How would **you** answer the question in the title? Make a short list of the things that you most regret, then compare your list with a partner's. Are your regrets mostly about things you **have** done or things you **haven't** done?

2 Quickly read the rest of the text and find answers to these questions.

1 What two types of regret have psychologists identified? How are they different?
2 Which type is more important in people's lives?
3 What do people express most regrets about?
4 What do people **not** regret?

2 Find these words and phrases and discuss with your partner what they mean. The context provides various clues. Look for:

- a definition or explanation.
- examples that clarify the meaning.
- repeated occurrences of the word(s).
- words in the text that have a similar or opposite meaning.

1 take stock of *(line 2) Compare line 97.*
2 foundered *(line 5) This is an example of 'things that failed'.*
3 failing to seize the day *(line 10) Look for an explanation in the same sentence and other occurrences in lines 83/98.*

4 over the long term *(line 12) Look for other related phrases in lines 53, 56, 72–3.*
5 inevitable *(line 32) Look for an explanation in the following sentence.*
6 figure prominently *(line 71) The word 'But' introduces a contrast with the previous sentence.*
7 cited *(line 75) Look for another occurrence in line 84 and an alternative word in line 89.*

3 For the multiple choice exercise, follow the last three steps in the Exam File. Be prepared to explain your answers and why the other options are incorrect. Question 1 has been done as an example.

1 What is emerging in new studies of regret?
A a confirmation of traditional beliefs
Incorrect. The text says that research 'findings are painting a new portrait of regret'.
B a recognition of the need for more education
Incorrect. The text refers to 'bad grades in school' as a possible cause of regret, but does not mention general educational standards.
C the importance of romance in people's lives
Incorrect. The reference to 'a romance that foundered' is just another example of a possible cause for regret.
D an enlarged view of this topic
Correct. The text refers to findings 'painting a new portrait' which 'is far more complex than once thought'.

2 According to Janet Landman, people are not keen to discuss regret because
A it can lead to negative feelings.
B it makes them feel embarrassed.
C it produces physical symptoms.
D it makes them feel inferior.

3 Psychologists view regret as something
A that should be accepted philosophically.
B that was avoidable in the past.
C that cannot be avoided in today's world.
D that takes different forms in various historical periods.

4 Research indicates that 'hot' regret
A is related to what other people do to you.
B is concerned with long-term effects.
C relates to physical actions.
D is less significant than 'wistful' regret.

5 According to research, people regret
A events that cause grief.
B the way they are treated by their families.
C chances that were not exploited.
D the way they were educated.

What do people most regret? – The paths they failed to take

When people sit back and take stock of their lives, do they regret the things that failed, such as a romance that foundered, the wrong career path chosen, bad grades in school? Or do they most regret what they failed to try?

A small but growing body of research points to inaction — failing to seize the day — as the leading cause of regret in people's lives over the long term. These findings are painting a new portrait of regret, an emotion proving to be far more complex than once thought.

Regret is a "more or less painful emotional state of feeling sorry for misfortunes, limitations, losses, transgressions, shortcomings or mistakes," says University of Michigan psychologist Janet Landman, author of several studies and a book on regret.

"As a culture, we are so afraid of regret, so allergic to it, often we don't even want to talk about it," Landman says. "The fear is that it will pull us down the slippery slope of depression and despair."

But psychologists say that regret is an inevitable fact of life.

"In today's world, in which people arguably exercise more choice than ever before in human history, it is exceedingly difficult to choose so consistently well that regret is avoided entirely," say Cornell University psychologists Thomas Gilovich and Victoria Medvec.

Regret involves two distinct types of emotion, what psychologists call 'hot' and 'wistful'. Hot regret is quick anger felt after discovering that you have made a mistake, like denting your car, accidentally dropping a prized vase and seeing it smash into a thousand pieces, or buying a share that suddenly plummets in price. This is when you want to kick yourself, and it is associated with a short-term perspective.

Wistful regret, on the other hand comes from having a longer range perspective. It is a bittersweet feeling that life might have been better or different if only certain actions had been taken. Typically, it means something that people should have done but didn't do. That might mean having the courage to follow a different career, gambling on starting a new business or pursuing what appears to be a risky romance.

Psychologists have focused on hot regret as the type most common to people's experience. But a growing body of research suggests that wistful regret may figure more prominently in people's lives over the long term.

Asked to describe their biggest regrets, participants most often cited things they failed to do. People said such things as, "I wish I had been more serious in college," "I regret that I never pursued my interest in dance," "I should have spent more time with my children."

In a study of 77 participants, the researchers found that failure to seize the moment was cited by a 2 to 1 ratio over other types of regret. The group, which included retired professors, nursing-home residents, undergraduates and staff members at Cornell University, listed more than 200 missed educational opportunities, romances and career paths, as well as failing to spend more time with relatives, pursue a special interest or take a chance.

"As troubling as regrettable actions might be initially, when people look back on their lives, it seems to be their regrettable failures to act that stand out and cause most grief." Gilovich and Medvec conclude.

Studies suggest that regrets about education are overwhelmingly the biggest. "Not getting enough education, or not taking it seriously enough, is a common regret even among highly educated people," says Janet Landman.

Tied for a distant second place are regrets about work or love. People talk about having gotten into the wrong occupation, marrying too young, or that they wish their parents had never divorced, or there were fewer conflicts in their family, or that their children had turned out better.

Many people also express regrets about themselves. They may wish they had been more disciplined or more assertive or had taken more risks. The best example of this kind of regret is the lament of one of Woody Allen's characters, "I have only one regret, and that is that I am not someone else."

What people don't regret, however, are events that seem to be beyond their control. Personal responsibility is central to the experience of regret, according to Gilovich and Medvec. "People might bemoan or curse their bad fate, but they rarely regret it in the sense that the term is typically understood."

Their studies found that older people expressed slightly more regrets than did young people. There is no solid evidence that regret increases as life goes on but regrets are likely to change throughout life.

For example, according to Janet Landman, young women are more likely to report family oriented regrets than young men. But by middle age men are more likely than women to regret not spending enough time with their families.

And what do middle-aged women regret? Marrying too early and not getting enough education.

Woody Allen: American comic actor and director

> **!** *Linking ideas: concession*
>
> In this extract from the text on page 37, the clause in italics introduces a contradiction to the idea in the main clause.
>
> (As) *troubling as regrettable actions might be initially,* when people look back on their lives, it seems to be their regrettable failures to act that stand out ... *(line 95)*
>
> Try rewriting the sentence using the link words a) *although* b) *but*. What happens to the position of the adjective *troubling*?

4 Discuss this question.

Think of important crossroads in your life. How might your life 'have been better or different if only certain actions had been taken'?

VOCABULARY

Collocation

1

1 Find and underline all the occurrences of the word *career* in the text on page 37. What other words does it collocate with? List all the combinations you can find under these headings.

Verb	+ Noun
....	a career

Adjective	+ Noun
....	career

Noun	+ Noun
career	....

Noun	+ Preposition + Noun
a career	in/as

2 Here are some more words that collocate with *career*. Add them to the appropriate tables above. Can you add more of your own?

strategy / film / successful / sacrifice / an actor / prospects / choice / political / pursue / developments / publishing / launch / medicine

2 Write some sentences about yourself using the word partnerships you have listed. For example:

I would like to pursue a career in/as ...

My career prospects are ...

3 Make a note of any other collocations from the text on page 37 that you think are useful and would like to learn.

Style and register

4 The text on page 37 is written in a fairly formal style. Match these phrases from the text with their less formal equivalents.

1 transgressions *(line 20)*
2 shortcomings *(line 20)*
3 pursue a special interest *(line 93)*
4 bemoan their fate *(line 133)*

A complain about their situation
B take up a new hobby
C wrong actions
D faults

5 The text below is written in a formal style. Rewrite it, replacing the words and phrases in italics with these informal expressions. Notice how the whole style of the text changes when you do this.

jumped at / dropped out of / handled / looked after / Talk about luck. / a mint / taking over / fancied / went bust / go up / pretty low / set up

I (1) *decided not to complete my studies at university* a few years ago and to (2) *establish* a business with a friend. He (3) *was responsible for* the financial side of things and I (4) *was in charge of* sales. He said we would make (5) *a large profit*, but we didn't have enough capital. Then interest rates started to (6) *increase* and the company (7) *became bankrupt* last year. I had been feeling (8) *quite depressed*, but then my girlfriend's father retired and he asked me if I (9) *would be interested in* (10) *becoming the manager* of his company. Of course, I (11) *welcomed* this opportunity. (12) *I was fortunate indeed.*

BANX

LISTENING 2

Exam file: Part 2, Note completion

Part 2 of the Listening Paper is often a monologue. It lasts about two minutes, and is heard only once. The task tests understanding of informational language, and answers can be numbers, dates, names and topic words. Here are some tips.

- Before listening, read through the notes and try to identify the type of information required. For example, is the answer a number?
- The information you need for your answer may be mentioned in two different ways in different parts of the recording, so you will get a second chance to check an answer you're not sure of. For example, if you hear '12 weeks' you may later hear the same information as '3 months'.

1 You will hear part of a radio programme about vacation work for students. First, discuss these questions.

1 Is it common for students to do vacation work in your country? What sort of jobs do students typically do?

2 Have you ever had a vacation job? Describe it.

2 📼 Before you listen, decide which type of answers are possible for questions 1—8 below. Then listen and complete the notes according to what you hear, using a word or number.

Vacation work for students

Film extra

No need to have (1) ....

Daily rate of pay: (2) ....

Costume and food provided

It's useful to have extra (3) ....

Nanny

Minimum length of contract: (4) ....

Includes board and lodging and free

(5) ....

Tourist Guide

Most important requirement is (6) ....

Minimum age: (7) ....

Geographical area: (8) ....

3 Discuss these questions.

1 If you had the chance, which of the vacation jobs mentioned in the recording would you prefer to do?

2 What are the advantages and disadvantages of each?

PRONUNCIATION

Weak forms

1 📼 Listen to the recording **Vacation work for students** again, and fill in the missing, unstressed words in these extracts. What kind of words are they?

1 Those .... us working on the Holiday Special Programme know .... many .... our student listeners .... always on the lookout .... that holiday with .... difference, something .... won't cost .... fortune

2 Have you ever wanted .... see .... name up in lights or .... least on the big screen .... the local cinema? There's .... demand .... people .... all shapes, sizes and ages .... walk-on parts

2

1 📼 Read these exchanges. Would you expect the words in italics to be weak or strong? Mark the stressed words, then listen to the recording and check.

1 **A:** Where are you *from*?
   B: I'm *from* South America.

2 **A:** How long *are* you planning *to* stay?
   B: I'll stay *as* long *as* I need *to*.

3 **A:** Who's the present *for*?
   B: It's *for* Peter.

4 **A:** What's *your* sweater made *of*?
   B: I think it's made *of* wool. What about *yours*?

5 **A:** Did you see *that* Western *that* was on TV last night?
   B: Yes, it's one *of* my favourite films.

6 **A:** Which job have you applied *for*?
   B: I've applied *for* the one *that's* well-paid!

2 Practise the exchanges with a partner, using the correct stress.

SPEAKING 2

1 Work in pairs. Look at the pictures and the captions. Imagine that three of these experiences are being offered as the first, second and third prizes in a talent competition for young people. The organisers of the competition have asked you to help them decide which prizes they should offer and in what order.

2 Report your decisions to the rest of the class. Say if you agreed or disagreed with each other.

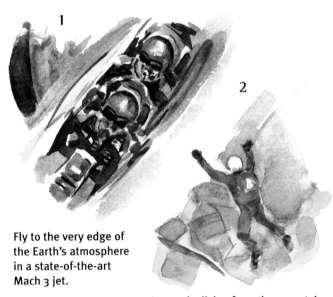

3

Fly to the very edge of the Earth's atmosphere in a state-of-the-art Mach 3 jet.

Learn skydiving from the experts!

A guaranteed role as an extra in a major Hollywood movie!

4

A one-year round the world voyage on a sailing yacht. Brave the dangers of the deep!

5

A one-year apprenticeship with a world-class expert in a field that interests you.

Language Bank

Asking for an opinion

What do you think? / What's your opinion?

Which one do you think would appeal most to young people?

Agreeing ...

Yes, that's what I think too. / I entirely agree with you. / That's a good point.

... and disagreeing

I'm not sure I agree with that.

I understand what you're saying, but ...

Wouldn't you say that ... / Don't you think that ...?

I'm afraid I don't agree at all.

I think we'll have to agree to differ!

Reporting conclusions

We've decided that the first prize should be ... because ... / We both felt that ...

ENGLISH IN USE

In Part 6 you have to re-insert six sentences, clauses or phrases into a text. You are given 10 options to choose from. This question tests how well you understand the text, your knowledge of grammatical patterns, and your understanding of cohesion (how relationships between different parts of a text are signalled in English).

When deciding if a sentence fits a particular gap in a text, ask yourself these questions:

- Does it make sense in the context?
- Is it grammatically correct? Does the correct structure come next? Does the punctuation help?
- Are there any vocabulary links between the sentences or clauses, e.g. repeated words, synonyms, antonyms?
- Are there any reference words like *he/it/this/that* referring to a previous sentence? Are there any link words like *However/In contrast* etc.?

The exercises below focus on using meaning and structure clues.

1 Decide which option (A, B or C) best completes each of these sentences. The first one has been done for you as an example.

1 When we first meet people we cannot avoid judging them
   A to form opinions about them.
   This is grammatically correct but doesn't make sense because it repeats the meaning of 'judging them'.
   B what kind of people they are.
   This is grammatically incorrect: you can use a pronoun or a clause as the object of 'judge' but not both together.
   C by their appearance.
   This is the only one which is grammatically correct and makes sense.

2 Often, people's facial expressions are a better guide than their words
   A to what they are saying.
   B to what they are feeling.
   C to what they are showing.

3 Research shows that we regard people as attractive
   A having faces that are symmetrical.
   B with symmetrical faces.
   C if their faces are symmetrical.

2 Read the article below, ignoring the gaps, to make sure you have a good idea of what it's about. What conclusions does it draw about the relationship between appearance and self-confidence?

3 Read the text again and choose from the list A—H the best phrase to fill the gaps 1—5. In this exercise, there are only five gaps and two phrases that don't fit, whereas in the exam there will be six gaps and four distractors. The first gap has been done for you as an example.

In Quest of the Ideal Image

Physical attractiveness can affect the personality. Of course, notions of what makes a person attractive have changed throughout history and from culture to culture. For instance, the Western ideal of beauty today is (0) .H. . It was not always so, nor is it likely to remain the same in the future. However, within the same culture at any given time, most people agree on (1) .... .

Most people also tend to think that someone with good looks is confident and socially adept. These perceptions do seem (2) .... . No doubt part of the explanation is that a person (3) .... tends to develop more self-confidence in dealing with others. In contrast, a less attractive person may seldom have experienced the same kind of ego-building feedback in social situations.

Differential treatment based on appearance seems to begin early in life. In one experiment, women were shown pictures (4) .... . The women saw the attractive children's behaviour as temporary, but judged the less attractive ones (5) .... .

A who has been treated as attractive
B why attractive people are self-confident
C to have serious behavioural problems
D of attractive and unattractive children misbehaving
E which individuals are more or less attractive
F to hold true up to a point
G depicting children of different ages
H to be tanned, slim and athletic

WRITING

Exam File: Part 1, Formal letter

In Part 1 of the Writing Paper, you have to base your answer on the input material provided. There can be up to three pieces of input material (no more than 400 words). Remember to read the instructions carefully and highlight the points you have to cover in your answer. When you are selecting ideas from the input material, make sure you:

- select only relevant information.
- paraphrase rather than copy whole sentences.
- use the correct register for your piece of writing, which may be different from the input.

Read the writing task on page 43 carefully and follow the **Steps to Writing** below.

Step 1 Task interpretation

Identify what the task requires. What text type do you have to produce? Who will read it? What is your purpose in writing? What will be the most appropriate register and tone? How will you begin and end it?

Step 2 Selecting and summarising

Read the input material, and decide what information you need to include.

1 Highlight the discrepancies between what the advertisement promised and the reality, as indicated by the diary entry and the handwritten notes. Which of these items will you complain about in your letter?

flight / Florida climate / cost / traffic / hotel amenities / hotel staff / airport transfers

2 Complete these notes.

Advertisement	Reality
bargain price moderately priced restaurants	lots of extra charges restaurants very expensive

Step 3 Layout and organisation

Organise your ideas into paragraphs. How many paragraphs will you need to write in your letter? What is the best order for the points you want to make?

Refer back to Unit 1, page 19, to check how a formal letter is laid out. Note down any useful vocabulary.

Step 4 Write

1 Think carefully about how to formulate your ideas when you write your letter. Remember that you should avoid 'lifting' phrases from the input. A change of register will be required when going from the language of the diary to the language of your letter.

2 Try to include a range of vocabulary and structures for interest and variety. Use linking words and phrases to connect your ideas.

1 How many ways can you think of to combine these sentences?

> I have just returned from a holiday. It was in Florida. It was organised by your company. Regrettably, the holiday did not meet my expectations. It was supposed to be a dream holiday. It turned out to be a nightmare.

2 What linking expressions can you use here?

> The hotel was not 'close' to the beach, . . . at least two miles away. . . ., the air conditioning didn't function properly . . . the fridge was always empty. . . . I complained to the hotel manager on numerous occasions, these problems were never remedied. . . . the manager was rude and unhelpful.

3 Now write your letter.

▶ Regret (page 34)
▶ Language Bank (page 43)

Step 5 Evaluate and edit

When you have finished, re-read and evaluate your work carefully. Make any necessary corrections.

▶ Writing checklist (page 214)

You recently went on a holiday to Florida, USA, arranged by Getaway Holiday Tours. However, the holiday did not turn out as you had expected. Some of the features offered in the company's advertisement were not available, and you were dissatisfied with other aspects.

Read the extract from your diary and the holiday advertisement with your handwritten comments. Then, using the information carefully, write a **letter** to the holiday company explaining why you are dissatisfied and asking them for compensation. You should use your own words as far as possible.

Write approximately 250 words. You do not need to include addresses.

Language Bank

Complaining, pointing out discrepancies

I regret to have to inform you that ...

Your advertisement offered ... /stated/claimed that ..., but in fact/as it turned out ...

Your advertisement failed to mention the fact that ...

As far as the hotel amenities are concerned, ... / As regards the hotel amenities, ...

I very much regret choosing ...

I feel that I am entitled to compensation for ...

I would be grateful if you would reply by return of post.

Link words: adding points

In addition, ... / On top of that, ... / To make matters worse, ...

Get away
from it all

Now's your chance to take your dream holiday in Florida at a genuine <u>bargain price</u>.

Stay in a luxury hotel with <u>three swimming pools</u>, choice of <u>moderately priced restaurants</u>, beautiful gardens and <u>helpful staff</u>.

Close to the beach.

Convenient comfortable transfer to <u>local airport</u>

<u>Budget car hire</u>

Call Getaway Holiday Tours

0014 375 3687

July

9 Thursday

Just arrived at the hotel — exhausted. Flight was delayed for twelve hours and the airline has lost one of my suitcases. This hotel is appalling — it overlooks a flyover. It's so hot and noisy and smelly. The air-conditioning doesn't help much. The beach seems to be miles away. I wish I'd never even thought of coming here. It's looking like a big mistake. If only I'd listened to my mum! I hope there is something good in the fridge because I'm desperate for a long, cold drink.
(Just had a look — totally empty!)

what about extra charges — there were a lot!

only one and it was dirty

actually very expensive

scruffy and impolite

200 km away

only expensive cars available

Amusing yourself

SPEAKING 1

1 Work in pairs. Take turns to talk about one of these cartoons. Answer these questions.

1 What is happening?

2 What point do you think the cartoon is making?

3 Do you find the cartoon funny? If you do, can you explain why? If you don't, is it because a) you can't see what's funny or b) you can see what's supposed to be funny, but you're not amused?

2 Comment on what your partner said. Do you agree? Say which cartoon you find funnier.

1

'OK – I'll hold'

3

2

1 In pairs, take turns to tell each other one of these jokes. Did your partner get the joke? Did the jokes make you laugh?

1 After their fourth defeat in succession, the players in the football team were so angry they threw their coach in the river. They had to bring a crane to get it out.

2 A man said to his friend, 'We have a real problem in our family. My brother thinks he's a chicken.'
His friend replied, 'Why don't you take him to see a psychiatrist so that he can be cured?'
'We can't do that,' said the man. 'We need the eggs.'

3 Patient: Nobody listens to anything I say.
Doctor: Next!

4 Question: Why did the chicken cross the football pitch?
Answer: Because the referee shouted 'foul'!

5 Question: How do you know when there is an elephant under your bed?
Answer: Your nose is touching the ceiling.

2 Which joke(s) relies on:
- one of the words having a double meaning?
- displacement, where an obvious conclusion is replaced by an unexpected one in the punchline?

VOCABULARY 1

Homophones

1 Homophones are words that have the same pronunciation but a different spelling and a different meaning. A lot of jokes are made with homophones, for example joke 4 above.

1 How many homophones can you think of for these words? Write them down.

1	roar [/rɔː/]	7	weigh [/weɪ/]
2	taut [/tɔːt/]	8	brake [/breɪk/]
3	meet [/miːt/]	9	pear [/peə/]
4	sea [/siː/]	10	heir [/eə/]
5	write [/raɪt/]	11	herd [/hɜːd/]
6	site [/saɪt/]	12	through [/θruː/]

2 Underline the different spellings that can be used to represent the same vowel sound. For example:

r<u>oar</u>   r<u>aw</u>   t<u>au</u>t

2 Read these pairs of words and decide if they are homophones or not. Then listen to the recording to check your answers.

1	soar	saw	8 wonder	wander
2	walk	work	9 role	roll
3	mood	mud	10 bear	beer
4	choose	chews	11 born	borne
5	hall	whole	12 advise	advice
6	lip	leap	13 lose	loose
7	real	reel	14 life	live

Words with more than one meaning

3 Many words have more than one meaning, and jokes often make use of the ambiguity that results, as in joke 1 opposite. Read these sentences. What is the meaning of the word in italics in the given context? What other meanings does the word have? Write a sentence to illustrate a different meaning.

1 Lara couldn't hurt anyone. It's not in her *nature* to be cruel.
2 What he told the police *bears* no relationship to what actually happened.
3 The play offers good *light* entertainment for all the family.
4 Alfred Nobel was the *founder* of the Nobel Prize.
5 Small and fat, Roger was the *butt* of many jokes at school.
6 She wore a diamond ring in a gold *setting*.
7 In American football, you're allowed to *tackle* members of the other team.
8 You can see my house in the *background* of the photograph.
9 'We're going to keep you in hospital under *observation* for a few more days.'
10 Susanna has a Master's *degree* in Business Administration.

READING

Exam File: Part 1, Multiple matching

One of the multiple matching questions in the Reading Paper may ask you to identify in which section of a text a particular item occurs. Follow this procedure.

- Skim read the text to get an idea of what it's about.
- Read the prompts, highlighting key words.
- Try to guess which section the prompt refers to, and scan that section first.

1 You are going to read a text about humour. Before you read, match these words and phrases with the appropriate definition below.

1 deride
2 malevolent
3 inhibitions
4 a taboo subject
5 subversive

A something that weakens an accepted belief
B something that isn't usually discussed
C wanting to cause harm
D feelings that make natural behaviour impossible
E make fun of in an unpleasant way

2

1 Read the first section of the text only (Introduction). What three different concepts of humour are described? Complete these sentences.

1 Plato believed that humour was ...
2 Sigmund Freud's view was that humour can ...
3 Recently, psychologists have emphasised ...

2 Now read the headings of the remaining sections. In which section do you expect to find a discussion of these concepts?

3 For the multiple matching exercise, follow the steps suggested in the Exam File. In this task, you have 11 items to match. In the exam, you will have to match 12 items or more.

Which part (A, B, C or D) refers to the following points?

the fact that comedians learn to be funny early in life	1 ....
a change in attitude over the centuries	2 ....
the effect being in a group has on the way a remark is perceived	3 ....
the personal factors that can affect the way an individual reacts to a joke	4 ....
the fundamental psychology of comedians	5 ....
how humour can help you gain influence over others	6 ....
the subversive nature of humour	7 ....
the unpredictability that is a characteristic of jokes	8 ....
criticism of those who make fun of others	9 ....
how subjects that are normally forbidden can be raised	10 ....
the benefits of humour in commercial transactions	11 ....

4 Find these words in the text and use the clues provided by the context to work out their meaning. Can you explain the meaning, using a synonym, a definition or examples?

1 incongruity *(line 20)*
2 rebound on *(line 37)*
3 lose face *(line 55)*
4 make/win concessions *(lines 55, 60)*
5 hilarious *(line 66)*
6 standing *(line 74)*
7 cope with *(lines 82, 101)*
8 defiance *(line 86)*

5 How far do you agree with the views expressed in section C? Can you describe any personal experiences which illustrate these views?

Raising a smile

Introduction (A)

HISTORICALLY, humour has often been seen in a very negative way. For example, about two and a half thousand years ago, Plato, the famous Greek philosopher, wrote about the 'malevolent nature of humour'. For him, it meant
5 trying to give yourself a sense of superiority by making fun of other people, and he taught that only people of lesser worth did this.

Modern psychology, however, regards humour with more respect. Sigmund Freud, the founder of
10 psychoanalysis, saw laughter as a means of safely discharging nervous energy. It provides relief and self-gratification and makes potentially damaging conflicts harmless. While this approach is still very influential, more recent work in psychology has also focused on the social
15 value of being funny, the useful role of the well-timed joke or light remark in everyday encounters.

What is a joke? (B)

What, exactly, is a joke? Why do we laugh at certain kinds of stories and what are the essential characteristics of being funny? For humour to exist, there must be an essential
20 incongruity — an unexpected conflict or inconsistency between two ideas which is resolved as a joke. This may come about because the punch line bears an unexpected relationship to the opening part of the story. This corny old joke also relies on a simple double meaning:

25 My dog has no nose.
Then how does he smell?
Terrible!

Another regular feature of humour is 'displacement'. Here the most obvious interpretation of the situation is displaced by a
30 less obvious or expected one. Take, for example, a typical psy-chiatrist joke:

Doctor, I keep thinking that there are two of me.
OK, but don't both speak at once.

Appreciation of humour depends very much on your
35 reference point. Group loyalties, political opinions and ethnic background all influence the way a joke is received and how funny people find it. Because of this, a joke can rebound on the teller. One story, for example, begins by making women the butt of a male chauvinist observation, but then the sting is in
40 the tail of the joke: 'Women are born without a sense of humour so that they can love men without laughing at them.'

The advantage of being funny (C)

Studies of persuasion have revealed that humorous people are perceived as being more likeable, and this in turn enables them to have greater influence. In one experiment, trained
45 psychology graduates played the role of sellers in a bargaining situation. They were to bargain with people over the price of a painting. Some were instructed to take a humorous approach, while others made no jokes at all and bargained in a straightforward, serious way. It was found that the dealers with
50 the more light-hearted attitude were able to get a significantly higher price for the painting. What humour does, in this context, is to reduce the buyer's feelings of threat and anxiety and to establish a more relaxed relationship with the seller. Both trust and attraction are increased and the buyer feels
55 able to make concessions without losing face.

The implications of this study are quite important. If humour can aid the salesman, then it can also work in a similar way with the buyer. Making jokes which do not threaten the self-esteem of the person who is trying to sell you a car or a
60 new refrigerator may allow you to win concessions. Humour can be used as a persuader in other social contexts and is useful in opening conversations with the opposite sex. Establishing a relaxed mood helps a relationship to develop quickly.

65 Remarks or actions that people would often not see as very funny are sometimes found quite hilarious in group settings. This is the result of an effect known as 'social facilitation'. If one person laughs, then this greatly increases the likelihood that others will, and — because they are laughing — members
70 of the group perceive the object of humour as funnier.

This illustrates one way in which you can increase your influence. If you can get people to laugh with you, then you have already established a degree of leadership that you can later build on. It can also improve your image and standing in
75 conversation with a group of friends.

Releasing and displacing emotions (D)

Many researchers believe that being genuinely funny can only be achieved by returning to a more childlike view of the world. This may be associated with the fact that comedians adopt humour early in life as a way of getting people to like
80 them, and then use it to maintain their attention.

Many comedians have reported that their use of humour developed in early schooldays and was a means of coping with anxiety-producing situations. Such strategies were rewarded with laughter by classmates who lacked the confidence
85 themselves to go against accepted values in the way that most humour requires. Defiance of convention continues into the adult life of comedians. The professionals tackle taboo subjects without inhibition and this gives them considerable social value. By encouraging us to laugh at the subjects that
90 give rise to our anxieties, they help us safely to discharge tensions.

Humour may also be a displacement of aggression. The professional comic is thought by psychoanalysts to be an angry person whose skills allow him to channel his aggression
95 in a socially acceptable and productive manner. Another psychoanalytic view of the personality of comedians suggests that they are depressed people, but with enough strength of character to transfer the depressed emotions into creative expression.
100 For all of us, humour is not only an invaluable social tool; it also provides a useful way of coping with personal frustrations and emotional difficulties. Making a joke about a problem enables us to communicate the nature of our true feelings to others. By laughing about them, we achieve a more relaxed
105 mood in which we are better able to understand and resolve conflicts.

male chauvinist: a man who doesn't respect women and believes they are inferior to men

LANGUAGE STUDY 1

Grammatical cohesion 1

Reference (Notes page 204)

1 In order to make the relationship and development of ideas as clear as possible, written English uses various grammatical devices to signal the links between clauses, sentences and paragraphs.

Pronouns *(he/she/it/our/their/this/that* etc.*)* are often used to refer back to something that has already been mentioned. Sometimes the reference is to a specific word, sometimes to a whole idea.

Find the following pronouns in the text on page 47 and decide what the pronoun refers to in each case.

1 *it* meant *(line 4)*
2 did *this (line 7)*
3 *It* provides *(line 11)*
4 *this* approach *(line 13)*
5 *This* may come about *(line 21)*
6 *this* in turn *(line 43)*
7 *This* is the result of *(line 67)*

2 Pronouns can be used not only to refer back to ideas within the same paragraph, but also to previous paragraphs. Look at these examples from the text and answer the questions.

1 Paragraph 6 (Section C) begins:

   'The implications of *this* study are quite important.'

   What study is being referred to? What conclusions are drawn in paragraph 6?

2 Paragraph 8 (Section C) begins:

   '*This* illustrates one way in which you can increase your influence.'

   What phenomenon is being referred to? What practical conclusion is drawn in paragraph 8?

Conjunction (Notes page 208)

3 Another method of signalling the type of relationship between sentences and ideas is to use conjunctions or link words. Answer these questions about the text on page 47.

1 Find link words in paragraphs 1 and 2 which:
   a. add another point.
   b. introduce an explanation of the previous statement.
   c. signal a contrasting idea.

2 In paragraphs 10 and 11, how many explanations are cited of the underlying psychology of comedians? What link words are used to signal the move from one to the next?

3 Can you think of other link words which perform the same functions?

❗ be to + infinitive

Look at these examples. What time is referred to by the verb *be* + infinitive?

They *were to* bargain with people ... *(text page 47)*

I'*m to* meet the new manager tomorrow.

The hero *was* never *to* see his native land again.

(Notes page 202)

VOCABULARY 2

Word formation

1 In this extract from the text on page 47, the words in italics have been made negative by the use of the prefix *in-*.

'For humour to exist, there must be an essential *incongruity* — an unexpected conflict or *inconsistency* between two ideas, which is resolved as a joke.'

Compare this extract. Does it mean that humour is valuable, very valuable or not valuable at all?

'... humour is an *invaluable* social tool ...'

2 The affixes *in-* and *-less* don't always have a negative meaning. Read these sentences and answer the questions. Can you rewrite the sentences to express the opposite meaning?

1 Your help has been invaluable. *(Would you be pleased if someone said this to you?)*
2 The island is inhabited. *(Are there people on it?)*
3 This liquid is inflammable. *(Will it catch fire?)*
4 This sculpture is priceless. *(Can you afford to buy it?)*

Idiomatic expressions

2 Can you explain or paraphrase these idiomatic expressions, which are all connected with the *face*?

1 I tried to *keep a straight face*, but I couldn't help laughing.
2 Wearing make-up makes me feel more confident. I never leave the house until I've *put my face on*.
3 He'd better not *show his face* round here again after what he did.
4 You've got to *face up to* your responsibilities instead of running away from them.
5 She finally realised her wildest dreams when she met her favourite film star *face to face*.
6 Bob was very upset at not getting a promotion, but he *put a brave face on it* and pretended he didn't mind.
7 His claim that he was abducted by aliens *flies in the face of* reason.

LISTENING 1

Exam File: Part 1, Note completion

In Part 1 of the Listening Paper you will be tested on your ability to take notes as well as complete sentences. Remember to:

- read the incomplete sentences and try to predict the missing words.
- listen for different ways of saying the same thing. The sentences in the task will summarise or rephrase the sentences in the recording.
- check that your sentence makes sense.

---

1 You will hear a radio talk about the positive relationship between humour and health. Before you listen, discuss these questions.

1 Think of reasons why an ability to 'see the funny side of things' might be good for you.
2 In what ways can humour be used to enhance relationships?
3 What do you think might go on at a 'Laughter Clinic'?

2 Now read the notes below, and see if you can predict what the missing information might be.

3 📼 Listen and complete the notes below according to the information you hear on the recording. Use one to three words in each gap.

Laughter, the best medicine

Immunity to diseases is improved by a
(1) ....
Blood pressure is reduced by (2) ....
Laughter clinic:
    first activity is (3) ....
    purpose of group activity is to (4) ....
    ....
    last activity is listening to (5) ....
    ....
Homework:
    spend two minutes thinking about (6) ....
    ....
Where to start each day:
    in front of (7) ....
Attitude of medical profession is (8) ....

4 What do you think of the activities prescribed by the Laughter Clinic? Try one out now. Work in groups. Each group member should try to recount an amusing incident that happened to them recently.

5 Discuss the following well-known sayings. Can you think of examples that show they are true?

1 Laugh and the world laughs with you; weep and you weep alone.
2 He who laughs last laughs longest.
3 A merry heart does good like a medicine.

LANGUAGE STUDY 2

Gerunds and infinitives

Prepositions followed by gerund (Notes page 202)

1 Read these examples. When a verb follows a preposition, what form must it take?

a. Laughter helps to relax the body *by reducing* blood pressure ...
b. Laughter is a way/means of safely *discharging* energy.
c. ... the buyer feels able to make concessions without *losing face* ...
d. It's not *worth getting* upset about things beyond your control.
e. Humorous people are perceived *as being* more likeable.

Choose an appropriate preposition and a verb from the lists to complete the following sentences. A preposition or verb may be used more than once.

by / with / in / without / of / about / to / from

drive / make / be / tell / become / sell / visit / learn / get

1 The comedian succeeded *in making* the audience roar with laughter.
2 John made himself popular .... funny stories.
3 I couldn't leave New York .... the World Trade Centre.
4 They claim that their method is the fastest way .... to speak a language.
5 The barriers across the street prevented me .... past the concert hall.
6 Have you ever thought .... a film extra?
7 I have a friend who's obsessed .... better and better at everything he does.
8 The man admitted .... tickets for the football game illegally.
9 Attractive people have a better chance .... promoted.

Verbs followed by gerund and/or infinitive
(Notes page 202)

2 When a verb is followed by another verb, the second verb must be either a bare infinitive (e.g. *can do*), a *to*-infinitive or a gerund. Some verbs are followed by a gerund but never by a *to*-infinitive. Others are followed by *to*-infinitive but never a gerund. Read these examples, and complete the notes below.

Verb + to-infinitive
a. She couldn't afford to buy a new dress.
b. I agreed to help him.
c. You promised to come, but you didn't.
d. We hope to arrive by 8 p.m.
e. We offered to give him a lift home.

Verb + gerund
f. I enjoy going for long walks at night.
g. We've finished checking the answers.
h. Why do you keep disturbing me?
i. Let's celebrate winning the match with a party.
j. Jack misses being with his friends.

- The .... frequently looks forward: the action of the verb in the .... form happens after the action of the main verb.
- The .... indicates either:
  a) an action or state prior to the action of the main verb, or
  b) the general idea of activity.

3 Underline the correct choice, *to*-infinitive or gerund.

1 He decided *not to rehearse/not rehearsing* his speech.
2 I refused *to lend/lending* him any more money.
3 They denied *to sell/selling* forged tickets.
4 Martin is planning *to change/changing* his job.
5 The film star wore a wig to avoid *to be recognised/being recognised*.
6 I must practise *to drive/driving* in the city.
7 I wanted to *help/helping* but he wouldn't let me.
8 The committee deferred *to make/making* a decision.

4 Some verbs can be followed by either the infinitive or the gerund, with little difference in meaning, for example: *hate, love, like, prefer, begin, continue, start*.

But there is a considerable difference in meaning with these verbs: *remember, forget, stop, try*.

Look at the examples below and identify the difference. Which of the actions/states described by the italicised words happened first?

1 a. He *stopped writing* in his notebook.
   b. He *stopped to write* in his notebook.

2 a. He definitely *remembered seeing* John arrive just after 10 a.m.
   b. Although I was busy, I *remembered to buy* a birthday card.

Which of the following sentences describes a goal? Which describes a course of action?

3 a. I've often *tried to give up* smoking.
   b. Have you *tried chewing gum* as a substitute?

5 Read this story and put the verbs in brackets into the correct form, gerund or *to*-infinitive.

As he walked along the street to the theatre, Tom stopped (1) .... (think) . Had he remembered (2) .... (bring) the tickets? He remembered (3) .... (buy) them a week ago but had he forgotten (4) .... (put) them in his pocket? He checked his pocket — the tickets were there!

Then another thought crept into his mind. Had he forgotten (5) .... (lock) the door of his house? He could remember (6) .... (switch off) the lights, but he had no memory of (7) .... (lock) the door.

At first he thought that he should stop (8) .... (worry) and continue (9) .... (walk) to the theatre, but then he realised that if the door was unlocked, he would regret (10) .... (go) on his way without (11) .... (check). He decided (12) .... (go) back.

Gerund and infinitive nominals (Notes page 203)

6 Gerunds and infinitives may be used as the subject of a sentence, or as complement after verbs such as *be*. For example:

a. *Making jokes* ... may allow you to win concessions.
b. *To know all* is *to forgive all*.
c. It's no use/good *crying over spilt milk*.
d. It isn't very nice *to make fun of other people*.

Note that an introductory *It* is preferred to a *to*-infinitive as subject of a sentence.

Read these sentences. Underline the gerund or infinitive subjects or complements and circle the main verb. Which sentence(s) can you rewrite beginning with *It*?

1 Establishing a relaxed mood helps a relationship to develop quickly.

2 Not getting enough education, or not taking it seriously enough, is a common regret even among highly educated people.

3 It requires courage to follow a different career, start a new business or pursue a risky romance.

4 Wishing someone else would come along and make your dreams come true is no use at all.

5 Not knowing what had happened to the comrades they had grown to love was the worst thing of all for the survivors of the wreck.

6 To be able to help other people in my job is really important to me.

7 Look at these examples. Can you explain

• why the *to*-infinitive is impossible in 1b.?
• why the *-ing* form is impossible in 2b.?

1 a. Winning the Gold Medal brought wealth and fame.
   b. *To win the Gold Medal brought wealth and fame.

2 a. My ambition is to write a best-selling novel.
   b. *My ambition is writing a best-selling novel.

8 Complete these sentences so they are true for you.

1 My favourite way of relaxing is to ...

2 Another way I relax is by ...

3 In my opinion, the best way of dealing with stress is ...

4 I think ... is a good way of making new friends.

LISTENING 2

Exam File: Part 3, Multiple choice questions

In Part 3, you may have to answer 5—7 multiple choice questions. These questions often test your understanding of gist and attitude. You may hear words from incorrect as well as correct options in the recording, so remember to listen carefully for the context. You will hear the recording twice.

Here is a suggested procedure.

* Before listening, read the multiple choice questions but not the options. You may need to turn some stems into questions yourself.

* While listening the first time, note down your answers.

* Before the second listening, read the options carefully and choose the one that best matches your answer.

1

1 You are going to hear someone discuss his hobby, photography. Match these words to the pictures below.

1 flash   2 prints   3 slides   4 projector
5 zoom lens   6 film

2 Now complete these tips for camera buyers. Use these words in the correct form.

wind / shutter / shoot / load

1 To take good pictures at night, use a slow .... speed.
2 Before you .... a picture, spend time composing it.
3 Buy a camera which will .... on your film automatically.
4 In daylight, always .... new film in the shade.

2 📟 Listen and choose the best answer to questions 1—6. Follow the steps in the Exam File and remember to listen carefully to the context.

1 The speaker became interested in the composition of pictures when
  A he began to look at photographs.
  B he did painting at school.
  C he received his first camera.
  D he realised how artificial pictures were.

2 The speaker says that his first camera
  A had been used by someone else.
  B failed to produce good photographs.
  C responded to different light conditions.
  D was difficult to use correctly.

3 The benefit of his second camera was that
  A he produced natural-looking photographs.
  B he developed technical skills.
  C he didn't need any extras.
  D he could use it without much preparation.

4 At school he was able to
  A use specialist facilities.
  B learn from skilled professionals.
  C enter photographic competitions.
  D receive criticism of his work.

5 The speaker recommends slide film if
  A your interest is in technical matters.
  B you want to save money.
  C you have the appropriate equipment.
  D you want to show your work to your friends.

6 The speaker's advice to young photographers is
  A to buy the best equipment you can.
  B to think before you take a picture.
  C to develop your own prints.
  D to get ideas from other enthusiasts.

3 The speaker uses adjectives and adverbs to modify his statements. Complete these extracts with a suitable modifier from the list.

obvious / major / virtually / fairly / extremely

1 My first camera was .... simple.
2 There were some .... disadvantages.
3 You had to be .... organised, too, when taking photographs.
4 A .... disadvantage of slides is that you need to be able to project them.
5 For a reasonable price, you can get a camera that does .... everything for you.

SPEAKING 2

Exam File: Part 2, Describe and compare

In Part 2 of the Speaking Test, you may have to describe and compare a number of pictures. You will have about one minute to talk, not only about the pictures themselves, but also about the themes and ideas suggested by the pictures. When you and your partner have both finished, you will be asked to comment on your partner's observations.

1 Work in pairs. Choose two pictures each and take it in turns to talk about them for about one minute. Answer these questions.

1 What different skills are required by each activity?
2 What kind of people would be attracted by each activity?
3 What are the advantages and disadvantages of each activity?

2 Do you agree or disagree with what your partner said? Justify your answer. Say which activity you would prefer to do and why.

3 Discuss these questions.

1 What are your favourite hobbies and pastimes?
2 What advice would you give to someone who wanted to take up similar hobbies and pastimes?

Language Bank

Describing

You need to be good with your hands/patient/physically fit for this activity.

The kind of person who would like this activity would be out-going/adventurous/sporty/intellectual.

This type of activity is for people who like being outdoors/enjoy competitive games.

Advantages and disadvantages

It gives you a great sense of achievement.

It's a great way of meeting people.

It wouldn't really be difficult to get started.

(Chess) needs very little equipment, whereas (hill-walking) ...

Compared with hill-walking, ...

... is much more intellectually demanding than ...

... is only suitable for people who are very fit.

The problem with ... is that ...

WRITING

Exam File: Part 2, Article

In Part 2 you will have to choose **one** task from a choice of **four**. One of the tasks may involve writing an **article**. An article

- can be informal or formal, depending on the target audience.
- has to appeal to a range of readers.
- has to catch the reader's attention and hold it to the end.

Follow this advice.

- Use a catchy title to attract the readers' attention.
- Make sure your first paragraph is interesting enough to make people want to read on.
- Use clearly differentiated paragraphs, each dealing with a different aspect of the topic. You may find it useful to highlight the key words in the question and base your paragraphs on these. In this way you can be sure that you have covered every aspect of the question. You don't have to give your paragraphs a heading, but if you can think of good ones, use them.
- Use a variety of interesting words and expressions, including adjectives and intensifying adverbs. Avoid boring words like *nice, good, very* etc.

Read the writing task and follow the **Steps to Writing** below.

An international magazine with a teens and twenties readership wants to publish articles by young people in different countries, describing the hobbies, sports or other leisure activities they enjoy doing. Write an **article** for the magazine, discussing the pleasures and challenges involved in your hobby, sport or leisure activity as well as any problems or disadvantages. Also include practical information that would help a person who is thinking of taking it up.

Write approximately 250 words.

Step 1 Task interpretation

Highlight the words in the question that tell you what form the writing will take and who will read it. What will be your purpose in writing? What will be the most appropriate register and tone?

Step 2 Generating ideas

1 What information do you have to include? Notice these key words:

'describe ... / pleasures and challenges / problems or disadvantages / include practical information'

2 Decide what hobby, sport or other leisure activity you are going to write about. If you prefer, you can choose from one of the hobbies below.

- photography
- computers
- playing a musical instrument
- watersports e.g. sailing, windsurfing, diving
- horse-riding

3 Make notes under headings suggested by the task, and list as many useful words and phrases as you can.

Step 3 Layout and organisation

1 How many paragraphs will you write? What order will the paragraphs follow? Here is one possible order.

Paragraph 1: Introduction to the activity — reasons for taking it up OR how you started
Paragraph 2: Examples of pleasures and challenges
Paragraph 3: Possible problems
Paragraph 4: Practical information about how to start, where to go, what to buy etc.

2 Think of a good, catchy title for your article. Can you guess what hobbies these titles are about?

Put yourself in the picture

Adventures on water

GOING DOWN IN THE WORLD

Sounds interesting!

A winter sport guaranteed to raise your temperature

Step 4 Write

1 Your opening paragraph should catch the readers' attention and make them want to read on. Compare these two opening paragraphs. Which do you prefer and why?

A *Have you ever considered taking up photography? If not, why not? Photography can provide you with hours of enjoyment both indoors and out of doors — and you don't have to be an expert to do it! All you need is a camera, some free time and a little creativity.*

B Photography is said to be one of the most rewarding pastimes. However, finding a suitable camera and the correct film can be a time-consuming and expensive business. Nevertheless, once all the necessary equipment has been purchased, it can be a highly enjoyable hobby.

2 Now write your article. Try to include a range of vocabulary and structures for interest and variety. Use linking words to connect your ideas.

▶ Grammatical cohesion (page 48)

▶ Language Bank

Step 5 Evaluate and edit
When you have finished, re-read and evaluate your work carefully. Make any necessary corrections.

▶ Writing checklist (page 214)

Language Bank

My introduction to … was …

I started … when I was …

… has always been a passion of mine.

Advantages and disadvantages

A particularly enjoyable aspect of this hobby is …

One major problem that all beginners have to overcome is …

At first, people are often put off by …

If you really take it seriously, you need to put in a lot of practice/the cost begins to mount up.

Practical information

More information is available from …

If you want expert help/lessons/more training, you can contact …

ENGLISH IN USE 1

Exam File: Part 3, Error correction

In Unit 2, you were introduced to a task type where you had to identify extra, wrong words in a text. Sometimes you may be asked to identify incorrect punctuation and spelling rather than extra words. The punctuation tested can be:

- capital letters for names of people, places etc.
- full stops at the end of sentences
- commas
- use of apostrophes e.g. Jane's bag; don't, wasn't
- punctuation of direct speech

The exercises below focus on the use of commas in English.

1 Combine the items below into a single sentence, adding or subtracting words as necessary. What features must a sentence have?

1 I went to Hollywood.
2 two years ago
3 To study acting.
4 I wanted to get a job as an actor.
5 home of the stars

Check your punctuation after doing the exercises below.

1 Read these examples — first silently, then aloud — and formulate a rule about the use of commas in this sort of sentence.

a. *Historically,* humour has often been seen in a negative way.
b. *If you can get people to laugh with you,* you have already established leadership.
c. *By laughing about our feelings,* we achieve a more relaxed mood.
d. *When I was growing up,* I became fascinated by visual images.
e. *In my teens,* I got my second camera.

2 A comma is less likely to be necessary with final elements. Try moving the introductory elements in the examples above to the end of the sentence, and saying the sentences aloud. Did you have to pause before the final element?

1 Now read the following examples and formulate a rule about the use of commas here.

Adverbial elements

a. I enjoy most sports. Boxing is one sport, *however*, that I don't like.
b. Chess is a game that, *until a friend introduced me to it*, I had always regarded as boring.
c. A good laugh, *it seems*, puts matters into perspective.

Adjective structures

d. Plato, *the famous Greek philosopher*, believed only inferior people used humour.
e. Dave, *a computer consultant*, was obsessed by his hobby.
f. Hollywood, *famous for its film industry*, is an exciting town.

2 What's the effect of the different punctuation in these examples?

a. People who can tell jokes are popular.
b. Susan and Ann, who can tell jokes, are popular.

4 Why are commas used in these examples?

a. I enjoy watching football, basketball, ice hockey and horse racing.
b. I don't like playing cards, playing chess or water-skiing.
c. I learned how to put together a picture, how to balance different shapes and how to create mood.

5

1 Read the text *A Stand-up Comedian* once straight through. What is a stand-up comedian? Why is Basile particularly successful?

2 Now read the text again, and insert the missing commas. There are 11 missing commas.

6 Look at the sentence you constructed in Exercise 1 on page 55. Do you want to make any changes?

A STAND-UP COMEDIAN

Stand-up comedian Basile has appeared on prime time television he's been heard on over 450 radio shows and he's played some of the biggest clubs across the United States. However comedy was not Basile's first career choice. This native New Yorker who now lives in North Carolina played semi-professional football before attending law school. In his final year needing a break from the stress he took a year off to pursue stand-up comedy. That was nine years ago. Since then Basile has used his wit improvisation skills and voice impersonations to build a fast-paced high-energy show. "My act is always on the edge," he says. "I never take it too seriously. I try to touch the inner child of every person. From the beginning to the end you're not sure of what's going to happen." No matter where he performs across the country Basile says he's always looking for the same response from his audience. "I'm not like one of those comedians who stand there with their hands in their pockets and get polite applause for witty remarks. I don't want that. When people are roaring with uncontrollable laughter that to me is what comedy is all about."

ENGLISH IN USE 2

Exam File: Part 1, Multiple choice cloze

The exercise in this section is an example of the Paper 3 multiple choice cloze. The cloze consists of a text with 15 one-word gaps and tests your knowledge of vocabulary and collocation. Here is a suggested procedure.

- Read the whole text first to get an idea of what it is about before reading the options.
- Consider carefully the words around each gap.
- Use your knowledge of collocates and fixed expressions.
- Think about precise words suitable for a particular context.
- Choose the best option for the context of the sentence.

1 Before you read the text below, discuss these questions in groups.

1 Find out how many hours of TV each member of the group watches on average per week.

2 What do you think are the positive benefits of TV? What negative effects can watching TV have? Make two lists.

2 Now read the text straight through. According to the article, what are the negative effects of watching TV?

3 Now read the text again and decide which word (A, B, C or D) best fits each space. Write one letter in each gap.
Note: In this first exercise, there are only 10 gaps, not 15 as in the exam.

Below are some clues to help you.
Question 1: Which **one** word can be followed by *from*?
Question 2: Which **one** word can follow *the*?
Question 3: Which word best fits the context? Read the first sentence again.
Question 4: Which verb collocates with a time phrase?
Question 5: You need a phrasal verb.
Question 6: The phrase is another collocation. Which noun collocates?

4 Discuss this question.

Do you agree with the ideas expressed in the article? Can you give any examples from your own experience that would support these ideas?

Teenage TV addicts prone to crime

TEENAGERS who watch more than four hours television a night are more prone to crime, drug-taking and becoming (1) .... from society, according to the (2) .... research. The (3) .... followed publication of a report which found that TV addicts — those who (4) .... at least four hours a night in front of the television — are more likely to have anti-social attitudes, (5) .... on badly with their parents and feel disillusioned. The researchers said that

these youngsters developed spectator mentalities which prevented them from taking an active (6) .... in life.

Of the 20,000 teenagers aged between 13 and 15 who participated in the (7) ...., more than a quarter said they watched at least four hours a night. After comparing their answers with those of the other respondents, the researchers said that their findings (8) .... a disturbing picture. Almost 50 per cent of the addict group dismissed school as boring compared

with fewer than 30 per cent of those who watched less television. TV addicts were also happier to accept that they might be unemployed after (9) .... school and more than 20 per cent would prefer it to work they did not like. More than one in ten condoned shoplifting, compared with one in twenty other teenagers, while one in five (10) .... graffiti as acceptable. TV addicts were also more tolerant of drug-taking.

1	A isolated	B distracted	C disappointed	D deprived
2	A current	B recent	C new	D latest
3	A notice	B warning	C saying	D advice
4	A use	B last	C relax	D spend
5	A get	B put	C go	D take
6	A play	B part	C place	D position
7	A report	B survey	C questionnaire	D examination
8	A displayed	B showed	C described	D painted
9	A graduating	B leaving	C abandoning	D stopping
10	A noticed	B observed	C remarked	D regarded

Creativity

SPEAKING 1

1 If you saw this advertisement in a magazine, would you be tempted to apply for one of the courses? How would you expect to benefit from such a course? Say why it would or wouldn't appeal to you.

You too can write a **blockbuster!**

An intensive weekend specifically designed to share the secrets of creating hugely successful books.

VENUE:
WESTON COURT CENTRE FOR THE CREATIVE ARTS, SHROPSHIRE

Other courses available include:
• How to write a film script
• How to paint a masterpiece
• How to improve your memory

Phone ARTSLINE 0800 505050 for further information!

2 Discuss these questions.

1 Is creativity something some people are born with or can it be developed?

2 If you think it can be developed, what kind of environment and activities could encourage creativity at school or in the workplace?

LISTENING 1

Exam File: Part 2, Note completion

The task in this section is another example of a Part 2 task, which is heard once only in the exam. Remember that the information you need for your answer concerns specific facts rather than interpretation and will be repeated during the recording, usually in a different way. Before you listen, don't forget to look at the gaps and predict the kind of information you need to note down.

1 You have decided to follow up on the Weston Court advert and phone for further information. You will hear an answerphone message. First, read through the notes below. Some of the information has already been completed for you. Use this to help you.

2 Listen and note down the main information. You will hear the recording only once.

Courses at Weston Court

Weekend courses start (1) ....

Finish (2) ....

Day courses start 9.15, finish 4.30

Save money by booking (3) ....

Full course information (4) ....

....

Difficulties choosing a course? Phone
(5) ....

Accommodation, with lake view, in (6) ....

....

£20 deposit (7) ....

Balance due (8) ....
before the course starts

Changes possible in course timing and
(9) ....

ENGLISH IN USE 1
Part 1, Multiple choice cloze

1 Read the text below, and decide what you think of the advice given on how to be creative. While you are reading, see if you can think what the missing words probably are.

2 Now read the text again and decide which word (A, B, C or D) best fits each space. Write one letter in each gap. Remember to:

- consider carefully the words around each gap.
- use your knowledge of collocates and fixed expressions.
- think about precise words suitable for a particular context.

HOW TO BE CREATIVE

Few human attributes are held in higher esteem than creativity. To be creative requires a form of flexible thinking that most people possess to some (1) .... . Contrary to popular (2) ...., creativity can be cultivated. Here are some (3) .... to set the stage.

- **Decide what you want to do.** It could be something as practical as living on your income, or getting a (4) .... of furniture through a doorway that is too (5) .... . It could be as ambitious as inventing a new device, or as personal as (6) .... yourself in poetry. (7) .... in mind that without a good idea of what to create, you can't be creative. It often helps to write down your objective.

- **Be positive** in your (8) .... . The solution may well be there for you if you work hard enough.

- **Learn all you can** about your subject. The more you know, the better (9) .... you are to find a solution.

- **Think.** Thinking is hard work, which is why we (10) .... away from it. Don't limit yourself to straight-line, logical thinking. Sneak up on your problem from a new (11) .... .

- **Incubate.** If the solution doesn't come after your (12) .... efforts, put the problem out of your (13) .... and let your subconscious work on it. Go back to it in a few days and see where you are.

- **Prune.** Review your ideas and set (14) .... the ones that have not worked. Make changes until you come up with your best.

- **Put your ideas to** (15) .... . That's the best way of testing them.

1	**A** degree	**B** stage	**C** proportion	**D** scale
2	**A** legend	**B** concept	**C** myth	**D** thought
3	**A** plans	**B** ways	**C** methods	**D** means
4	**A** section	**B** part	**C** bit	**D** piece
5	**A** close	**B** tight	**C** straight	**D** narrow
6	**A** expressing	**B** showing	**C** telling	**D** representing
7	**A** Believe	**B** Get	**C** Bear	**D** Maintain
8	**A** attitude	**B** spirit	**C** feeling	**D** opinion
9	**A** supplied	**B** provided	**C** equipped	**D** furnished
10	**A** start	**B** shy	**C** draw	**D** shrink
11	**A** angle	**B** edge	**C** point	**D** approach
12	**A** early	**B** primary	**C** opening	**D** initial
13	**A** head	**B** mind	**C** brain	**D** thought
14	**A** about	**B** off	**C** out	**D** aside
15	**A** perform	**B** run	**C** work	**D** produce

READING
Part 3, Multiple choice questions

1 You are going to read about a contemporary English poet. Before you do so, talk about your country's most famous poet. Use these questions to guide you.

Is he/she living or dead?
What is he/she particularly famous for?
What kind of life does/did he/she lead?
What is his/her public image?
What subjects are his/her poems about?

2

1 Below is a list of events from the life of the poet and journalist James Fenton. Read the magazine article opposite, underlining key dates and place names as you read, and write when each event happened on the left.

Date	Event
last year	gave a reading from his new poetry collection
....	lost job as librettist on musical *Les Miserables*
....	published *Memory of War*
....	became Far East correspondent in the Philippines
....	bought a farm in Philippines with some friends; started to write *Out of Danger*
....	was born
after school	studied at Oxford University
....	published first volume of poetry, which won an award
....	lives on farm near Oxford

2 The article is a biographical account of Fenton's career, but events are not related in chronological order. At what point in time does it begin and end? Why is this?

3 Read the article again and answer the multiple choice questions that follow. Choose the best option (A, B, C or D) according to the information in the text. Remember, one approach is to read the questions and look for the answer before reading the four options.

1 Fenton's public readings are unusual because of the
  A quality of the poetry.
  B personal reminiscence.
  C passionate delivery.
  D feeling for the audience.

2 Fenton's involvement in *Les Miserables*
  A continued until the first performance.
  B brought professional praise.
  C has made him famous all round the world.
  D was well-rewarded.

3 Peter Porter attributes Fenton's success to
  A his choice of themes familiar to his readers.
  B his involvement in real issues.
  C his commitment to poetic language.
  D his international themes.

4 When asked who he wrote the love poems in *Out of Danger* for, Fenton is
  A evasive.
  B convincing.
  C contradictory.
  D irritated.

5 After university, Fenton got a job as Anthony Thwaite's assistant because
  A he knew a number of poets.
  B his poetry had impressed Thwaite.
  C he already had some journalistic experience.
  D Auden had advised him to apply.

6 Fenton decided not to pursue a career as a literary journalist because he
  A anticipated more success as a poet.
  B thought poetry would provide sufficient income.
  C wanted to write in a non-literary area.
  D felt it would limit his potential experiences.

7 How does the writer of the article react to Fenton's home?
  A He accepts Fenton's view of it.
  B He doubts if Fenton is truly settled.
  C He is critical of the design.
  D He is envious of what he sees.

4 Discuss these questions.

1 What impression do you get of Fenton as a person from the article?
2 In what ways does or doesn't he conform to the typical image of a poet?

James Fenton gave a poetry reading last year. He started with 'Out of the East', the epic poem that opens Part 2 of his new collection *Out of Danger*. Much of what Fenton had experienced as a journalist in Indo-China is infused into the poem like a bloodstain. "It's a far cry. / It's a war cry./ Cry for the war that can do this thing," Fenton read — or rather sang. It was not just what he read, it was how he read it. Fenton punched the air, spoke his lines as if they were burning his mouth, and pranced around dramatically. It was the most electrifying stage performance I've ever seen — and it was just a poetry reading.

"James," says Christopher Reid, poetry editor at Faber and Faber, "is the nearest thing we have to a rap artist. When he reads, he doesn't mumble in the way we university poets are meant to."

But James Fenton is not how poets are meant to be. Poets are not meant to be rich. They are meant to be wild, drunk, aesthetically penniless. Fenton, described as "the most talented poet of his generation" a decade ago, defies this cliché. He is very rich, though his wealth has little to do with his verse. Fenton is rich because of a musical. When he was fired as librettist of the musical *Les Miserables* in 1985, it was thought only fair that he should gain some reward for the work he had already done. His agent negotiated a percentage.

Given that *Les Miserables* has played all around the globe, this must amount to a very large sum of money indeed.

On the proceeds, Fenton has bought property. He owns a flat near the Adelphi Theatre in London and a farm four miles outside Oxford. The money has also brought him independence. "When I work now," he says, "it is only because I want to." It's been a long wait since Fenton's last volume, *The Memory of War and Children in Exile* was published in 1983. Acclaim for the book was led by another poet, Peter Porter; his view of Fenton hasn't changed. "He is a spasmodic poet, but also very popular — it's the way he writes, with a mixture of poetic language and real directness. But the important thing about him is that he doesn't indulge himself in poetry every morning. He's devoted to the outside world."

In the Seventies, this devotion took Fenton to most points east — Vietnam, Cambodia and in 1986 to the Philippines, where he became Far East correspondent for a newspaper. In the late Eighties, he bought a prawn farm with a group of friends out there, and spent a lot of time in the remote countryside. He settled down to write many of the poems collected in *Out of Danger*.

Fans will not be disappointed. The qualities of the last volume — narrative skill, wit, a taste for fantasy — are on display in abundance. There's also a new tone, a new preoccupation. At least five of the poems are achingly tender love lyrics. Presumably these are addressed to someone?

"I wouldn't presume anything," Fenton answers briskly. "The point is, with a lyric, you have to write about what you are feeling, but also about what one generally feels in such situations. That's what makes the poem, not a particular person. So I wouldn't presume anything at all if I were you."

Fenton was born in 1949, the son of a theologian. His interest in English literature began only when he took his school-leaving exams. He had written to W H Auden, and the poet visited the school. "He talked to us and we were absolutely tongue-tied," says Fenton. "He was particularly nice to me." Auden's influence was decisive. When Fenton went up to Oxford to read English, Auden

would take him out to lunch.

After Oxford, Fenton considered journalism. He wrote to every newspaper north of Birmingham, but no job was forthcoming. The poet Anthony Thwaite, then literary editor of the *New Statesman*, came to the rescue. Fenton had been doing monthly book reviews for him: when Thwaite needed an assistant, Fenton got the job.

His first volume of poetry was published in 1972. "The book was well-received," says Fenton, "and I was convinced that I wanted to be a poet. But the point was: how to live as poet? I didn't want to live off poetry and I didn't want to be a literary journalist. If all you worked on was books, and you wanted to write them, I figured you'd end up constantly referring to your own reading."

A rich man in his garden

The book won an award and he used the money to go to Vietnam. Why Indochina? "I knew I wanted to travel, either to Africa or Indo-China." His account of his trips to Vietnam just after the US had pulled out, and of the fall of Saigon, remain one of the great pieces of modern reportage.

Currently, he is a poet-landowner. On returning to England, he felt he had to be near Oxford. So he bought the farm, restored the house, created the library and set to work on a design for the garden. The result is a vegetable plot of geometrical orderliness, a rose garden, flower beds and a wide, carefully-tended lawn. But it's a far cry from the East — and it's hard to believe Fenton is going to stick around. "Well," he says, "it does fulfil the ideals I set myself when I started this. I thought I was going to buy a house but it was the garden that was what I wanted to do next. It's a way of saying: I'm going to be here for a long time."

rap artist: a singer who chants the words of a song to a melody with a strong rhythmic beat

Faber and Faber: a publishing company

The New Statesman: a political magazine

LANGUAGE STUDY 1

Lexical cohesion

1 Grammatical devices such as reference and conjunction are used to signal the relationship between elements in a text. This is called grammatical cohesion (see Unit 4 page 48). Another feature of texts is lexical cohesion. This refers to the way vocabulary items are repeated or, more frequently, replaced with a synonym or paraphrase as the topic is developed.

Underline the related words in these extracts from the article on page 61.

1 He is very rich, though his wealth has little to do with his verse. Fenton is rich because of a musical. *(para 3)*

2 It's been a long wait since Fenton's last volume *The Memory of War*. Acclaim for the book was led by another poet, Peter Porter. *(para 4)*

3 At least five of the poems are achingly tender love lyrics. *(para 6)*

4 He had written to W H Auden and the poet visited the school. *(para 8)*

2 Lexical links also help to make the relationships between paragraphs in a text clear. Paragraphs usually contain a transitional sentence, which points forward to the next paragraph or backwards to the previous paragraph. The transitional sentences usually occur at the end of one paragraph and the beginning of the next. Answer these questions about the article.

1 Read the first sentence of paragraph 3. What words echo the last sentence of paragraph 2? How is paragraph 3 developed?

2 Paragraph 4 begins: 'On the proceeds, Fenton has bought property.' What event in paragraph 3 does this refer to?

3 Paragraph 4 ends: 'He's devoted to the outside world.' Which word is echoed in the first sentence of paragraph 5?

4 Paragraph 6 begins: 'Fans will not be disappointed.' What won't they be disappointed with?

5 Who asked the question at the end of paragraph 6? What makes it clear that the first sentence of paragraph 7 is in answer to the question?

6 Which words in the first paragraph are echoed in the concluding paragraph?

VOCABULARY

Phrasal verbs with *off*

1 Complete the sentences below with one of these verbs in the correct form.

put (x2) / sell / send / stop / see / wear / fork / break / call

1 Jack .... off a piece of chocolate and gave it to me.

2 Take the road that .... off to the right.

3 The company's assets were .... off at a knock-down price.

4 They went to the airport to .... their daughter off.

5 After a few hours, the anaesthetic .... off and my tooth began to ache again.

6 On my way to Australia I .... off in Hong Kong.

7 Write the letter now. Don't .... it off till tomorrow.

8 When I saw the advertisement, I .... off for a free sample.

9 Don't be .... off by the cover. It's a really good novel.

10 The strike has been .... off because the management have offered a better deal.

2 In Unit 2 you looked at phrasal verbs with metaphorical meanings. Knowing the literal meaning of the main word helped you work out the meaning of the phrasal verb. Another way of identifying meaning is through the definition of the particle or preposition. Can you work out a definition for *off* on the basis of the examples above?

2 Use verbs from Exercise 1 to complete these sentences.

1 I should have done my homework by now, but ....

2 I have to go to the station to ....

3 The CD was very expensive, which ....

4 The video they were offering in the advert was free, so I ....

5 I was late home because I ....

LANGUAGE STUDY 2

Confusible structures (Notes page 203)

as/like, as if/as though

1 The words *as* and *like* function as prepositions and conjunctions, and are often confused. Read this information about how they are used, then do the exercise below.

> The prepositions *as* and *like* are both used to compare, but their meanings are different.
>
> - We use *as* in the sense of 'in the role of' and *like* to compare two different things.
>   Compare:
>   *As* your friend, I advise you to be careful.
>   (= I am your friend.)
>   *Like* your friend, I advise you to be careful.
>   (= I agree with your friend.)
>
> - *as* is also used in the following pattern:
>   Humorous people are perceived *as* (being) more likeable.
>
> - *as* and *like* can be conjunctions and introduce clauses of manner. For example:
>   He gave an excellent performance *as* we expected.
>   I wish I could write poetry *like* he does. (informal)
>
> - Clauses of manner can also be introduced by the conjunctions *as if/as though*. For example:
>   It looks *as if/as though* it's going to rain.

Fill in the gaps in these sentences with *as, like, as if, as though*.

1 It's hard to earn a living .... a poet.
2 Fenton joined the *Guardian* .... German Correspondent.
3 Craig Raine is a poet, ... Fenton.
4 I don't feel .... going out tonight.
5 He feels .... he's going to be here for a long time.
6 Fenton is described .... 'the most talented poet of his generation'.
7 .... most people, I hate war.
8 She looks very .... her mother.

used to / be, get used to / use

2 It's important to distinguish between the preposition *to*, which can be followed by a noun or *-ing* form, and the infinitive particle *to*, which is followed by an infinitive verb. The following verbs are often confused. Read the examples and answer the questions below.

a. Auden *used* to take Fenton out for lunch.
b. Fenton *used* his award money to go to Vietnam.
c. After a while I *got used* to living in a big city.
d. We *are used* to getting up early.

1 Rephrase each example using *would, be/get accustomed*, or *make use of*.
2 Which italicised verb in the examples is followed by:
   - a direct object?   • an infinitive?
   - a prepositional phrase?
3 What happens to the italicised verbs when you turn the statements into questions?

3 Complete these sentences using the words in brackets in the correct form.

1 I'll never get used to ... . (operate this machine)
2 Have you got used to ... ? (be famous)
3 Didn't you use to .... ? (work at the British Museum)
4 He used a credit card ... . (buy the tickets)
5 It might take a long time for you to become used to ... . (work in such a busy office)

suppose / be supposed to

4 The following verbs are also easily confused. Read the examples and answer the questions below.

a. The situation is not as bad as people *suppose*.
b. I *suppose* (that) you'll be coming by car?
c. We all *supposed* him to be a great artist.
d. *Aren't* you *supposed* to be in bed!
e. They *weren't supposed* to know about this.
f. What's that *supposed* to mean?
g. Did you really *suppose* I would agree to your demands?

1 Rephrase the examples using *think/consider* or *be meant to* as appropriate.
2 What structures can follow *suppose*? What structure follows *be supposed to*?

5 Complete these sentences with *suppose* or *be supposed to* in the correct form.

1 It's getting late. I .... I'd better be going.

2 What are you doing here? You .... be in London!

3 When are you going to finish your report? You .... have handed it in by now.

4 I don't .... you could lend me £10?

5 When .... they will make up their minds?

6 I don't know how I .... finish this in time.

ENGLISH IN USE 2

Exam File: Part 2, Structural cloze

In Part 2, you have to fill in 15 gaps in a text with one suitable word. No options are given, but the missing words will always be ones you know. They are mainly small 'grammatical' words and may include prepositions and particles (in phrasal verbs), determiners and pronouns, and conjunctions. Some gaps may require a verb, modal verb or verbal auxiliary. The aim is to test your understanding of the way sentences are formed in English. Follow this procedure.

• Always read the text all the way through at least once, so you understand what it's about.

• Before writing a word in the gap, read the whole sentence carefully, as well as the one before and after. Think about what type of word is required.

• Where a verb is missing, think about
a) the verb pattern: is it followed by a preposition, a gerund or an infinitive?
b) collocation: what verb is normally found in that context?

• Make sure the word you write is grammatically correct and **makes sense** in the context.

1 Read the following text quickly, ignoring the gaps, to find out what it's about. What does the title refer to?

2 Read the text again and complete each gap with **one word** only. When you have finished, compare your answers with a partner.

The difference a day made

Free and happy and broke in Paris — that was the moment he knew he was a poet.

Brian Patten, 50, poet, performer and children's writer was born in Liverpool and edited a poetry magazine, Underdog, when he was sixteen. He explains how he became a poet.

After leaving school (1) .... fifteen, I had joined a local newspaper (2) .... a junior reporter. In April 1963, when I was seventeen, I resigned. I was dissatisfied (3) .... my daily job. I remember that one day, when I was delivering some photographic blocks to the block-maker, which I (4) .... to do every week, I just sat at the railway station, looking at the tracks and wishing I could follow (5) ....

In June, I set (6) .... with a friend to hitch-hike to Paris, not sure how long we would be staying. We didn't have a lot of money, but you didn't need (7) .... then. So, one morning in July, I was sitting with my friend near Notre Dame, eating banana sandwiches and drinking goats' milk. We (8) .... supposed to start hitch-hiking back to get the ferry to England, and I decided (9) ...., despite having no money left, I didn't want to go back. My friend left (10) .... hitch home alone.

I began sleeping rough under the bridges of the Seine and to get money I joined the pavement artists. I (11) .... coloured chalk to write out short poems on the pavements. I suppose I was the first and the last pavement poet. I had a great feeling of liberation, of euphoria. I had absolutely (12) .... doubt that I had done the right thing, and felt as (13) .... all things were possible. I realise now that it was (14) .... day when I totally committed myself to (15) .... a poet.

pavement poet: this is a play on the expression 'pavement artist' i.e. someone who draws pictures on pavements with chalk as a way of getting money.

SPEAKING 2

Part 3, Discuss and select; Part 4, Report decisions

1 Look at the photographs and use some of these words to describe the works of art.

sculpture / sculptor
abstract/representational painting / still life /
portrait / landscape
oil painting / sketch / water colour / Old Master
frame / canvas / brush / stroke / palette
intense / brilliant / subtle colours
depict / portray

2

1 Work with a partner or in groups of three. Your school or college has decided to buy a work of art — a painting or piece of sculpture — to display in the reception area. A committee has been set up to choose what to buy, and the four pieces in the photographs have been shortlisted. As members of the committee, you have been asked to make a final recommendation. Discuss which work of art you would like your school to buy. Give your reasons.

2 Report your decision to the rest of the class. Say if you found it easy or difficult to make your choice.

Language Bank

Negotiating

My first choice would be the sculpture.

I really think ... is excellent/outstanding/very original, don't you?

I couldn't agree more — I particularly like the vibrant colours/the use of ...

X is a/an brilliant/extremely talented sculptor/painter.

It's all right if you like that kind of thing, but I don't think it will appeal to everyone.

Personally, I'm not too keen on/I don't think much of abstract art.

Shouldn't we choose something that will be acceptable to a majority?

After all/I mean, most people prefer paintings they can understand.

Well, what do you think of the still-life, then?

Reporting decisions

We've decided to recommend the painting by ...

All things considered, we feel that ...

3 Discuss these questions.

1 Do you like going to art galleries?
2 Do you think 'public art' is important? Should the state support art in the community?
3 Do you like abstract art? Do you think art should always be easy to understand? Why?
4 Do you have any favourite artists? Say why you like them.

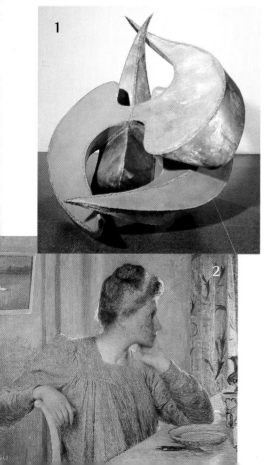

ENGLISH IN USE 3
Part 4, Word formation

1 Read the text below, ignoring the gaps, and work out the meaning of the title.

2 Now complete the gaps with the correct form of the base words below. Think about these points.

- What part of speech is needed to fill the gap?
- Should the missing word be positive or negative? If it's a noun, should it be singular or plural?

A pachyderm Picasso

A collection of abstract painting, the (1) .... of a Canadian zoo elephant are to be auctioned next month. Kamala, a 19-year-old Indian elephant, holds a brush with her trunk and paints pictures which have amazed art experts. The elephant learned to paint as part of the zoo's behavioural (2) .... programme, under which animals are given various (3) .... to stimulate their intelligence. "We sort of monkeyed around with all of our elephants but Kamala was the only one that had the (4) .... and interest to keep painting," said Dave Percival, her keeper. "As soon as we set up the easel and get the paints out, her ears start flapping because she gets really (5) .... about it. She's got real (6) .... talent. Currently, she's one of the zoo's most popular (7) .... If she were human, she could make a living out of it." Six of Kamala's best paintings are expected to fetch thousands of dollars at next month's public auction.

(1) CREATE	**(5)** ENTHUSE
(2) RICH	**(6)** ART
(3) ACTIVE	**(7)** ATTRACT
(4) DEXTROUS	

3 Discuss these questions.

1 Is it really possible for an animal to be creative?
2 Can you describe any similar examples of animals being creative or inventive?

LISTENING 2
Part 1, Note completion

1 People who devote their lives to art, such as writers, painters or musicians often suffer health problems related to their chosen activity. You are going to hear a report on some of the health problems suffered by musicians. Here are some of the problems mentioned in the recording. Discuss what they might be caused by.

muscle fatigue	deafness
anxiety	allergies
muscle cramps	stage fright
dermatitis (skin disease)	

2 Read the notes below. How many string instruments can you name? How many wind instruments?

3 🔊 Now listen and complete the notes according to the information you hear in the recording. Use one to three words in each gap. Make sure the words fit grammatically.

Suffering for your art

Physical complaints
suffered by all players:
(1) .... and
(2) ....
suffered by players of string instruments:
(3) ....
caused by (4) .... and
(5) ....
suffered by players of wind instruments:
(6) ....

Psychological problems
two commonest (7) ....
and (8) ....
Depression caused by (9) ....
Help now available from (10) ....
....

LANGUAGE STUDY 3

Present participle clauses (Notes pages 203—204)

1 Read this information about present participle clauses.

We can use present participles
- to replace *and* + coordinate clause.
  a. I just sat at the railway station and I looked at the tracks and I wished I could follow them.
  ▶ I just sat at the railway station, *looking* at the tracks *and wishing* I could follow them.
  b. I was sitting with my friend, I was eating banana sandwiches and I was drinking goats' milk.
  ▶ I was sitting with my friend, *eating* banana sandwiches *and drinking* goats' milk.

- to replace adverbial clauses of time, contrast/concession, reason, result.
  c. After I left school at 15, I had joined a local newspaper.
  ▶ *After leaving* school at 15, I joined a local newspaper.
  d. I decided that, although I had no money left, I didn't want to go back.
  ▶ I decided that, *despite having* no money left, I didn't want to go back.
  e. He wrote to every newspaper north of Birmingham because he hoped to get a job as a journalist.
  ▶ He wrote to every newspaper north of Birmingham, *hoping to get* a job ...

- to replace a relative clause.
  f. *War and Peace*, which stars Woody Allen and Diane Keaton, is one of my favourite films.
  ▶ *War and Peace, starring* Woody Allen and Diane Keaton, is one of my favourite films.

2 Rewrite these sentences, which contain participle clauses, using the link words in brackets.

1 The film is about five young men hanging around Los Angeles, hoping to become actors. (who, because)

2 Not wanting to be late for the theatre, I took a taxi. (so)

3 John sat in the park, reading a book. (and)

4 The story, beginning in the 1920s, is about a Chicago gangster. (which)

5 Failing to convince the police that a crime has occurred, the hero looks for more evidence. (so)

3 Read this text and combine the following sentences, using participle clauses.

Sentences 3 + 4
Sentences 5 + 6 (use *before*)
Sentences 8 + 9
Sentences 10 + 11
Sentences 12 + 13 (start with *Despite*)
Sentences 14 + 15

Maestro for the millennium

(1) Simon Rattle, born in Liverpool in 1955, is one of Britain's most famous musicians and conductors. (2) He has changed the face of classical music in this country. (3) At a time when classical music was opening out to a new public, Rattle came along. (4) He caught the imagination of the public in a way no other British conductor of his generation has achieved.

(5) He worked with various symphony orchestras. (6) Then he joined the City of Birmingham Symphony Orchestra as principal conductor. (7) This was the start of a long and fruitful partnership. (8) He turned down offers from other orchestras at home and abroad. (9) He concentrated instead on transforming the CBSO's standing and international reputation. (10) In partnership with Birmingham City council, he led the CBSO from the Victorian Town Hall to its ultramodern new concert hall in the International Convention Centre. (11) Thus he decisively expanded the classical music audience of the city.

(12) Rattle left his full-time post with the CBSO in 1998 and handed over the reins to his successor, Sakari Oramo. (13) Despite this, he returns regularly as guest conductor. (14) He also works with a number of other orchestras. (15) He divides his time between Birmingham, Vienna and Berlin.

WRITING

Exam File: Part 2, Review

In Part 2 you may be asked to write a review of something you have seen (e.g. a film or play), or read (e.g. a novel).

Follow this advice.

- Use a fairly formal style — don't be too informal and chatty.
- Don't assume the reader knows the story — summarise it clearly and concisely.
- Avoid using *I think* and *in my opinion* — try to be objective.
- Always make a final recommendation.

Remember, your review doesn't necessarily have to be about something you liked or enjoyed.

1 Discuss these questions.

1 Where do you expect to find reviews of books, films etc.?
2 What is their purpose?
3 What do you expect a review to contain?
4 Do you read reviews? If yes, do you take any notice of them?

2 Read the review of the film *Tin Cup* and answer these questions.

1 Who is the director? Who does the film star?
2 What type of film is it?
3 Who does Kevin Costner play?
4 Where is the film set? What is it about? Paraphrase the story briefly. (Notice the use of the present tense.)
5 What is the reviewer's opinion of the film? of the performances?
6 How would you describe the style and register of the review? Quite formal or chatty? Personal and subjective or impersonal and objective?
7 What is the effect of the review on you? Would you like to see the film? Why/why not?

3 Here are some words that can be used to talk about films. Check you know what they mean, and add more from the review of *Tin Cup*. Then discuss the questions below.

thriller / horror film / epic / animated film / science fiction
director / scriptwriter / star / leading man / supporting cast / extra / stunt man
screenplay / dialogue / sound track / special effects
a box-office success/flop

1 What's your favourite type of film?
2 Who's your favourite director? actor?
3 Can you name a recent box-office success?
4 Can you name any famous films that rely on special effects?

4 Here are some adjectives often found in reviews. Put the adjectives into two groups, positive and negative.

moving / predictable / funny / sophisticated / clichéd / stylish / atmospheric / (un)sentimental / entertaining / spine-chilling / spectacular / over-hyped / disappointing / heavy-handed

Which adjectives could you use to describe the genres and films you discussed in Exercise 3?

TIN CUP

★★★

DIRECTED BY RON SHELTON
STARRING KEVIN COSTNER
 RENÉ RUSSO
 DON JOHNSON

Kevin Costner returns to a genre he's adept at, namely romantic comedy, teaming up with director Ron Shelton for a film that reconfirms his position as both modern cinema's finest romantic leading man and a gifted comedy actor.

Costner stars as Ron 'Tin Cup' McAvoy, an ex-college golfing champion whose stubbornness hampered his natural ability to swing a club and consequently kept him off the professional touring circuit. He trades on his former glories, giving lessons on a run-down driving range in the middle of rural Texas.

But when the new psychiatrist in town (played by René Russo, never better) turns up one evening for a lesson, McAvoy is immediately smitten with love for her. He sets out to woo her, but after his normal romantic technique fails to convince, he decides that only a grand gesture will do and he sets out to win the US Open. So determined is he to succeed in sport and love that he makes some extraordinary, and hilarious, changes in his personality and style of play.

Tin Cup is a deliciously witty, profound and sly exploration of love, redemption and one man's quest for immortality. Shelton uses the ritual and metaphors of sport to relate the complexities of love and relationships. The performances throughout are spot on, with Costner once again on top form. Quite wonderful. I can thoroughly recommend it.

5 In reviews, adverbs are often used to intensify adjectives upwards or downwards. They fall into the following groups.

- adverbs like *very,* used for extra emphasis.
- adverbs like *absolutely, completely, entirely, totally,* which mean *in every way*
- adverbs that collocate with particular adjectives, e.g.:
  utterly ridiculous/delightful/enchanting
  highly successful/improbable
  hugely successful/expensive
- adverbs like *quite* (= *moderately/rather/fairly*) tone an adjective down.

Use an appropriate adverb from these groups to modify the adjectives in Exercise 4. For example:

totally predictable

6 Work in pairs or groups. Tell each other about a film you have seen recently, using the vocabulary in Exercises 3, 4 and 5. Give a summary of the story and your opinion of the film.

7 Read the writing task and follow the **Steps to Writing** below.

> Choose a film or a book that you have enjoyed (or not enjoyed) recently and write a **review** of it for a student magazine. Give details of the content and your assessment of it. Say whether you would recommend it to your fellow students.
> Write approximately 250 words.

Step 1 Task interpretation
Who will read your review? What is your purpose in writing? What will be the most appropriate register and tone?

Step 2 Generating ideas
Decide if you are going to write about a film or a book. Use questions 1—5 in Exercise 2 to guide you, and jot down your answers in note form.

Step 3 Layout and organisation
Organise your ideas into paragraphs. How many paragraphs will you need?

Step 4 Write
1 Remember to use a range of vocabulary and structures for interest and variety. The following paragraph describes a thriller. How many different ways can you think of to combine the sentences?

> The book is about Mark Fletcher. He is searching for his elder brother, Stephen. Stephen disappeared five years ago. Mark is convinced that he's still alive. Mark begins his search in London. He bravely confronts the many dangers and difficulties that lie in his path. Mark finally finds his brother. He discovers the bitter truth.

2 Write your review.
▶ Participle clauses (page 67)
▶ Language Bank

Step 5 Evaluate and edit
When you have finished, re-read and evaluate your work carefully.
▶ Writing checklist (page 214)

Language Bank

Describing
The film/book is produced/written/published by ...
It's set in .../It deals with/tells the story of ...
The story describes/portrays/is about ...
The story is based on/taken from the novel by ...
The starring role/female lead is played by ...

Assessing
The special effects are marvellous. However, the plot is not always convincing.
Although X is excellent, the acting is generally rather wooden.

Making a recommendation
Nevertheless, this is a book/film well worth considering.
If you enjoy spectacular epics, this is the film for you.
Predictable and heavy-handed, this is definitely one to miss!

Exam Practice 1

READING

Part 1

For questions **1—14**, answer by choosing from the list **(A—D)** on the right below. Some of the choices may be required more than once.

Which athlete

expresses dissatisfaction with a university?	**1**		
complains about travelling?	**2**	**3**	
describes the study habits of fellow students?	**4**		**A** Paula Radcliffe
received special help from the university?	**5**	**6**	**B** Andrew Gomersall
has a fairly clear idea of how long he/she will continue with his/her sport?	**7**		**C** John Crawley
found sports training mentally refreshing?	**8**	**9**	**D** Sian Lewis
had time for a social life?	**10**	**11**	
spent long periods abroad?	**12**	**13**	
wanted to stay at university longer than was possible?	**14**		

SPORTING COURSES

The only exercise many students are likely to take during their years at university is lifting a cup of coffee. But what about those who take sport more seriously? The ones who want to compete at the highest levels? How do they combine studying and training for their chosen sport?

Paula Radcliffe

In Loughborough, it's made easier for you because all the facilities are on campus, so you don't waste time travelling. It's a brilliant place to do a degree. On a typical day, I got up in the morning at seven and trained for an hour. Then I went to lectures from nine to one, had an hour off for lunch and then back to lectures or studying from two to six and then I'd go training for a couple of hours. This still left plenty of time for socialising.

It was difficult during last year's exams — I was getting up at six instead of seven. I couldn't have kept that up for long. Serious training didn't get in the way of my studying. It can't have done because I ended up getting a first-class degree. I just had to be very organised. In fact, I think training actually helped my academic work. When you've been studying all day, your head feels woozy and it feels wonderful to run it all off.

I didn't have allowances made for me in my academic work because of my sport. You do get special treatment if you do the sports science degree, but as languages have nothing to do with sport I didn't get special consideration. I thought of sports as my leisure.

Now I've finished my degree, I still train at Loughborough. I also do some part-time translation work. I want to keep up my languages — when I'm past running I want to go into international marketing. But as long as I'm fit I'll keep on running for at least another ten years.

Andrew Gomersall

When I first went to Oxford Brookes University, I had no idea I would become a professional rugby-player although I had set my heart on getting as far in the game as I could. I started doing Estate Management, but I gave up after the first year as I found it too hard to combine with training. The lectures and seminars were all at fixed times and if they clashed with my training I had to miss them. So I switched to Marketing, Management and Tourism, principally because this was a modular course and I could select my options to fit in with my rugby.

For the first two years, I managed to balance things quite well. I would go to lectures in the morning and then drive to the rugby ground in the afternoon. In the evenings, I would catch up with my coursework. It was an exhausting regime, especially with two hours' driving each day, but I coped —and even got a bit of a social life too.

When I was selected to play for England, things got a bit out of hand as I had to put my rugby first. I was on tour in Argentina during the summer term. I bought myself a laptop computer to try and keep up with the course work but I never used it.

The university has been very helpful and given me an extension to complete my degree. The way things are going I may have to ask for another extension. It's been a hard slog, juggling my studies and my sport, but I've no regrets.

John Crawley

I had played professional cricket before I went up to Cambridge, so I always had it in mind to make cricket my first career. But I didn't want to abandon my studies as I thought it would be useful to have a second string to my bow. I also thought I would be more relaxed about my cricket if I had something else to rely on but, in fact, it didn't have this effect at all. My first year was the most difficult. I missed the whole of the second term when I was chosen to tour New Zealand with the England Under 19s. I took some work with me but I didn't really keep up with it.

The university insisted that sportsmen and sportswomen kept up with their studies and I didn't get any preferential treatment. It was worst in the summer, when we play a lot of cricket, sometimes six days a week. Some people would get up really early and get their work done before play started. Others would try to do their academic work at the end of the day. I found it impossible to work like this and would just try to fit all the work into the day when we weren't playing. The pressure on me during the final exams was immense. We finished playing cricket on May 16 and the exams began a week later. Still, I came away with a good degree, so I have no regrets about my time in Cambridge.

Sian Lewis

I started off doing statistics at Glasgow. But after two years, and purely because of my sport, I transferred to Bath to do the last two years of my degree. I wasn't getting enough support at Glasgow. Nobody was moderating my training apart from myself. I just ticked away and did my own thing. But it was hard going. As modern pentathlon is five sports, you have to do a lot of training. At Glasgow it took ages to get to the swimming pool. At Bath, I walk 100 metres across the sports field and dive into the new pool. It's great because I'm allowed to train with Olympic swimmers. I really like having sporty people around me. The only thing I have to travel for is fencing.

I'm glad I did my degree in statistics because I think it will improve my chances of getting a job. I would have liked to have got a sports scholarship to extend my degree for another year, but pentathlon is so expensive it's rare to get one. However, the university has been very supportive. For example, last year the world championships coincided with my exams, so I was allowed to take them in August instead of June. Sport and using your brain go well together. I particularly enjoyed my training when I was revising for my exams— it was good to get away from all the stress of studying.

ENGLISH IN USE

Part 1

For questions **1—15**, read the text and then decide which word (A, B, C or D) best fits each space. Put the letter you choose for each question **(A—D)** in the gap. The exercise begins with an example **(0)**.

Example: | 0 | A |

CYCLING FURIOUSLY

An obscure, 150-year-old law, originally intended to **(0)** .... with horsemen riding too quickly has **(1)** .... an unlikely victim — a cyclist who was not even speeding. Tony Adams was prosecuted for "cycling furiously" after police in Cambridge spotted him, in training for a world record **(2)** ...., cruising at 40kph in a 50kph **(3)** .... . A police car **(4)** .... after him through the city centre, in what must have been one of the slowest pursuits on record, before he was arrested. Now he is **(5)** .... up to three months in jail after refusing to pay the £120 fine **(6)** .... for breaking the law, which **(7)** .... back to 1847 when bicycles as we know them today did not exist. "I couldn't believe it," he said. "I was riding along and there was this police car behind me, **(8)** .... its lights."

Mr Adams, 24, was spotted by officers on foot patrol in the early hours on one of his nightly training **(9)** ...., which are designed to improve his **(10)** .... of beating the world record. **(11)** ...., this is 55 kilometres in a one-hour time trial. He insists he was **(12)** .... no more than 40kph when police signalled to him to stop. Thinking they were waving to encourage him, he **(13)** .... on. He was then pulled over by the police car.

A police spokesman admitted the law was rarely **(14)** .... but said it was the only one which could be used to prosecute speeding cyclists. He added, "I do think that if people are training for world records, a city centre is not the most **(15)** .... place to do it."

0	A deal	B act	C prevent	D control
1	A claimed	B taken	C demanded	D chosen
2	A try	B effort	C go	D attempt
3	A part	B zone	C place	D district
4	A slowed	B moved	C crawled	D rolled
5	A regarding	B facing	C looking	D considering
6	A expected	B given	C made	D imposed
7	A dates	B passes	C turns	D originates
8	A displaying	B showing	C dazzling	D flashing
9	A practices	B rehearsals	C sessions	D preparations
10	A chances	B options	C likelihood	D possibility
11	A Actually	B Currently	C Instantly	D Momentarily
12	A moving	B riding	C going	D doing
13	A carried	B took	C passed	D continued
14	A forced	B effected	C applied	D exercised
15	A suited	B relevant	C appropriate	D applicable

ENGLISH IN USE

Part 2

For questions **16—30** complete the following article by writing each missing word in the correct space. **Write only one word for each space.** The exercise begins with an example **(0)**.

Example: | **0** | at |

GROWING PAINS

At the age of thirteen, Zara Long became the youngest athlete to represent her country **(0)** .... the 1984 Los Angeles Olympics. By twenty-one, she **(16)** .... had enough. "I'd **(17)** .... stick pins in my eyes than go swimming now. I want to do normal things in my life. I want to commute." **(18)** .... twenty-six, Zara works as a sports administrator. It has been a struggle to find a job she enjoys. "When you have got accustomed to that level of achievement, when you have got so far **(19)** .... early, it's hard not to feel unproductive."

Long accepts that she was ill-equipped to deal **(20)** .... the social and educational consequences of her time-consuming and lonely training regime. "It just gradually creeps up on you at **(21)** .... age," she explains, "and it seems like the **(22)** .... normal thing in the world. The other kids thought I was mad." In **(23)** .... early twenties, Long admits that she experienced some resentment **(24)** .... her parents. "I missed out on so **(25)** .... Education was always second best. No-one ever suggested I wouldn't be a swimmer for the rest of my life." She believes that because of the intensity of her coaching she has been left **(26)** .... personal discipline. "I find **(27)** .... hard to do things for **(28)** .... because I'm so **(29)** .... to people dangling a carrot in front of me. Regret is the wrong word, but I do wonder **(30)** .... would have happened if things had been different."

Commitments

SPEAKING

1 Work in pairs. Choose two photographs each and take turns to answer these questions.

1 What commitments do the people in the photographs have to each other?

2 What could happen if these people had no sense of commitment?

3 What conflicts could arise between their commitments and other things they might want to do?

2 Do you agree with what your partner has said?

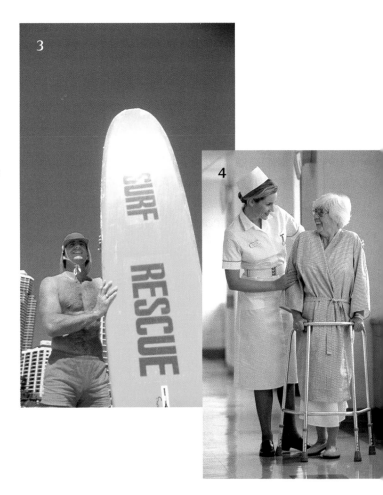

Language Bank

Describing

They have a responsibility towards other team members/their patients/their children.

They probably have a strong sense of loyalty/duty.

They have to pull their weight.

They can't afford to let people down.

He's/They're there to protect/save lives.

Others depend/rely on him/them.

Parents have to put their children first.

They're under an obligation to bring up/protect/look after ...

Speculating

There could be an accident.

It would probably/most certainly be difficult to ...

2 In certain situations, commitments to family and friends may be difficult to keep. Do the following quiz. Decide what **you** would do in each situation, choosing from options A—C.

Then compare and discuss your answers with other students. Give reasons for your choices.

quiz

①You go shopping with a new friend. After visiting a department store, your friend proudly shows you a lipstick she has stolen from the cosmetics department. Would you:
A try to persuade her to take it back?
B say nothing?
C tell her parents?

②You have a friend whose family seem to have a much more interesting lifestyle than your own family. They have a spare room in their house where you could stay and their house is much nearer to the college where you have to go every day. Would you:
A move to your friend's house?
B stay at home but visit your friend a lot?
C find another place to live nearer to college?

③Both you and your brother/sister are unemployed and are desperately looking for a job, of a similar kind. One day, you are at home alone and the phone rings. It's an employer inviting your brother/sister to an interview. Would you:
A go instead and say nothing to your brother/sister?
B give the message to your brother/sister?
C ask the employer if there is a second vacancy?

④You belong to a sports team and have been chosen to play in a match on Saturday in another town, so the whole day will be taken up. You have a really important exam to take on Monday and need the time to revise. Would you:
A stay at home and revise?
B play in the match?
C revise during the journey to and from the match?

ENGLISH IN USE
Part 4, Word formation

1 Read the text below. How do we choose our friends according to the text?

2 Complete the text by putting words 1—7 into the correct form. Consider the context carefully and think about the part of speech needed to fill each gap. Check whether the word you need should be singular or plural.

How we choose our friends

The words *friend* and *free* come from the same root word, suggesting that one aspect of friendship is the freedom to be (1) .... in the company of another person.

Most friendships begin with shared interests or (2) ...., which gradually develop into mutual trust, openness, affection and (3) .... We like people who share our attitudes and values. When someone agrees with us or makes the same (4) .... we have made, we gain confidence in our own views.

There is also a (5) .... for people to enjoy the companionship of those of the same (6) .... status and level of education. Friends may also share an altruistic goal, such as a concern for (7) .... or the cultivation of the arts.

---

(1) OUR	**(5)** TEND
(2) ACTIVE	**(6)** ECONOMY
(3) LOYAL	**(7)** JUST
(4) CHOOSE	

3 Discuss these questions.

1 The text suggests that we choose friends who are like us. Can you think of examples of friends who are very different from each other? Why do you think they became, and remain, friends?

2 What kind of things might bring a friendship to an end?

READING 1
Part 4, Multiple matching

1 You are going to read an article in which four fathers talk about their experiences.

1 Read the headline and try to predict what difficulties might be mentioned in the article.

2 Skim-read each section to find out:
- what arrangements each father/couple has made for childcare.
- the effect on each father's career.

2 Match each of the statements below to the father (A, B, C or D) it refers to. Notice how the prompts paraphrase the language of the article. (See Unit 2, page 22, for advice on how to approach this type of task.)

A David Batup
B George Beattie
C Tom Spenser
D Stephen Lowe

He had a *physical indication* that all was not well. **1** ....

His company provides *on-site care* for employees' children. **2** ....

He acknowledges the *help* of friends. **3** ....

He is aware that his child/ren *react to him differently* when he has more time. **4** ....

He appreciates *understanding* attitudes at work. **5** .... **6** ....

His wife *plays the major role* in child care. **7** ....

He is aware that being a man *limits his chances to socialise* with other parents. **8** ....

He admits to *worrying about work* while involved in childcare. **9** ....

His experience of childcare has *made him more aware of the feelings of others*. **10** ....

He has suffered from *sleep deprivation*. **11** ....

He is *not satisfied with* his relationship with his children. **12** ....

Sometimes he feels *out of place* among his colleagues. **13** ....

He refused the chance of *advancement* at work. **14** ....

What price more time with the children?

Men who try to balance the demands of family life and career face difficult choices. We report on how four of them are coping.

A

*When **David Batup** separated from his wife, his children lived with him after he was given custody. David continued to work full time.*

WE CAME home from a family holiday and the next thing, my wife had left me. It came as a complete shock. I felt panic. I was on my own with two children, aged nine and thirteen, while trying to hold down a job as a senior manager with responsibility for a large budget in a computer company. Not only did we have practical problems to sort out, but we were overwhelmed by our emotions.

Friends gave me a lot of support. For the first few weeks they helped me collect and deliver the children while I was at work. They helped me find an *au pair*. And they gave me a listening ear.

The emotional upheaval was the most difficult aspect to come to terms with. I had always helped with the housework and was quite domesticated. I had also been involved with the children and we were close. But it was a whole new ball game having primary responsibility for home and children.

My manager was very supportive. As long as I achieved my work goals, he was satisfied. My secretary was brilliant, too. She knew where I was at all times and the children always had access to me.

The time following the separation was painful for all of us. But I have learnt to express my feelings and empathise with other people. It has taught me how to be a better manager, too. I know how to play a supportive role to members of my staff who have been through personal crises, in the way my boss did for me.

B

George Beattie, *46, works nights as a senior supervisor with a large parcels delivery company while his wife, Lynn, works days in the catering industry.*

WE PUT our plan into action when our children were four and two. The big question was: would I be able to manage on a maximum of five hours' sleep per night? Well, five years on we are still doing it, so it must have been all right ... but at times it was hard.

We had a tight schedule. Lynn would leave home at 8.30 in the morning and was back by 5.30, just in time to take over while I went out fifteen minutes later to start my night shift at 6pm.

At one point, I began having stomach pains. I was going to bed at 3.15 in the morning, when I got home from work, and the next thing I knew, a bump would wake me up at 6am when one of the children jumped on me. Lynn would take the children downstairs so that I could get more sleep. But I could hear the chit chat and would only doze, if I was lucky. So you can imagine how exhausted I felt with the children during the day.

When Robert started playgroup, I took my turn on the rota to look after the children. But it's not that easy being a man in a world of mothers with their young children. Often you feel excluded by conversations, and you just can't go round to other people's houses for a cup of coffee like other mums do.

Three years ago, the manager put pressure on me to go for the night manager's job, which would have included daytime meetings on top of my night shift. I wasn't interested because I valued my time at home with the children so much. I did not want to miss out on collecting them and having that couple of hours with them before Lynn came home from work. And with Lynn's well-paid job, we could afford my passing up promotion. Some of my colleagues thought I should go for the promotion, but I stuck to my guns and I am pleased that I did.

C

Tom Spenser, *43, is a consultant physician. His wife, Penny, works three days a week as a paediatrician and looks after their two children on the other days.*

FROM Monday to Friday, I only see the children for an hour at the end of the day. They are not at their best because it's just before their bedtime, when they are tired.

In the holidays, the children have time to adjust to having Dad around and get to know him again. They become more spontaneous with their cuddles and seem to feel more able to talk about the things that are important to them.

Penny and I decided before starting a family that I would be the one who would make work my focus and she would focus on the children. Over the years, there have been many periods of a few days when I have 'played at' being househusband because Penny's work has taken her away. I found it frustrating, knowing that my work was piling up at the hospital while I was at home. In such a situation, you can't get work out of your mind, so you aren't fully with the children.

I do have some regrets that I haven't spent as much time with the children as I would have liked. The shortage of quality time together obviously affects my relationship with them.

D

Stephen Lowe, *36, and his wife, Janet, work at management level in multinational companies. When Janet had a child, they both wanted to continue their careers.*

JANET and I had decided to place Hannah in my workplace nursery because it was the most practical solution. I have experienced a side of my daughter's life I would never have seen, and that I doubt most fathers who work full time ever see.

I love the joy on her face when she recognises me coming in the distance and I also value watching her play with other children when she hasn't seen me coming. At the same time, I feel like a fish out of water in the nursery, because I am the only dad who drops off and collects his child — the others are all mums.

Before I became a father, I was ambitious and single-minded about my career. I had a great deal of job satisfaction and career progression. Janet and I were very happy when she became pregnant. We both wanted to continue our careers. I went to my company's childcare information service for advice. They helped us to make the decision to put our baby into their workplace nursery.

I have had the odd telephone call in the time Hannah has been there. My first reaction is "Damn!" because it won't be good news. There is potentially a conflict between Hannah's needs and the demands of my work, but I would always put my daughter first. The fact that senior management is sympathetic makes a big difference.

3 Compare your answers with other students. Read out the parts of the text which gave you the answers and identify the words and expressions that are paraphrased in the prompts. For example:

Question 5/6: *understanding*

Text: supportive, sympathetic

4 Find idiomatic expressions, phrasal verbs and collocations in the article that mean the following:

Text A
1 manage to keep
2 learn to accept
3 a completely novel situation

Text B
4 informal conversation about unimportant things
5 lose an opportunity to do something
6 refuse to change plans even when others try to influence you

Text C
7 increase in quantity

Text D
8 feel out of place
9 opposite of *collect someone/pick someone up*
10 a few, not so many as to be important

5 Discuss these questions.

1 When a couple have children, who do you think should have responsibility for childcare?
2 Which of the parents in the article do you think have made the most satisfactory arrangements?
3 What does a person who looks after his or her own children gain from the experience?
4 Which do you consider more important, children or career? Do you think your views may change in the future?

VOCABULARY

Prepositions

Complete these expressions, based on what you have read, with the correct preposition. Each preposition may be used more than once.

to / on / for / of / with / into

1 It took Dave a while to adjust .... being a househusband.
2 Kathy would rather focus .... her job than spend time with her family.

3 If you're a working parent, it helps if you have access .... a company nursery.
4 Doctors have responsibility .... their patients' well-being.
5 It took them five years to put their plan .... action.
6 His boss put pressure .... him to accept the promotion.
7 At the weekends, he found it difficult to relax — he couldn't get work out .... his mind.
8 She never really came to terms .... the fact that she had given up her career for her family.

PRONUNCIATION

Elision (disappearing sounds)

1 📼 A typical feature of fluent, connected speech in English is the disappearance of sounds within and between words. This is called *elision*.

Say these words, then listen to the way they are said on the recording. Which letters are not pronounced? Cross them out.

1	postman	5	windmill
2	Westminster	6	family
3	grandmother	7	interesting
4	handsome	8	history

2 📼 Now say and listen to these words. There are two possible pronunciations. Cross out the letters that can disappear.

1	asked	4	necessary
2	clothes	5	secretary
3	often		

3 📼 Now say and listen to these groups of words. Some are extracted from the talk on social trends in the next listening section.

1	next week	5	he loved tennis
2	compact disc	6	they seemed nice
3	strict parents	7	it looked good
4	latest survey	8	have increased slightly

You will have noticed that when there is a sequence of three (or more) consonant sounds and the middle one is *t* or *d*, it is not pronounced, unless you speak very, very slowly.

LISTENING 1

Part 1, Note completion

1 Look at the two family photographs. Which photograph illustrates a 'nuclear family'? Which illustrates an 'extended family'? Which picture is closest to the typical family situation in your country?

2 You are going to hear part of a radio programme about the results of a recent survey on social trends in Britain. Can you explain the meaning of the following words and expressions, some of which you will hear in the recording?

1 dependent children
2 lone parent
3 step-family, step-parents, step-children
4 childminder
5 carer

3 🖭 Listen and complete the notes with one word or a number. Remember that the notes may summarise or rephrase words in the recording.

Social trends

Percentage of
one person households (1) ....
households with married couples plus two
children (2) ....
households with one parent plus dependent
children (3) ....
unmarried women (4) ....

People are getting married (5) ....

More women are having children (6) ....
....

In the last ten years there has been a rise in
(7) ....

Percentage of children living in step-families
(8) ....

In extended families, an important role is
played by (9) ....

The report emphasises how (10) ....
the family is.

4 Can you think of reasons for the changes mentioned in the survey? Use these ways of expressing reasons and causes.

The increase/fall in marriage rates is probably due to/the result of *changes in lifestyle*.

Marriage rates may have fallen as a result of/because of *increased expectations on the part of women*.

One of the reasons why fewer couples are having children/more women are staying single may be because ...

5 Compare the results of this survey with the situation in your country.

1 Have there been similar changes in the way families live in your country compared with previous generations?

2 Is it more common for people to live alone? What are the benefits and drawbacks of living alone?

WRITING 1

Exam File: Parts 1 and 2, Report writing

In Paper 2, Part 1 or 2, you may be asked to write a report. This may include:

1 supplying information for the benefit of others, e.g. about a course you have attended.

2 supplying a description and analysis of a situation or problem together with a recommendation for action, e.g. about a local environmental problem.

Follow this advice.

- Use a neutral or formal register. Avoid expressing personal opinions except in your conclusion or recommendation.
- Begin by stating the subject of your report clearly.
- Present your ideas concisely and in a logical sequence.
- Use clearly differentiated paragraphs with headings where appropriate to indicate the main points.
- End with a summary, recommendation or conclusion depending on the type of report.
- Don't begin or end your report like a letter.

Read the writing task carefully. Then follow the **Steps to Writing** below.

An international organisation has asked you to write a **report** for a survey it is carrying out into key social changes around the world. They would like you to describe the typical family situation in your country today, any important changes that have occurred over the last 25 years and the probable reasons for these changes. They have asked you to conclude by giving your opinion of the importance of the family unit today in your society.

Write your report in about 250 words.

Step 1 Task interpretation
Who are you writing for? What is your purpose in writing?

Step 2 Generating ideas
Make notes for each area you have to write about. For example, you could make a list of points comparing today with 25 years ago.

	today	25 years ago	reason for changes
typical family size			
number of generations under one roof			
age when women get married			
age when men get married			

Step 3 Layout and organisation
Look at the notes you jotted down in Step 2. Use these headings to help you plan your report. (You may want to change these headings during this stage, but the ones suggested are a useful starting point.)

Introduction
Explain the purpose of the report.

The family today
Describe the typical family.

How the family has changed
Describe the changes that have occurred. If you feel there has been very little change, explain this with reference to the situation 25 years ago.

Reasons for the changes
Explain what you consider to be the causes of the changes you have described.

Conclusion
Comment on the role and importance of the family unit today.

Step 4 Write
1 Remember to state the purpose of your report clearly in your introduction.

Which of these introductory paragraphs do you think is better? Why?

A

The aim of this report is to describe the typical family situation in [country] today, and to outline the major changes that have occurred in relation to the family over the last 25 years. It will consider the reasons for these changes and summarise how they have affected the role of the family unit in society.

B

In my country the family situation has changed a lot, and I'm going to describe these changes in this report. I'm also going to say why I think they have happened. I don't think the family is less important now than it was before.

2 Write your report. Try to use a range of vocabulary and structures. However, avoid over-long sentences — remember that you must present your information in a clear and easily accessible way.

▶ Present perfect tense (see page 16)
▶ Language Bank

Step 5 Evaluate and edit

▶ Writing checklist (page 214)

Language Bank

Introduction
The aim of this report is to ...
This report describes/discusses ...

Describing trends
Typically, the family consists of ...
There has been an increase/decrease in the number of ...
The proportion of ... has fallen/risen to/by ... per cent.
Women/Men/Couples are tending to ...
By comparison with/Compared with 25 years ago, ...
This is due to / a result of ...

Conclusion
In conclusion, / To sum up, ...
It appears/seems that ...
For the majority of people ...

READING 2

Exam File: Part 2, Gapped text

The second text in Paper 1 is a 'gapped' text. Several paragraphs have been taken out, and you have to decide where they fit. There is also an extra paragraph that doesn't fit at all. To do this task, you need to understand the logical development of the argument, or if the text is a narrative, the sequence of events. Here is a suggested procedure for a narrative.

• Read the main part of the text first.
• Highlight words that refer to people and places, and any time references.
• Make sure you understand the order of events in the story. Note down the main events.
• Read the paragraphs that have been removed.
• Look for grammatical and lexical links between paragraphs to help you decide where the missing paragraphs fit.

1 In Britain, it's quite common for young people to take a year 'out' between passing their A-levels (school-leaving exams) and going to university. This is called a 'gap year'. Many of them go abroad and take a variety of jobs. Girls often work as an *au pair* with a family. You are going to read an article about a girl who did this, and what happened to her. Before you read, make a list of the benefits of the gap year and a list of the possible drawbacks for the young person and his or her family. For example:

Benefits
gain work experience
learn another language/culture

Drawbacks
feel homesick
lose contact with friends

2 Now read the base text on page 82, ignoring the gaps. What happened in the case of this girl? Summarise the story briefly.

The au pair's tale

Amanda Harrison was 18 and had just left school. She wanted a year out — a year of fun, travel and excitement far from home. America beckoned and like many girls in the gap year, she signed up to be an *au pair* with a family in Boston.

(The first paragraph mentions a family in Boston. The next paragraph will probably give you more information about them.)

(1)

She had been told by the agency to expect a new-born baby. She was puzzled when she found that there was no baby in the house and the lady was obviously not pregnant. This made her feel a little apprehensive and she found it difficult to settle down. She remembers receiving a lot of flattering comments at this time about her accent, dress sense and general behaviour which put her at her ease, to some extent.

(The paragraph above says that there was no baby. The paragraph after the gap mentions a baby. Which paragraph links these two?)

(2)

"The couple behaved as if they had a new toy," said Amanda. "For the first few weeks, they were buying expensive outfits for the baby to wear. They would wheel me and the baby out to show us off." But it was she, the young British student with no childcare qualifications and experience limited to babysitting and voluntary work in a primary school, who was left holding the baby.

(Which paragraph gives further information about how Amanda cared for the baby?)

(3)

When the two of them were brought in to be shown off to friends and the adoptive mother would pick up the child, "she would crane her neck around trying to watch me". The baby would cry. "Your natural instinct is to pick her up." But when Amanda did, and the baby quietened, the mother did not like it. "The mother wasn't really interested in the child at all. The baby screamed when she went near. It was like psychological warfare between me and the mother."

(The paragraph above says that Amanda was not getting on with the mother. What about the father? The paragraph after the gap mentions 'the new car'. Where is this mentioned first?)

(4)

Amanda was certainly not allowed to use the new car, or either of the other two the couple owned, which made it difficult to get out of the house. So much for the 45 hours' work and alternate free weekends written into the contract. She knew what was happening was not right but took the blame on herself. "I just thought it was my fault because I didn't know any better. And I was too proud to admit that I had made a mistake. After moving away from home and going to America, I just didn't want to accept that things were not going well. I just didn't know what to do."

(The paragraph above tells you that Amanda did not know what to do. Does she find a solution to her problem?)

(5)

Leaving the child was hard for Amanda. "It was such a wrench to leave her after four months because I felt as if she was my baby. I felt guilty about severing the close bond I had with her. It was lacerating. I felt a great sense of loss. Thank God I was fine with her and loved her, but they should have had somebody with loads of experience with new-born babies."

A Luckily, she knew another *au pair* not far away to whom she voiced her fears. This girl told the agency's local representative what was going on. "She had a chat with me and said, 'Right — we're getting you out of there now.' She picked me up and I was out." She had been with the family for four months. The agency placed another girl with them after that. She lasted five months. She pretty much had a nervous breakdown. They made her wash the dogs and clean out the swimming pool. I dread to think how the baby felt, losing two carers in less than a year."

B A week after her arrival, an adopted new-born baby was delivered to the house. Amanda was very surprised, but so were all the couple's friends. The couple seemed to enjoy surprising everybody. She had been initially introduced to their circle as 'the daughter of a British friend'. And then ... guess what! Suddenly they had a baby and she was the nanny.

C "The mother expected me to do everything. I had to, because she didn't return from work until late in the evening. I was looking after the baby 24 hours a day. She was sleeping in my bed for about the first two months. I had total responsibility. I was the one getting up in the night. What was the child to think? It was like I was her mother."

D The couple she was sent to were in the medical profession. The husband was a doctor and the wife an anaesthetist. They had a huge house with a swimming pool. "It was quite awesome," said Amanda. "Everything made a big impression on me."

E Amanda wasn't getting on with the husband either. "The car of the season was a Jaguar. The man said it was a beautiful car. Then he told me he had a toy in the garage. It was a new black Jag. I said my father had one just like it. He didn't talk to me for a week. He must have thought that I came from a poor family." In fact, as Amanda later realised, he did think that anyone taking such a job must be poor. "It was just one example of the lack of communication and understanding between us," said Amanda bleakly.

 3

1 Now read the base text **and** the missing paragraphs. Try to decide where the missing paragraphs fit. The clues in brackets will help you. Note that there are only five gaps and five missing paragraphs for this text, but in the exam there will always be six or seven gaps and one paragraph that doesn't fit anywhere.

2 Check your answers by reading the whole article in sequence. Does it make sense?

4 The article is an account of an emotional experience, and the writer describes in some detail how Amanda and other characters felt about what was happening. Find adjectives and expressions that describe:

1 how Amanda felt when she first arrived in Boston.
2 the effect on Amanda of the flattering comments.
3 the adoptive parents' feelings about the baby.
4 Amanda's relationship with the adoptive mother.
5 Amanda's feelings when she realised things were not right.
6 how she felt when she had to leave the baby behind.

5 Read these examples. Then complete the sentences below using *fault* or *blame* in the appropriate form.

a. [Amanda] *took the blame* on herself ...
b. Amanda felt she was *to blame* ...
c. She *blamed* herself for the situation.
d. "I just thought it was my *fault* ..."

1 No one is .... It was an accident.

2 I am not going to take .... for this. It wasn't my ....

3 Are you suggesting that everything was Tom's .... ?

4 It's not a question of .... anyone. We just want to know what happened.

6 Discuss these questions.

1 Who do you think bears the biggest responsibility for what happened to Amanda?

• her parents, for letting her go
• the agency, for not vetting the couple
• the American couple

2 How could situations like this be avoided?

LANGUAGE STUDY 1

Grammatical cohesion 2 (Notes page 204)

Substitution

1 Look at these examples from the text on pages 76—77. What words does *do* refer back to?

a. I know how to play a supportive role to members of my staff ... in the way my boss *did* for me. *(line 31)*

b. You just can't go round to other people's houses for a cup of coffee like other mums *do*. *(line 71)*

c. Some of my colleagues thought I should go for the promotion, but I stuck to my guns, and I am pleased that I *did*. *(line 86)*

The verb *do* is used to avoid repeating an earlier phrase or clause. This is one of various ways you can avoid repetition in English. Read the sentences below and highlight the words which substitute for:

- a noun   • a verb   • a clause

1 [In jokes,] the most obvious interpretation of the situation is replaced by a less obvious one. *(text page 47)*

2 Amanda was very surprised, but so were all the couple's friends. *(text page 82)*

3 My wife thinks it's important that I spend time with the children, and I feel the same.

4 A: Has he seen the film?
B: He may have done. If not, I'll tell him not to miss it.

5 If I have to put my family before my work, I'll do so.

Omission

2 In English it is important to express yourself as economically as possible. Another way of avoiding repetition is by omitting words.

Can you identify the words that have been omitted in these extracts from the text on page 82?

a. The husband was a doctor and the wife an anaesthetist. *(para D)*

b. Amanda certainly wasn't allowed to use the new car or either of the other two the couple owned. *(para 6)*

Now read the following sentences and identify an omitted

- noun phrase   • (auxiliary) verb   • clause

1 'When I work now, it is only because I want to.' *(text page 61)*

2 '[Fenton] is a spasmodic poet, but also very popular.' *(text page 61)*

3 He promised he'd finish the report by today and he has.

4 'They could have been held up.'
'I suppose they could.'

5 Mary accepted the invitation but not John.

LISTENING 2

Exam File: Part 3, Sentence completion

Part 3 tasks test your understanding of the text as a whole, as well as directly stated information, and they often require you to identify and understand opinion and attitude. One of the task types in Part 3 may involve completing sentences with up to three words. The words you need to write don't necessarily appear in the recording. You may need different words to complete the sentences in a way that is grammatically correct and expresses the same ideas that you hear.

1 Some children like to rebel against their parents when they get older and break away, while others may follow closely in their parents' footsteps. Discuss the ways in which you are similar to or different from your parents. Think about:

- your character and temperament
- chosen/likely career and interests
- beliefs and attitudes

2 You will hear an extract from a radio programme in which a father and son, Martin and Sebastian, both professional musicians, talk to an interviewer about their lives. Read sentences 1—10 on page 85 carefully. Then listen and complete the sentences according to the ideas and opinions expressed in the recording using up to three words. You will hear the recording twice.

3 Discuss these questions.

1 How would you describe the relationship between Sebastian and his father, Martin? Do they get on well or not? Justify your answers.

2 What are the advantages and disadvantages of following the same profession as your father or mother? Is this something you would like to do?

Like father, like son?

Comparing Sebastian as a child and an adult, Martin says he is now less (1) ....

He also thinks Sebastian has become much more (2) ....

Sebastian complains that his father's attitude to him is now more (3) ....

Compared with Sebastian, Martin's approach to music is (4) ....

When he heard about the rock group, Martin reacted very (5) ....

He reacted in this way partly because of a (6) ....

Just one pop record seems to have made Sebastian both (7) ....

Concerning work, Martin is pleased that his son has much more (8) ....

They had a big argument about what Sebastian (9) .... at a concert.

As for the incident with the press photographers, Martin thinks Sebastian was (10) ....

LANGUAGE STUDY 2

Making suggestions and recommendations
(Notes page 204)

1 Read these sentences and identify the ones which are **not** correct. Then answer the questions below.

1 I suggest that you should apply for another job.
2 If you're not sure, I suggest you to ask Peter.
3 The receptionist suggested that he should take a taxi to the airport.
4 Sally suggested going to the Piccolo restaurant after the theatre.
5 Jack suggested to buy the tickets today because they were cheaper.
6 I suggested to George that he wait a few more days.

a) When can we use *to* after *suggest* and when is it incorrect to do so?
b) Which words can we omit from sentences 1 and 3?

c) What do you notice about the form of the verb after *suggest* in sentences 3 and 6?
d) Which two correct patterns are frequently used after *suggest*?
e) Try substituting *recommend* for *suggest* in each correct sentence. Can it take the same structures?

Giving advice (Notes page 205)

2 Identify the grammatically incorrect responses to this request for advice, and correct them. Then answer the questions below.

'I've just finished my exams and I've got a place at university. Now I've been invited by a theatre company to tour with them for a year. I love acting but my parents don't want me to be an actor, as they say it's very insecure. Should I accept the invitation or take up my university place and forget acting?'

1 I advise to go to university and get more qualifications.
2 Let me give you some good advices: don't become an actor!
3 My advice is not to take the job offer — acting is such a risky profession.
4 I'd advise you accepting the offer. After all, you can go to university later if it doesn't work out.
5 No one can advise you what to do — you have to make up your own mind.

a) What structures can follow the verb *advise*?
b) What's the spelling difference between the verb and the noun? Can you think of more examples where the noun and verb have a similar spelling difference?
c) Which response do you agree with? What advice would **you** give in this situation?

3 Complete these sentences using *suggest*, *recommend* and *advise*. Then compare your ideas with the class.

1 If you have an important exam tomorrow, I advise ....
2 If you are unhappy in your job, I suggest ....
3 If you want to improve your English, I recommend ....
4 If you want a career which offers security, ...

Giving warnings (Notes page 205)

4 Complete these sentences with the correct form of *warn*. What is the difference in meaning between *warn* and *advise*?

1 David's wife left him without any ....

2 George recognised his stomach pains were a .... sign of stress.

3 Sam's parents .... him against becoming an actor.

4 They felt they had to .... him of the high risk of failure in a competitive field.

5 This is your final .... One more mistake and you're fired!

6 The meteorological office has issued gale .... for tomorrow.

7 I'm .... you — if you do that again, you'll be in deep trouble!

8 There were police notices .... people to be on the lookout for pickpockets.

Concession (Notes page 205)

5 When you give people advice or make suggestions, you may sometimes want to acknowledge, or concede, that there are good reasons for taking a different course of action.

1 Look at this example.

A: Attending this course will help me get a better job, but it's expensive. What should I do?

B: *Even if/though* the course costs a lot, I'd advise you to apply for it.

How can you express the same idea using these expressions?

In spite of the fact that ...
In spite of/Despite + noun

2 Rewrite the following sentences, using the words in brackets at the end of the sentence.

1 Even though you have failed your exams, I suggest you carry on with the course. (In spite of the fact that)

2 Despite the difficulties in your life at the moment, my advice is to be patient. (Even though)

3 Even though the journey to work will be very long, I'd advise you to accept the job. (Despite)

4 Even though it could be dangerous, I think you should take the risk. (In spite of)

6 Here are some more ways of expressing concession.

a. The course *may* be expensive, *but* I still suggest you apply for it.

b. *However much* the course costs, I think you should apply for it.

c. No *matter how* expensive the course is, I recommend applying for it.

Use an appropriate structure to rewrite these sentences.

1 Even though you think you are well-prepared, I warn you not to travel in that part of the desert.

2 Hitch-hiking is an opportunity to travel around cheaply, but I advise against it because of the risks.

3 Even if you've travelled abroad many times, you can still get homesick.

4 Even if you are very tired, you should never fall asleep when you're travelling alone.

7 Work in pairs or groups. Discuss or roleplay the following situations, using the language you have practised.

1 You are a receptionist at a hotel in your town. An English-speaking tourist asks you to recommend some things to do and see in your town. What do you recommend? What places do you suggest avoiding? What do you warn him/her not to do? (For example, is it safe to walk everywhere, even at night?)

2 You're on a business trip with a colleague and you're flying back home to London tomorrow. Your colleague tells you this story. 'A really nice man I met in the disco has asked me to deliver a small parcel to his sister, who lives in London. He's offered me £50 for my time and trouble. It seems all right to do that, don't you think?' How do you respond?

WRITING 2

Exam File: Part 1, Informal letter

In Part 1 of the Writing Paper, you have to base your answer on the input material provided. You can add points of your own, but your answer must be based on what you read on the paper. Remember to:

- read the instructions carefully and highlight the points you have to cover in your answer.
- select only relevant information.
- paraphrase rather than copy whole sentences.
- use the correct register for your piece of writing — it may be different from the input.

Read this writing task and follow the **Steps to Writing** on page 88.

You have received a letter from an English friend asking for advice about whether or not to take a year out before university. You have also received an e-mail message from another friend who you haven't heard from for some time. Using the information in both texts, reply to the **letter** from your friend, offering appropriate advice.

Write approximately 250 words.

You'll be pleased to hear I've just passed my school-leaving exams! I'm so relieved!
Now I'm thinking about taking a year out before I go to university. Yes, I'm going to spend a year travelling round the world by myself. I've already bought my 'Globetrotter' ticket, which is valid for twelve months. I've got lots of addresses in other countries of people I have met and I can stay with them (I hope!). Of course, Mum and Dad have hit the roof about me leaving school and not going to university. They go on and on about how I don't know what I'm doing and I'm running all these risks, but I just can't see it myself. I've already been abroad several times, although only for a few weeks. I know there won't be any problems that I can't handle. If the money runs out (which it might because Mum and Dad have refused to give me any) I can just get jobs wherever I happen to be. I'm sure there's no problem living cheaply once you know how to cope.
I bet you're envious and, unlike Mum and Dad, I'm sure you'll agree I'm doing the right thing. I know it will be the adventure of a lifetime. But when I leave, I'd like Mum and Dad to feel a bit more relaxed. Any advice about how I can reassure them? Write soon because I'm leaving as soon as I can.

Love Francesca

```
I bet you're surprised to hear from me after so
long! Luckily some kind person let me use their
terminal. Can you reply as soon as possible? It's
bad news, I'm afraid. My journey — my so-called
adventure of a lifetime — isn't going well at all.
Last night I took a long bus journey — over 12
hours — to this city near the border. Foolishly,
I fell asleep — a dangerous thing to do when
you're travelling alone. Someone cut open my bag
and stole my passport and all my travel cheques —
the whole lot! I've just got enough money in my
pocket to get back to the capital. Please get in
touch with my parents urgently and ask them to
transfer some money immediately — they know how to
organise it. I've only got enough left for two
days — if I don't eat.
```

Step 1 Task interpretation

1 What type of writing do you have to produce? What is your purpose in writing? What register is suitable for this letter? How will you begin and end it?

2 Your letter will need to offer advice in a tactful way. Underline the phrases that convey Francesca's attitude. Use this information to decide on the tone of your letter. Will it be serious or light-hearted? Friendly or stern? Persuasive or reassuring?

Step 2 Selecting and summarising

Read the input on page 87 again and underline words and phrases which give you information about factual details. Decide what advice you will give. Are you in favour of Francesca's plan or against it? Will you:

- try to persuade her not to go?
- advise her to go?
- write about the pros and cons and leave the final decision to her?

Note down some ideas, for example:

Pros	Cons
new experiences	might be robbed
make new friends	might fall ill

Step 3 Layout and organisation

Organise your ideas into paragraphs. Here is a possible plan.

Paragraph 1: Greeting and reaction to good news about exams
Paragraphs 2/3: Re-statement of problem and comments/advice
Concluding paragraph: Ending

Step 4 Write

Write your letter. Remember to include a range of vocabulary and structures for interest and variety, and to show what you can say in English.

▶ Suggestions, advice, warnings, concession (pages 85–86)
▶ Language Bank

Step 5 Evaluate and edit

▶ Writing checklist (page 214)

Language Bank

Introduction

It was lovely to hear from you.

I'm so pleased to hear that ... /about ...

Pros and cons

You asked for/want my advice about going to ...

Obviously there are advantages and disadvantages.

On the one hand, ...

... have you thought about how your studies will be affected?

... do you really think it's a good idea to ...?

What if you end up alone in a strange place/are robbed?

On the other hand, ...

... if things don't work out, you could always ...

... if the worst comes to the worst ...

Recommendation

Personally, I think you should ...

If I were you/In your place, I would/wouldn't ...

Conclusion

Do let me know what you decide in the end.

In the meantime, give my love/regards to ...

Best wishes / Love ...

7 Home sweet home

SPEAKING 1

1 Work in pairs. Look at the photographs and discuss these questions.

1 Compared with 100 years ago, how has daily life in the home changed?

2 What has brought these changes about? Think about social and economic changes, technological advances, labour-saving devices.

3 In what ways are the changes an improvement?

2 Look at this list of household chores. Which ones do you consider important? Which ones do you think are mainly done by women?

- dusting
- vacuuming/hoovering
- mopping the kitchen floor
- polishing furniture
- doing the washing
- doing the ironing
- cleaning the fridge
- wiping down paintwork
- wiping skirting boards
- cleaning tiled surfaces
- wiping down the fridge door

3 Now read these quotations about housework from men. What's your reaction to the ideas expressed?

OPINIONS

'I'm one of the old school. I don't do a thing. No, I don't have a slave who does it all for me, but I have a girlfriend, which is just about the same thing, isn't it? Sometimes she gets really tough with me — I remember last Christmas she made me put some plates in the dishwasher.'

'I do everything because my girlfriend is slovenly and I'm given no alternative. I do all my cooking and day-to-day upkeep. Girls always seem to be the most untidy, but they do have other virtues.'

'Men have a responsibility to do their share, and not let women slip into doing it all because they are conditioned to do it. But I do as little as possible.'

'I think I share things evenly with my girlfriend, but I don't see mess in the same way. There are better things to do in life than clean the flat.'

4 Who does the chores in your household?

READING

Part 1, Multiple matching

 Skim the article opposite to find out what it's about.

According to the text ...

1 who does most of the housework today, men or women?
2 how do most women feel about household chores?
   They enjoy doing them.
   They feel guilty if they don't do them.
   They feel guilty if they do them.
3 why do women feel cleaning the house is important?

2 In which part(s) of the house would you find the following items mentioned in the text?

hob / laminated surfaces / sink / U-bend / chrome fixtures / food processor

3

1 The multiple matching task in this unit is similar to that in Unit 1. You have to match prompts with names of people spread through the article. Scan the text and highlight their names. This will help you to locate the relevant parts of the text.

2 Match each statement below with the person to whom it refers.

A The writer	**E** Sue Halliday
B Jane Harrap	**F** Jane Ussher
C Juliet Steele	**G** Nick Emler
D Fran Hepworth	**H** Daniel Wright

This person:

outlines the repetitive nature of housework.	**1** ....
is critical of the claims of manufacturers.	**2** ....
refers to people not realising the difference between their beliefs and actions.	**3** .... **4** ....
thinks a partner is helped not to accept responsibility for household tasks.	**5** ....
avoids housework by working outside the home.	**6** ....
points out a link between good housekeeping and the opinion others have of a homemaker.	**7** ....
mentions things of which a partner is unaware.	**8** .... **9** ....
blames another if the house is not spotless.	**10** ....
stresses the individuality of reactions to cleaning.	**11** ....
resents a failure to maintain an approach learnt from friends.	**12** ....
has mixed feelings about cleaning.	**13** ....
refers to an early age at which attitudes to housework become fixed.	**14** .... **15** ....

4 Discuss these questions.

1 How much sympathy do you have with the writer of the article? Do you think she is making a lot of fuss about nothing?

2 How does your experience compare with hers?

5 Find idiomatic expressions, phrasal verbs and collocations in the article that mean the following:

Paragraph 1
1 roughly similar

Paragraph 3
2 as far as housework is concerned
3 continue doing something

Paragraph 6
4 very greasy/dusty

Paragraph 9
5 untidy
6 behave according to stereotype

Paragraph 11
7 not much influence
8 depend on
9 put up with

Paragraph 15
10 still in good condition

Still cleaning after all these years

UNDER my kitchen sink I have cream cleaner, hob cleaner, carpet cleaner and three separate cleaners for laminates, ceramics and chrome. I have detergents which claim to differentiate between bathrooms and kitchens, though the surfaces look pretty much the same to me.

I buy all these plastic bottles of detergent to make myself feel better about not doing much housework. The marketing messages imply that they will save me effort, even while they conspicuously increase the number of jobs I am supposed to be doing. So they sit there, getting dirty and silently reproaching me for not being able to remember when I last cleaned the bath.

I am not especially eccentric. Volume sales of household cleaning products rose 15 per cent last year. Practically all this work is still being done by women. Women may be company directors, go on assertiveness training courses, enter politics and talk about equality, but when it comes to housework, it appears from the latest research that they just carry on getting out the Hoover.

A recent survey found that 77 per cent of women vacuum and 75 per cent dust at least every two or three days, while 45 per cent wash the kitchen floor at least twice a week. More than one in three women all over Britain spend more than ten hours a week cleaning.

Sexual politics has passed by on the other side. Another survey found that 62 per cent of women do all their household's dusting, cleaning and vacuuming, compared with only 3 per cent of men. Doing the washing defeats men almost entirely: only one per cent of men manages to do the washing and two per cent to iron the family's clothes.

"I SUPPOSE Toby must have done his own washing before he moved in with me," says Jane Harrap, a 30-year-old teacher, "but you wouldn't know it. I sometimes wonder if I encourage his incompetence, because it makes me think he needs me. But if I didn't wipe down the fridge door, noone would, because he just wouldn't notice it was thick with grease and dust."

"A MAJOR reason I have a job outside the home is that I know that otherwise I'd spend all day wiping my skirting boards," says Juliet Steele, a 34-year-old journalist. "But the skirting boards still make me feel anxious. I employ a cleaner three times a week, so I can think it's her fault if the paintwork is grimy."

FRAN Hepworth, 62, stayed at home when her two daughters were growing up. "Housework then was my life's work, which was demoralising. In other jobs, work may pile up for tomorrow, but at least what you've done today still stands. There is something very depressing about performing a task only so that it can be messed up."

Sue Halliday, a 35-year-old doctor, believes feelings about social class confuse her attitude to housework. "I grew up in a lower middle-class household where my mother cleaned and tidied up manically and my parents were always having their friends round to admire their home improvements. Then at university I met all these messy people who didn't see their houses as the centre of their lives, merely as the background to a vivid social and intellectual life. The older I get, the more I find myself reverting to type, and worrying about my home. But I despise myself for it."

JANE Ussher, psychology lecturer, believes that "the pressure to keep your house clean doesn't just come from your mother, or those neighbours in advertisements who comment on your kitchen floor. It's internal. Men simply don't think or care about a lot of these jobs.

Feminism has had so little impact on housework partly because it's a very personal, individual matter — we don't even discuss it, so it all comes down to whether you personally can live with a dirty sink, and if not, is it quicker to do it yourself than argue about it?"

Professor Nick Emler of Dundee University has just been studying the domestic contributions of boys and girls aged between six and fourteen, and found that girls continue to do significantly more, despite professed beliefs in sexual equality among both sexes. "Boys can choose not to do housework. They aren't really aware of the gap between their beliefs and their behaviour." Professor Emler believes domestic attitudes are impressed on children very early.

Daniel Wright, an anthropologist, recently studied a former mining village with high unemployment and found the community was strongly stratified, not on the basis of income but 'respectability'. Women were the guardians of this respectability, and their ability to keep the house smart was a key factor. "It mattered whether they had aspirations to renew their furniture, whether the house was kept tidy, the grass mown, the children had new clothes."

For the women I spoke to, these moral overtones are creating considerable strain. Most of them said they feel inadequate in the face of their never-ending housework, the plethora of jobs they are now required to do. And all too often, labour-saving devices simply create more surfaces to clean. The time you used to spend beating eggs, you now spend cleaning the crevices on your food processor.

I wish I didn't feel guilty about housework. But I still rush around nervously cleaning sinks before people come to visit. Meanwhile, all those bottles under my sink show a deep emotional need to see myself as someone who can keep her surfaces sparkling and her U-bends as good as new.

ENGLISH IN USE 1
Part 3, Error correction

1 In Part 3 of Paper 3, you may have to identify and correct incorrect spelling and punctuation. The following exercises focus on typical spelling mistakes to look out for. You can find the Spelling Rules in the Notes on page 213.

1 Similar-looking words
Complete these sentences with one of these words:

although / through / thought / throughout / thorough

1 The inspector's report was extremely ....

2 I .... it would take us about two hours to walk .... the tunnel.

3 .... the train left late, it arrived on time.

4 The book is illustrated with colour photographs ....

5 The company has branch offices .... the United Kingdom.

2 *i* before *e*
Say these words aloud.

p*ie*ce / ach*ie*vement / bel*ie*f / n*ie*ce

Exceptions:
1 after *c*: rec*ei*ve, dec*ei*t
2 s*ei*ze, K*ei*th, N*ei*l

When do we use the *i* before *e* spelling?

3 Doubling final consonants
Which of these words double the final consonant when we add *-ing* or *-ed*? Cross out the ones that don't. What's the rule?

slim / drop / chop / bake / leak / deal / omit / occur

4 Final *-e*
Look at these sets of words. What's the rule for dropping *e* before an added syllable?

• take + *-ing* = taking
• advertise + *-ing* = advertising
• arrive + *-al* = arrival

Exceptions:
notice + *-able* = noticeable; change + *-able* = changeable

• advertise + *-ment* = advertisement
• care + *-ful* = careful

5 Homophones (see Unit 4 page 45)
Homophones have the same sound but different spelling and meaning. Check the context carefully. Choose the right word from each pair to complete these sentences.

1 I don't know what to .... for the party. (wear/where)

2 The ball's in your .... (court/caught)

3 Could you help me .... up this report? (write/right)

4 The city centre is an ideal .... for the company's new offices. (site/sight)

6 Silent letters
Remember that many words have letters which are never pronounced but must be spelt. Identify the silent letters in these examples.

bombed / debt / castle / chemical

Can you think of any more?

7 Suffixes
Identify which **one** word in each of these sets is spelt wrongly and correct the spelling.

A independence / confident / confidant / intelligence / acceptence

B hunter / gardener / supervisor / inventer / conductor / investigator

2 Underline ten spelling mistakes in the text below and correct them. After you have read the text once, read the lines again from right to left. This will make you concentrate on each separate word. You can easily overlook spelling errors through focussing on meaning rather than form.

Forked-tongue toaster drama

A young woman fled her home when a snake poped out of her kitchen toaster. Shelley Bovington, aged 20, ran to a nieghbour for help and the reptile was cought in a towel and taken to the local Natural History Museum. Ms Bovington, who works as a security gard said, "I saw the snake's head pop out of the toaster. At first, I thought it was a fake. I couldn't beleive it when it moved. I just screemed and ran." Experts are trying to identify the brown and red reptile and it is not yet known if it is poisoinous. Council officials are makeing a thourough search of the flat in case their are others.

3 When looking for punctuation errors, check these areas carefully:

- full stops and commas
- capital letters
- apostrophes
- brackets: make sure the second bracket is there.

Can you identify and correct the punctuation errors in these sentences?

1 'I hate doing the housework, said Helen Butler. It's so boring.'
2 Is this Jane's bag? No, it isnt, it's mine.
3 It's a beautiful dog, but I don't like the colour of it's fur.
4 Do you like my new mexican rug?

4 In this exercise, you must identify spelling and punctuation mistakes.

1 Read the text below straight through. Can you explain the pun in the title?

2 Some lines are correct. Mark these with a tick. When you find a spelling error, write out the correct spelling of the word. When you find a punctuation error, write the correct punctuation mark and the words on either side of it. Study these examples carefully.

0 *Simon Coley's front*
0 ✓
0 *creatures*

3 Compare your answers in pairs. What type of mistakes did you find?

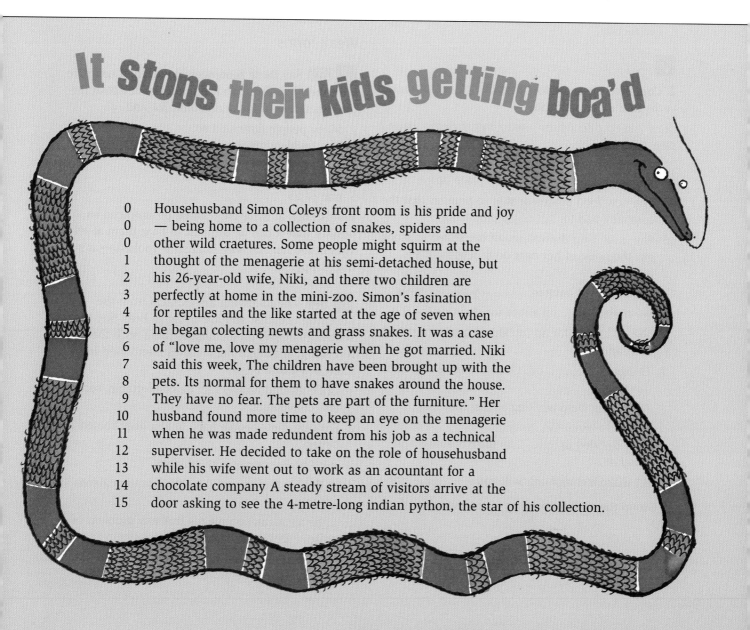

It stops their kids getting boa'd

0 Househusband Simon Coleys front room is his pride and joy
0 — being home to a collection of snakes, spiders and
0 other wild craetures. Some people might squirm at the
1 thought of the menagerie at his semi-detached house, but
2 his 26-year-old wife, Niki, and there two children are
3 perfectly at home in the mini-zoo. Simon's fasination
4 for reptiles and the like started at the age of seven when
5 he began colecting newts and grass snakes. It was a case
6 of "love me, love my menagerie when he got married. Niki
7 said this week, The children have been brought up with the
8 pets. Its normal for them to have snakes around the house.
9 They have no fear. The pets are part of the furniture." Her
10 husband found more time to keep an eye on the menagerie
11 when he was made redundent from his job as a technical
12 superviser. He decided to take on the role of househusband
13 while his wife went out to work as an acountant for a
14 chocolate company A steady stream of visitors arrive at the
15 door asking to see the 4-metre-long indian python, the star of his collection.

VOCABULARY 1
Phrasal verbs with *up*

1 Identify the phrasal verbs in these extracts from the article on page 91 and explain what they mean. Can you match the meanings of *up* to the definitions below?

1 ... work may pile up for tomorrow, but at least what you've done today still stands.

2 There is something very depressing about performing a task only so that it can be messed up.

3 I grew up in a lower middle-class household where my mother cleaned and tidied up manically.

A *up* indicates progress to a higher or superior position, growth, increase.

B *up* acts as an intensifier, implying completion or destruction.

2

1 Complete the sentences below with one of these verbs in the correct form.

draw / keep / do / turn / sell / sign / clear / back / step / look

1 The house we've bought is in poor condition, but we're going to .... the place up.

2 The new food processor was so popular that the company had to .... up production.

3 She .... up the volume of her stereo to block out the noise of her next-door neighbour's hoover.

4 Someone will have to .... up all this mess.

5 We must .... up a rota for cleaning the flat.

6 She .... up for an intensive course in interior decorating.

7 Things are .... up. Our sales increased 25% this year.

8 The others were working so fast that Jack couldn't .... up.

9 They decided to .... up their business and emigrate.

10 If I make a complaint, will you .... me up?

2 Group the verbs according to the meaning of *up*.

PRONUNCIATION
Linking words up

1 📻 How do you say these phrases? Say them aloud, then listen to the recording.

A
1 he's always
2 he did amazing things
3 almost all

B
1 my own car
2 the other day
3 way out

C
1 her own home
2 for hours
3 we're always
4 their instruments

D
1 go in
2 slow up

Notice how the pronunciation changes when a word beginning with a vowel is preceded by

- a word that ends in a consonant.
- a word that ends in a vowel.

Weak forms

2 📻 Say these sentences aloud, then compare with the recording. What do you notice about the pronunciation of *have, are, that, for* and *of*?

1 Many people *have* said so.
2 The builders *are* nearly finished.
3 It's the one *that* comes on Monday.
4 It's *for* you.
5 one *of* us

Words such as *have* etc. can be pronounced so weakly that it can be difficult to hear them at all. This is the normal way English is spoken — it's not sloppy!

3 📻 The following are extracts from the Listening text that you are going to hear. Say the sentences aloud, then compare them with the recording. Highlight the features mentioned in Exercises 1 and 2.

1 Underground houses can be comfortable, secure and convenient.

2 For centuries, people have held a deep-rooted belief ...

3 such houses are energy efficient

4 ... double the level of density of houses above ground ...

5 ... better insulation means that any problem of noise ... is virtually non-existent ...

6 ... cinemas and libraries are all making profitable use of space underground ...

LISTENING
Part 1, Note completion

1 You will hear a talk about houses of the future. Before you listen, discuss what you think would be the benefits and drawbacks of living underground.

2

1 Read the notes below, and see if you can predict what the missing information might be.

2 Listen and complete the notes with one to three words in each gap. Remember that the notes may summarise or rephrase words in the recording.

Buildings underground

Traditional attitude characterised by
(1) ....

Underground houses considered to be
(2) .... and ....
Benefits of such houses:
    can hardly be (3) ....
    heating costs reduced by (4) ....
    roofs are partly made of (5) ....
    owners can enjoy astonishing (6) ....
    ....

Attitudes changing because of success of
(7) ....

Public buildings being built underground due to (8) ....

Claustrophobia reduced by (9) ....
.... and improved lighting.

3 Answer these questions based on the information in the recording. Use the words given.

1 Why are underground houses so energy efficient?
dense / high thermal mass / poor conductor / solar panels

2 Why is building below ground so useful in cities?
space / level of density / insulation

4 Discuss this question.

Now that you know more about underground houses, does that way of living appeal to you?

SPEAKING 2
Part 3, Express priorities; Part 4, Report conclusions

1 Work in pairs. Look at the pictures and discuss these questions.

1 What do you think would be the best and the worst aspects of living in such places? Which of these words and phrases would you use to describe them?

draughty / light and airy / impersonal / not very cosy / full of character / spacious / stylish / dilapidated / ramshackle

2 If you had to live in these places, how would you change them? What would be your priorities?

2 Tell the rest of the class what you have decided. Say if you found it easy or difficult to agree on your priorities.

LANGUAGE STUDY

Talking about the future

(Notes page 205—206)

1 Read the text opposite and underline examples of the following tenses.

1 Future Perfect
2 Future Simple
3 Present Continuous with future reference
4 'going to' future
5 Future Continuous
6 Present Simple with future reference

2 Now match these uses of the various future forms with the examples you found in the text.

1 a spontaneous decision
2 a prediction ('pure' future)
3 certainty based on present evidence
4 a future event already scheduled now
5 an existing personal arrangement
6 a point in the future when something will be completed
7 a planned event in progress in the future

3 Read these extracts from the text. What effect does the use of the modal verbs have? Are these events very likely? probable? possible?

1 'It may even be possible for one wall to contain tropical fish.'
2 'It could be the house of the future.'

House of Glass

Believe it or not, Tom Hardy <u>is having</u> a house built entirely of glass! Yes, the external and internal walls, the roof, the floor, everything, will be glass. And it is for him, not his tropical plants.

"As soon as I saw the architect's model, I said 'I'll take it!' I knew it was for me."

Tom has a plot of land and the builders arrive next Monday — they will have finished the construction by the end of August. Until the house is ready, Tom is living in a tent on the site so that he can watch the builders at work.

"In just six months' time I'll be living in one of the most futuristic houses in the world," says Tom. "I can hardly wait. People are going to be really amazed, I'm sure of that. Journalists are coming round to see me all the time. I'll get visitors from all over the world. Once it's finished, I'll be moving in straightaway."

Of course, it's no ordinary glass. It won't break if you throw stones at it because it is thick and flexible. And you won't be able to see in because this glass automatically goes dark when night falls — there is no need for curtains. What's more, the glass can conduct electricity in such a way that pockets of gas within the glass change shape and colour to create a visual display. You can 're-decorate' at the flick of a switch! No need to use a paint brush ever again. Even better, this glass repels dust, so there is no need to clean.

One wall will function as a television and computer screen. You'll be able to download famous paintings from the Internet and turn your house into an art gallery. It may even be possible for one wall to contain tropical fish — even sharks and octopuses! Because the glass provides good insulation, there is no heating system. All the heat comes from the sun.

By the end of the decade, the architect, Shigeru Kawabata, will have designed ten houses of this type. It could be the house of the future.

2 Categorise the sentences below into three groups, according to the likelihood of them happening.

Group 1: very likely/certain
Group 2: probable
Group 3: possible

1 He'll be arriving in five minutes.
2 I'll be here at the same time tomorrow.
3 We should have nice weather tomorrow.
4 There could be a manned mission to Mars in the next thirty years.
5 We may be able to help you.
6 The match will start at 3 p.m.
7 I'm going to see that new play next week.
8 The minister is about to speak.
9 Your flight leaves at 7.55 tomorrow.
10 Jack is bound to win the race.
11 We might be living in a different country this time next year.
12 The government is to introduce tough new legislation.

Future time in subordinate clauses (Notes page 206)

3 Read these examples and identify the main clause and the subordinate clause. Then answer the questions below.

a. Once the house is finished, I'll be moving in straightaway.
b. We're going to wait until Tom arrives.
c. I'll phone you when we get there.
d. I'll cook the dinner while you take a shower.
e. We'll let you know as soon as we have arrived.
f. By the time you've finished, we will have left.

1 What time is referred to in each clause?
2 What tense form is used in each clause?
3 Why is the verb in the subordinate clause not a future although it refers to the future?
4 What does the use of the present perfect indicate about the sequence of events?

4

1 Put the verbs in brackets into the correct form.

1 I .... (phone) you as soon as I .... (get) the results.
2 He .... (not be) satisfied until he .... (get) all his money back.
3 Once he .... (win) the gold medal he .... (retire).
4 After you .... (pass) the test, you .... (receive) a certificate.

2 Write four sentences about yourself beginning with the words given.

1 By the time ...
2 As soon as ...
3 Once I have ...
4 Until ...

Speculating about future trends

5 Read the following predictions about lifestyle trends over the next 50 years. Decide if you agree, disagree or partly agree with them. Comment on each statement, expressing your own opinion and giving a reason. For example:

'I very much doubt if there will be permanent colonies on Mars by 2050. It would be too expensive.'

'By 2050, there will be permanent colonies on Mars.'

'I think it's quite likely that there will be permanent colonies by then. We've already sent a space probe there.'

WORK
❝There will be a big increase in the number of people who choose to work from home.❞
❝The majority of people will retire at age 40.❞

HOMES
❝As families get smaller, houses are likely to get smaller.❞
❝More people will employ servants in their homes so that they can concentrate on their careers.❞

TRAVEL AND COMMUNICATIONS
❝Traffic congestion will no longer be a problem because most people will work from home.❞
❝There might well be trips into space for tourists.❞

LEISURE AND SHOPPING
❝By the middle of the 21st century, printed books will have disappeared.❞
❝Everyone will be able to shop from home.❞

HEALTH AND MEDICINE
❝Scientists may not be able to control dangerous new diseases.❞
❝People may well be able to choose whether their children will be boys or girls.❞

RELATIONSHIPS
❝More men will choose to become househusbands while their wives go out to work.❞
❝Most people will live alone.❞

BANX

6 Now add your own predictions and speculations about future developments in the areas above.

WRITING 1
Part 2, Article

Read the writing task and follow the **Steps to Writing** below.

An international student magazine has asked you to contribute an **article** to a series entitled 'Lifestyle Trends in My Country'. You have been asked to write about the kind of homes people will live in fifty years from now. You should mention these points: location, design, labour-saving devices and home entertainment.
Write approximately 250 words.

Step 1 Task interpretation
What text type do you have to produce? Who will read it? What is the purpose of the task — to advise, to entertain, to inform? What register will be appropriate?

Step 2 Generating ideas
You have to write about changes in the home. Think about the situation now, then imagine which things may have changed in 50 years time.

Think about the different types of house described in listening and reading texts earlier in the unit. Are these realistic possibilities?

Step 3 Layout and organisation
Since this is an article for a magazine, it is appropriate to have a main heading and subheadings for each section. For this article, the headings could correspond to the four topics mentioned in the task, e.g.:

Homes of the future

Where will they be?

What will they look like?

More help around the house means ... more time to relax!

By basing the headings on key words in the task, you can be sure that you have covered every aspect of the question.

Step 4 Write
Write your article. Give your own opinion about how likely it is that something will happen, or how soon it will happen. Try to use a range of vocabulary and structures for variety.

▶ Talking about the future (pages 96—97)

Step 5 Evaluate and edit
▶ Writing checklist (page 214)

ENGLISH IN USE 2

Exam File: Part 5, Register cloze

Part 5 of Paper 3 consists of two short texts in contrasting registers. The first text could be in a formal style, followed by a gapped text in an informal style, or vice versa. The gaps in the second text must be completed with the information in the first text but in a **style** appropriate to the second text.

Here is a suggested procedure.
- Read both texts to get an idea of what they are about.
- Highlight the words and phrases in the first text that you have to re-express in a different style.
- Make sure the information in the gapped text is the same and the grammar is correct.

1 Use one or two words to complete the second sentence so that it means the same as the first, but in an informal style. You will need to change the italicised words.

1 All this rubbish has to be *disposed of*.
We must *get rid of* all this rubbish.

2 Tom started to learn to play golf but soon *abandoned the attempt*.
Tom started to learn golf but soon ....

3 Can you tell me *the arrival time* of the train at Paddington?
When does the train .... Paddington?

4 Are *matters proceeding* in a satisfactory manner?
How .... ?

5 Very few people *attended* the meeting.
Hardly anyone ....

6 If you arrive early, you will *be able to buy* our products at a 20% *discount*.
Turn up bright and early and you will .... 20% off everything.

7 Mike took *full advantage* of his three-day absence from work.
Mike made .... of his time off.

8 *Admission* is by ticket only.
You can't .... without a ticket.

2 Now complete this task.

You recently spent a holiday with three friends in a cottage near the sea. You signed the rental agreement on behalf of your friends and returned home before the last day of the holiday. You have now received a letter from a solicitor.

Read the letter from the solicitor and use the information in it to complete the numbered gaps in the letter to a friend. The words and phrases that you need to pay special attention to have been highlighted. Use no more than one or two words for each gap. Remember, the words you need for the gaps do not occur in the first letter.

LETTER FROM A SOLICITOR

CHEETHAM & OWEN

6-8 High Street Lyme Regis Dorset DT4 6LY

Dear Mr Collins

On the instructions of my client, Mr Philip Knightly, I am writing to you *with regard to* your rental of 'Seaview Cottage' Coombe Lane, Lyme Regis, Dorset *during the period 1—15 August* this year. Mr Knightly, *the owner*, *inspected* the cottage after the departure of you and your three companions, and was very distressed at the *appalling condition* in which you had left it. To begin with, the key had been left in the front door, *which was open*, and not, as stated in the rental agreement, returned to the caretaker, *Mrs Anne Parker*, who lives *in close proximity* to the cottage and who *admitted* you to the property on your arrival. Furthermore, Mr Knightly reports that a large amount of *crockery* was cracked or broken and a great deal of cutlery was missing. By checking the inventory, he discovered that some blankets were also missing. He formed the impression that *no cleaning had taken place* during the time that you occupied the cottage.

Consequently, he has had to employ, at his own expense, a professional cleaning service in order to restore the cottage to a state that *will be acceptable* to future tenants.

In view of these matters, Mr Knightly *expects compensation* of £400. Please forward a cheque for this amount to the address at the top of this letter, to arrive *on 30 September at the latest*. Otherwise, further action may be taken.

Yours sincerely

Philip Cheetham

Philip Cheetham

LETTER TO FRIENDS

Dear Jack and Steve,

I've just got a letter (0) ..about.. that cottage we rented for those (1) .... in August. The guy it (2) .... has complained to his solicitor and he's sent me a nasty letter. Apparently, when Mr K. thought it was in a (4) .... He says the front door wasn't (5) .... and we hadn't given the key to the (6) .... who lives (7) ...., the one who (8) .... in when we arrived. He also says that a lot of the (9) .... are broken and several knives and forks are missing. He checked the list of things in the cottage and says that some blankets are missing too.

Mr K. says the cottage was (10) .... (I thought we agreed to tidy up, etc., on the last day?) and he had to employ cleaners to sort everything out so that the next tenants won't (11) ....

As you know, I left the day before you and the others, so what happened? Mr K. wants us (or me, since I signed the form) to (12) .... £400 and to do this before the (13) .... of this month. What do you suggest? If we don't pay, this problem won't go away.

Best wishes,

Tim

VOCABULARY 2

Still

1 Look at this example from the article on page 91.

... all this work is *still* being done by women ...

It tells us not only that this work continues to be done by women, but also expresses the writer's irritation with this fact. In which of these sentences does *still* express irritation?

1 Jack still doesn't know how to load the dishwasher.
2 It's a pity about the result. Still, better luck next year.
3 There were still five minutes to go before the final whistle.
4 It was bad news. But still worse was to come.
5 Tom still hasn't replied to my letter.

2 What could you say to express irritation in the following situations, using *still*?

1 You want to use the phone and someone is making a very long call.
2 You go to Poste Restante but the letter you are expecting is not there.
3 You don't join a queue for tickets, thinking it will get shorter later in the day. When you return it is just as long.

It's time

2 Sometimes we use *It's time* + past tense verb to express impatience or irritation with people. For example:

A: I don't know how this machine works.
B: Well, it's (about/high) time you did.

Respond to these remarks using *It's time* ...

1 I don't know how to drive.
2 Jack has been reading that book for months.
3 Sarah is still unemployed.
4 I don't know this aspect of English grammar.

WRITING 2

Part 2, Informal letter

Read the writing task and follow the **Steps to Writing**.

> You have been sharing your flat with a flatmate for the last three months. Recently, you have been getting very irritated by their inconsiderate behaviour. Unfortunately, your hints about how you are feeling have not produced any change. Write a **letter** to another friend, describing the situation and asking for helpful advice. Write approximately 250 words. You do not need to include addresses.

Step 1 Task interpretation
You are writing a letter to a friend. What two things does the task ask you to do? What register would be suitable — formal, informal or semi-formal?

Step 2 Generating ideas
1 You have to describe the situation. Make a list of the things your flatmate may have done. Can you add to the list of possible problems below?

<u>Problems</u>

isn't doing his/her share of the work

washing up is always left to me

plays loud music when I need to work

2 Now note down your feelings, and say what you want to happen.

Step 3 Layout and organisation
Organise your ideas into paragraphs.

Step 4 Write
1 Look at this extract from a letter complaining about a friend's behaviour. Pick out the structures that are useful for complaining.

Honestly, we'd get on much better if only Alasdair didn't keep leaving his dirty dishes in the sink! Didn't his parents ever train him how to clear up? I'm sure they're to blame for all this. And I wish he'd be a bit more considerate about noise. He just can't be quiet, even first thing in the morning. What on earth can I do to get him to be more considerate? You've had plenty of experience. What are your words of wisdom?

2 Write your letter.
▶ *wish, if only* (page 34); advice (page 85)

Step 5 Evaluate and edit
▶ Writing checklist (page 214)

Honesty, the best policy

SPEAKING

1 Work in pairs. Look at the photographs, which illustrate different methods of crime prevention, and discuss which method you think is the most/least effective.

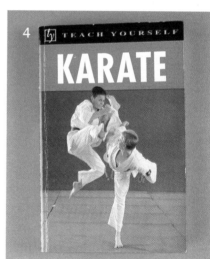

2 Can you suggest other ways in which ordinary citizens can protect themselves against crime? Think about safety measures you could take both at home and on the streets.

3 If you saw a crime in progress, or people behaving suspiciously, would you:
- call the police / dial 999 (in UK)?
- decide it's none of your business and turn a blind eye?
- try to get other bystanders involved?

Language Bank

Comparing and contrasting

I'd say that ... is more effective, because ...

... would be less of a deterrent than ..., but on the other hand ...

I think you probably need a combination of methods. I mean, ...

Speculating

I might feel too frightened to ...

If I ..., I could/might get hurt.

It could/may be dangerous to get involved.

I'd have no qualms about ... + -ing

It depends on the circumstances, but perhaps I'd ...

Reading 1

1 Read the title and the first few paragraphs of the article opposite as far as 'But she was convinced about one thing.' What do you think the article is about? Can you predict what Sylvia will do?

Read quickly to the end to see if your prediction was correct.

2 This text contains a lot of colloquial language relating to police work and crime. Match the colloquial expressions with their equivalent meanings A—F.

1 a villain *(line 27)*   A an informer
2 a shooter *(line 23)*   B in prison
3 a copper's nark *(line 119)* C inform
4 behind bars *(line 143)*   D very silly
5 grass *(line 136)*   E a gun
6 pretty daft *(line 133)*   F a criminal

3 Read the text again and answer the multiple choice questions. Follow the advice in the Exam File. Question 1 has been done for you.

1 As she sat on the bed, what were Sylvia's thoughts about Bernie?
  A He was relaxing with friends.
  B His behaviour was suspicious.
  C He was planning a robbery.
  D His friends were being noisy.

All the options are true and there is support for them in the text.

'Bernie was sitting at the kitchen table, drinking with a few of his friends.' *This supports A.*

'What was he up to?' *This supports B.*

'"Vince'll have the sawn-off shotgun," her cousin was saying, "I'll have a shooter …" She had no idea he was involved in armed robbery.' *These sentences support C.*

'She was wide-awake, listening to voices from downstairs.' *This supports D.*

However, the only answer that is correct is B, because this answers the question asked in the stem, and tells us what Sylvia was thinking. To select the right answer, make sure that the stem and the option together provide what is required.

2 When Sylvia heard guns mentioned, she
  A showed her displeasure.
  B was taken by surprise.
  C was worried about the danger.
  D rushed to make a phone-call.

3 After learning the result of her giving information to the police, Sylvia
  A wished she had acted differently.
  B realised how useful she could be.
  C congratulated herself on her actions.
  D realised her conscience was clear.

4 What makes Sylvia useful to the police?
  A She does not take risks.
  B Her family has a bad reputation.
  C She does not stand out.
  D Her abilities have developed.

5 When threatened, Sylvia
  A is especially careful.
  B reports events to the police.
  C ignores what is said.
  D is given extra protection.

6 Sylvia considers what she does is justifiable because
  A she is fulfilling an ambition.
  B she thinks some of her family will benefit.
  C she wants to punish wrong-doers.
  D she get considerable financial rewards.

4 Discuss these questions.

1 Do you admire Sylvia? In what ways is her behaviour admirable? How might she regret what she has done?

2 If you were in Sylvia's position, would you behave in a similar way? Justify your answer.

The woman who dare not show her face

Sylvia sat on the edge of the bed. Although it was late, she was wide awake, listening to voices from downstairs. Her cousin
5 Bernie was staying with her, but what was he up to at this hour of the night?

'I think I'll see what's going on,' she thought, wrapping her
10 dressing gown tightly around her.

Bernie was sitting at the kitchen table, drinking with a few of his friends. He looked up,
15 startled.

'Sylv, why did you get up?' he asked. 'Sorry about this. You know all the guys, don't you?'

As she walked over to the sink
20 for a glass of water, they started talking again. 'Vince'll have the sawn-off shotgun,' her cousin was saying, 'I'll have a shooter ...'

25 Sylvia couldn't believe what she was hearing. She knew Bernie was a bit of a villain, but she thought his activities were limited to break-ins and stealing
30 cars. She had no idea he was involved in armed robbery.

But she was convinced about one thing — she'd have to do something about it.

35 The next morning, Sylvia rushed to the public phone box near her house. Nervously, she dialled 999. 'Police, please,' she said, anxiously looking around
40 her. 'I want to tell you about an armed robbery.'

The police knew what she was talking about. 'We know that your cousin was watching
45 the security van. We just didn't know when it was going to happen,' they said.

Sylvia replied, 'It's today ... and they've got a gun.'

50 The police only had minutes to get to the scene of the robbery. It was exactly as Sylvia had explained. Some of the gang were waiting in a van, another
55 two were in a car. 'Quick, move!' they yelled to each other, as soon as they saw the police cars screech up. Half the gang managed to get away, but,
60 thanks to Sylvia, the crime was averted.

> 'I've tried to turn a blind eye, but the guilt is too much. I have to inform.'

Even though she'd informed on a member of her family, Sylvia felt no remorse. More
65 important was the fact that she'd never have been able to live with herself if anyone had been hurt. Knowing that she had probably saved the security guard's life
70 made it all worthwhile.

A few weeks later, the doorbell rang. 'Hello, Sylvia. Mind if I come in?' A police officer, in plain clothes, had
75 brought her a carton of her favourite cigarettes as a thank you. As they sat drinking a cup of tea, he showed her some photos of stolen goods. 'Perhaps
80 you can help us trace these?' he suggested.

It was the start of a fruitful partnership. Going about her daily business, Sylvia looked like
85 every other middle-aged housewife on the estate where she lived. No-one could have realised she was a sharp-eyed crime spotter.

90 Codenamed 'Penny Black', Sylvia was an ideal informer. She was genuinely interested in helping the police detect crime — a reward wasn't important to
95 her. She was close to criminals and her information was accurate. She'd even wanted to join the police when she left school, but her family had such
100 a bad reputation that her application was refused. She knows the risk she is running, but her attitude is, 'If I'm caught, that's tough.'

105 She remembers with a shudder the morning the phone rang and a threatening voice told her, 'I know it was you. It couldn't have been anyone else
110 ... I'll do your bloody kneecaps in.'

But those sorts of threats won't stop Sylvia informing. It's ten years since she first gave
115 information to the police. Even today her family don't know. She's well aware of her perilous position. 'I know what I am — a copper's nark. I'm not proud of
120 it. I could be killed for it, but I can't ignore what I see going on around me,' she explains. 'I have no qualms about informing on thieves. I've tried to turn a blind
125 eye, but the guilt is too much. I have to inform.'

'Where I live, I'm surrounded by crime. I see the comings and goings outside my door, and I
130 know what's going on. Besides, you can always tell a villain when you've been brought up by one. You've got to be pretty daft if you can't.'

135 'They can accuse me of grassing, but I have to put it at the back of my mind. I know I've done some good,' she says. 'If I can prevent my children
140 growing up in a world of crime, then I'll do so.' Sylvia (not her real name) has helped put twenty villains behind bars.

Listening 1

Part 1, Note completion

1 You are going to hear a talk about a British detective agency that specialises in investigating the background of potential husbands. Before you listen, discuss these questions.

1 Would you use a private detective to investigate a person you are thinking of marrying?
2 What kind of information would make you have second thoughts about marrying someone?

2 The following descriptions of people may occur in the recording. Which ones sound like a good person to marry? Which would you not recommend marrying? Why?

charismatic and debonair / cold and calculating / weak and selfish / a lout / bookish and reserved / ruthless and ambitious / two-faced / conventional

3 Listen and complete the information using a number or a short phrase. Remember that notes may summarise or replace words in the recording.

Awful wedded husbands

The idea for a special service came from
(1) ....
Package designed especially for women who
are (2) ....
Investigators check previous marriages,
name changes (3) ....
This may be followed by (4) ....
Female clients talk to (5) ....
Service especially popular with (6) ....
....
% of dishonest men who are calculating (7) .....
Requests for investigation not accepted from
(8) ....
Typical age of clients (9) ....
Ms Hodges limits her comments to (10) ....
....

4 Now you've heard the recording, what do you think of the idea of an agency?

Vocabulary 1

Informal expressions with *be* + particle

1 A number of informal expressions are formed using the verb *be* + particle/preposition. Match these expressions with their meanings.

***be* + off**	A published/available
1 They're off.	B it's your decision/ responsibility
2 She's off today.	
3 The meeting's off.	C what's wrong
4 The milk's off.	D cancelled
***be* + out**	E doing
5 It's out now.	F not capable
6 He's out cold.	G not at work
***be* + over**	H have left their starting point
7 It's all over.	
8 She's not over him yet.	I unconscious
***be* + up**	J still loves him
9 It's up to you.	K sour
10 What's he up to?	L finished
11 What's up with her?	
12 He's not up to it.	

Nouns formed from phrasal verbs

2 Phrasal verbs can be used to form nouns and adjectives, for example:

break in — a break-in; saw off — sawn-off

Use these words to write a sentence similar in meaning to the sentences below.

turn-out / write-off / sell-out / slip-up / work-out / (make a) stop-over / tip-off

1 We bought a *meal at the restaurant and ate it at home.*
 We bought a <u>take-away</u> *meal.*
2 The police received a warning that an armed robbery was going to take place.
3 We can't repair this car because it is too badly damaged.
4 More people came to the meeting than I expected.
5 Jack likes nothing better than a good session at the gym.
6 When we flew to Australia, we stayed for two nights in Singapore.
7 It's just a small mistake.
8 All the tickets for the play have been sold.

ENGLISH IN USE 1

Part 5, Register cloze

This question is another example of a register cloze, like the one you did in Unit 7. This time you have to read a letter to a friend written in an informal style and use the information to complete a letter to an insurance company, which is written in a formal style.

1 Quickly read the first letter to get an idea of what it is about. What two unfortunate incidents does the writer mention?

2 Fill in the gaps in the second letter, using no more than one or two words for each gap. Remember to:

- underline the words and phrases that you need to change.
- make sure that the information is the same.
- check that the grammar is correct and the style suitable.

EXTRACT FROM LETTER TO A FRIEND

A week ago, I parked my car in the street, which I don't normally do, instead of in the car park where I work. On that day I wanted to make a quick start to my journey home. At 5 o'clock, when I got to my car, I couldn't believe it – someone had smashed into it. Actually, the damage wasn't too bad - it wasn't a write-off - and the car would still go. Then I spotted an envelope tucked under the wipers. At first, I thought it would contain the name and address of the driver who had done the damage but I was mistaken. There was a note saying sorry and two tickets for the best seats at that musical that's been sold out for months. The tickets are like gold dust so I wasn't complaining! Mary and I went the next night and we had a great time.

When we got back home, we found that burglars had robbed us of thousands of pounds worth of valuables and left a note saying, 'Hope you enjoyed the show.' Clearly, they knew we would be out and had made the most of the situation!

EXTRACT FROM LETTER TO INSURANCE COMPANY

On 12 December, contrary to my (0) ......usual...... practice, which is to park my car in the (1) .... car park, I left it in the street next to the car park. On that particular day I wished to commence my homeward journey without (2) .... At 5 p.m. I left my office and walked to the car. To my (3) ...., it had, while parked, been involved in a (4) .... with another vehicle. There was some damage, fairly (5) ...., to the front of the car, but it could still be (6) ....

I observed, under the windscreen wipers, a white envelope. My (7) .... assumption that it would contain the name and address of the driver who had damaged my car proved to be (8) .... There was no name and address but there was a note of (9) .... and, as compensation, two (10) .... tickets to a popular musical — for which tickets are almost (11) .... These tickets seemed a suitable recompense for the damage to the car. The next evening I attended the theatre, accompanied by my wife, and enjoyed the show very much.

You can imagine our horror when, on (12) .... home late at night, we found that our house had been burgled and thousands of pounds' worth of valuables had been stolen. There was also another note, obviously from the burglars which said, 'Hope you enjoyed the show.' Clearly they had taken (13) .... of the certain knowledge that we would be out of the house in order to perpetrate this crime.

LISTENING 2

1 You are going to listen to three people discussing why children tell lies. Before you listen, discuss these questions.

1 Why do you think children tell lies? How do you think their parents should react?

2 How serious do you think lying is? Does it depend on the age of the child or the type of lie?

2 ▣ Before you listen, read through the notes below and try to predict the missing words. Then listen to the recording and complete the notes according to the information you hear. Use one, two or three words.

Why do children tell lies?

Major problem: adults send children (1) ....
When children are about four, parents regard lies as a kind of (2) ....
Parents take (3) .... very seriously.
Age three: beginning of the development of (4) ....
Children may lie to show (5) .... to friends.
Children need to know that good relationships are based on (6) ....
Teenagers are especially critical of (7) ....
Psychologists are against (8) .... for lying.
Teenage lying may be a reaction against parental (9) ....
....

3 Are there any situations in which you think it would be acceptable to tell a lie? For example, is it acceptable to lie in order to:

- avoid doing an unpleasant task, e.g. doing the housework?
- protect a friend from trouble, e.g. if you saw them shoplifting?
- help someone who's depressed feel good about themselves?

LANGUAGE STUDY 1

Nominal clauses after thinking verbs (Notes page 206)

1 Verbs denoting mental processes, such as *think, believe, know, wonder, imagine, understand* are often followed by nominal clauses. Nominal clauses are introduced by *that* or *wh-*words, *if* and *whether*, which indicate indirect questions.

1 In which of these examples can the introductory word be omitted without a change of meaning?

a. Sylvia couldn't believe *what* she was hearing. *(text page 103)*
b. The police didn't know *when* the robbery was going to happen. *(text page 103)*
c. Children need to know *that* telling other people the truth is the basis of a good relationship. *(Listening 2)*
d. Parents should try to understand *why* their children are telling lies. *(Listening 2)*
e. Some parents wonder *if* punishment is a good thing when children lie.

2 Re-express these sentences beginning with a nominal clause.

1 Is it right to punish a child for lying?
I don't believe ....
2 Should I always tell a friend the truth?
I don't know ....
3 Why do you never talk to me?
I don't understand ....
4 77% of women vacuum every 2—3 days.
Did you know .... ?
5 Did you lock the door behind you when you left the house?
Can you remember .... ?
6 How could I forget our anniversary?
I can't imagine ....

Nominal clauses in indirect speech (Notes pages 206—207)

2 Nominal clauses are also used after reporting verbs in indirect speech. Read these examples and identify the changes that occur after a past tense reporting verb. When does the 'sequence of tenses' rule apply?

1 a. 'Sylvia, why did you get up?' he asked.
  b. He asked Sylvia why she had got up.

2 a. 'The robbery will take place tomorrow,' she told the police.
  b. She told the police that the robbery would take place the next day.

3 a. 'Can I come in?' he asked.
  b. He asked if he could come in.

4 a. 'I'm not proud of being an informer,' she explains.
  b. She explained that she isn't proud of being an informer.

5 a. 'Honesty is the best policy,' my mother always said.
  b. My mother always said that honesty is the best policy.

3 We don't always have to use *say* or *tell* to introduce indirect statements. Other reporting verbs that are followed by a nominal clause include:

complain / conclude / declare / reply / insist that / assure / convince / remind someone that / admit / announce / explain (to someone) that

Report these statements using an appropriate verb from the list above.

1 'I'll never let you down!' he said.
  He assured me that ...

2 'I've got a new boyfriend!' she told her parents proudly.

3 'I'm very sorry Mrs Smith-Brown, it was I who broke your Ming vase,' he said.

4 'You never buy me flowers any more!' she said.

5 'He must have gone home,' we said.

6 'It's your Mother's birthday this Saturday,' he said to Mary.

7 'The battle is over and we have won!' he told the General.

Other verb patterns after reporting verbs (Notes page 207)

4 Here are some more verbs that can be used to report what people say.

1 Which of the verb patterns A—D can follow these sets of verbs?

1 admit / deny / suggest
2 advise / insist / recommend / request
3 agree / offer / promise / threaten
4 beg / order / persuade / urge / warn

A to do something
B someone (not) to do something
C doing something
D that someone (should) do something

2 Fill in the gaps with the correct preposition.

A: I do apologise .... breaking your vase.

B: I will never forgive you .... being so clumsy! I insist .... your buying me a new one now!

A: But it's priceless! Shouldn't you blame yourself .... not keeping it in a safe place?

5 Use appropriate verbs from Exercise 4 to report the direct speech. You don't need to report every word. Invent the situation and the speakers yourself.

1 'Please forgive me! I can't imagine how I could have forgotten your birthday. I'll never do it again!'

2 'You look tired. Why don't you take a few days off? It'll do you good.'

3 'You must come and visit us soon, I won't take no for an answer!'

4 'Promise me you won't tell anyone what I've just told you? It'll be our little secret, won't it?'

5 'You shouldn't go climbing in this weather. It's too dangerous!'

6 'I tell you it wasn't me! I was at home reading a book when it happened!'

READING 2

Exam File: Part 2, Gapped text

When answering this question, remember:

- read the main part of the text first.
- the 'gapped' text may tell a story. If so, make sure you understand the order of the main events.
- highlight linking and referencing words to help you put the paragraphs in the right place.
- look for grammatical and lexical links between paragraphs.
- check your answers by reading the whole text again in sequence. Does it make sense?

1 Discuss these questions before you read the article below.

1 What do you think of hitchhiking? Have you ever done it?
2 What are the possible dangers a) for the hitchhiker? b) for the driver of the vehicle?

2 Read the base text, ignoring the gaps. Complete these notes, which summarise the main events of the story.

Writer picks up hitchhiker at ... Hitchhiker tells sad story about ... Writer takes him home ... Takes him back to London ... Writer discovers that hitchhiker ...

Innocents abroad

LAST TIME I went to Devon, I stopped at Heston service station and picked up a shabby, unshaven, shivering image of desolation. "You don't often get picked up by a woman," he said. Now that I owned a car, I explained, I wanted to repay some of the hospitality I had enjoyed in my own hitchhiking days.

(1)

Every hitchhiker has a story. David's was an innocent abroad's nightmare, which had begun when his plane from Australia landed hours late on Wednesday night. Too late for him to pick up the camper van that was to be his home throughout a five-week tour of the British Isles. He booked into a small hotel in London. On his return from the shower, he found that his rucksack, containing money, traveller's cheques, clothes, camcorder, passport and driving licence had vanished. Stripped of everything, he reported the theft to the hotel manager and the police. He then shivered for hours before a sergeant took him to the Salvation Army in order to get some clothes. Thursday at the Australian High Commission was a bureaucratic blur of quadruple form-filling, faxes, telexes and emergency applications for replacement papers.

(2)

I was surprised that David wasn't interested in Stonehenge. "We've got prehistoric stone circles in Australia too, you know, much older than this." But when we reached the seaside, Buddleigh Salterton and Portland Bill lifted his spirits. We found him some trousers and shoes, a shirt and socks, a couple of old jumpers that had been Dad's. Our reward was to see him regaining energy and enthusiasm and talking more about himself.

(3)

In the local pub, he met my friends, played pool, talked politics. We planned a picnic for the weekend before he flew home. He was a good and grateful guest. He tightened the wheel nuts on my car, chatted amiably with my family and friends, and spent the money I had lent him on a miniature rose for my mother and lunch on Portland Bill.

(4)

Monday was very tiring. After conducting interviews all day, I hardly felt in the mood for a wild night out. Which was just as well, because David didn't show. He had booked out of the hotel that morning. When I phoned the Australian High Commission, the

consular section told me they had a file on him going back to 1992. Richard Stevenson, *aka* David Walsh *aka* several other names, is not even an Australian. He is a UK citizen who has been fined for deception. Apparently, he has a penchant for soft-hearted saps from the South West.

(5)

At least other liberal softies can learn from my mistake. Don't believe a word of it! Deny your better instincts and if 'David' should happen to hitch a lift from you, dump him on a B-road to nowhere!

Devon: a county on the south-west coast of England

The Salvation Army: a Christian organisation who work to help the poor

aka: abbreviation for 'also known as'

A He *told us* about the farm his parents had left him, which he ran with his sister, helped and hindered by ten ex-psychiatric patients. Even the disasters had their funny side. One disaster was a tragedy, though; a mother and child had been killed when the driver of a massive truck suffered a heart attack and ploughed into their car. They were David's wife and three-year-old son. That was three years ago. Now it was time to take a holiday, get a fresh perspective. David didn't want to dwell on the past, near or distant. "My holiday started," he declared, "when you stopped your car."

B It wasn't all bad. The police were pretty sure who the thief was. It was just a matter of finding him. The lawyer at the *High Commission* assured David that the insurance money would come through by Monday. And the van hire people were holding the camper for him, waiving charges for the first five days' hire that they had lost. The only problem was how to get through a weekend in London with no money, no cheques, no plastic and no ID. A fruit farmer, accustomed to surfing off his own five-mile stretch of coast in north-west Australia, he had naturally headed away from the grime of London.

C Some did not escape as lightly as I. Some lost their hearts as well as their money. They were too chagrined to report the fraud to the police. I did report it, not because I thought I'd ever see my money again, but in the hope that further frauds might be prevented. The police took a written statement from me but they were not really interested.

D I did not at first reveal my destination to *my passenger*, having learnt from past experience of sharing long journeys with surly, smelly strangers. But as we hit the A303, my mind was made up. I phoned ahead to my mother in Exeter and asked her if I might bring my hitchhiker home for the weekend. After hearing the drift of David's tale, she agreed.

E After a wet, dark journey back to London on *Sunday evening*, I booked him in to a small hotel in Kings Cross. We both had a long day ahead of us. For me, four long *interviews for a housing survey*. For him, picking up the threads of his holiday at the Australian High Commission. But we had *Monday evening* to look forward to. David was going to take me out for a meal at a restaurant of my choice, pay me back the money I'd lent him, drink a toast to his forthcoming tour of Britain — and plan the visit I was going to make to his farm next Christmas.

plastic: a reference to 'plastic money' or credit cards
A303, B-road: roads connecting towns and/or villages. B roads are smaller, less important roads.

3 Now read the base text **and** the paragraphs that have been removed, and decide where they fit in the main part of the text. Lexical clues have been italicised to help you.
Note that there are only five missing paragraphs for this text, but in the exam there will always be six or seven missing paragraphs plus an extra paragraph that doesn't fit anywhere.

4 Can you explain these words and expressions from the article which the writer uses to describe herself and the hitchhiker?

1 an image of desolation *(main text)*
2 an innocent abroad *(main text)*
3 amiably *(main text)*
4 a soft-hearted sap *(main text)*
5 a liberal softy *(main text)*
6 chagrined *(para C)*
7 surly *(para D)*

5 Like the one in Unit 1, this article uses a mixture of direct and indirect speech. The third paragraph (beginning 'Every hitchhiker has a story ...') is a report of what 'David' told the writer. What do you think his actual words were? Can you find any other extended passages of indirect speech like this?

6 Discuss these questions.

1 What do you think David's motives were for behaving in this way?
2 What do you think the writer has learnt from this experience?
3 What is the double meaning of the title?
4 Have you ever made a similar error of judgement about a person? Explain what happened.

VOCABULARY 2

Word formation

1 Complete the sentences with the words below.

trustworthy / trusted / trusting / mistrust / untrustworthy

1 John hated the atmosphere of hostility and .... in his office.
2 He is entirely .... — you can ask him to deliver the diamonds for you and be confident that they will arrive safely.
3 Sarah has a very .... nature and believes the hard-luck stories that people tell her.
4 The President discussed the matter with his most .... advisers.
5 His record of petty crime shows that he is completely ....

Abbreviations

2 What do these abbreviations stand for? How do you say them?

1 You don't have to carry an *ID* card in Britain.
2 The boxer was *KO*'d in the first round.
3 This programme will run on a *PC*.
4 Please reply *asap*.
5 The flight's *ETA* was 12.10, so it's 30 minutes overdue.
6 You can pay for the package *COD*.

Expressions to do with honesty/dishonesty

3 What is meant by these expressions, which are all connected with honesty and dishonesty?

1 In his speech, the politician *trod a fine line* between truth and falsehood.
2 The conspiracy remained a secret until someone decided to *spill the beans*.
3 The prosecution accused the defence witness of being *a pathological liar*.
4 If you've done something wrong, it's always best to *own up* and tell the truth.
5 You can't trust Gill. Everything she says is *a pack of lies*.
6 The jury found the criminal guilty. The expression on his face *gave the game away*.

WRITING

> **Exam File: Parts 1 and 2, Report writing**
>
> In Parts 1 or 2 of Paper 2 you may be asked to write a recommendation report. This could involve analysing problems and suggesting solutions. Remember to:
> • state the subject of your report clearly.
> • present your ideas in a logical sequence.
> • use headings to indicate the main points.
> • end with a clear recommendation.

Read the writing task on page 111 and follow the **Steps to Writing** below.

Step 1 Task interpretation
You are writing a report for the principal of your college. What **two** things does the task ask you to do? What register and tone would be suitable?

Step 2 Selecting and summarising
1 Decide what information you need to include. Look at the article and memo and complete this list of problems mentioned.

Safety problems	Security problems
litter everywhere	computer equipment stolen

2 Now look at the suggestions made in the annotations. Remember that your report will be 250 words, so you won't be able to include them all. Add suggestions to the list below, selecting only the most useful and adding any of your own.

Recommendations
fine students for dropping litter
chain computers to desks ...

Step 3 Layout and organisation
Look at the notes you made in Step 2. Think about how you are going to organise your report. Use these headings to help you plan.

Introduction
Safety and security in the college
What we can do about it

Step 4 Write

1 Read this conclusion to a report about crime prevention. How could it be improved? Rewrite it in a suitable register, using these words and phrases:

In conclusion, we must take urgent steps to … I would strongly advise … .

```
Crime in local neighbourhoods
is on the increase, and we
have to do something to stop
it — now! I myself was
burgled last June! Things
just can't go on like this!
I really think that one of
the best ways to discourage
crime is to set up a
Neighbourhood Watch group.
```

2 Now write your report.
▶ Recommending (page 85)
▶ Language Bank

Step 5 Evaluate and edit
▶ Writing checklist (page 214)

Language Bank

Introduction
This report outlines/deals with/looks at/considers …

It is based on …

Describing problems
The college has suffered a number of break-ins …

Many students are concerned about their safety …

Another cause for concern is …

Many accidents are caused by …

Making recommendations
To discourage people from littering …

To improve security …

As an additional security measure, …
you should consider installing video cameras.

Another solution would be to …

The Principal of your college has asked you to write a report entitled 'Safety and Security in the College', from the students' point of view. He has sent you a newspaper article that he is very concerned about, and a memo from the caretaker of the college which he has annotated.

Read the newspaper report and the memo. Then, using the information carefully, write a **report** describing safety and security problems from a student's point of view, and suggesting some solutions.

students complain about missing equipment and lost files

aradise for thieves

and the college's accounts reveal that over £50,000 of computer equipment has been stolen from the college in the last six months. Apparently, thieves posing as students have just walked out with it in broad daylight! Twice recently students have been violently attacked when they challenged suspicious characters carrying computers.

chain computers to desks? employ security guards?

memo

```
TO       The principal
FROM     John Briggs, caretaker
SUBJECT  Your request for information
DATE     22/5

Thanks for your note. The problems we
encounter include:
```

• missing keys — people don't return them *new system?*
• doors not locked when there is valuable equipment in the room *replace?*
• too much litter — can cause accidents (a lot of litter bins have disappeared)
• students not carrying identity cards *make carrying IDs compulsory?*
• coffee spilt on floor (not just in cafeteria) — causes accidents, sometimes serious ones *restrict to cafeteria?*
• too many exits and entrances to the building — difficult to check who's coming in

video cameras?

111

LANGUAGE STUDY 2

Verbs with two objects (Notes pages 207—208)

Many verbs that take two objects can appear in the following patterns. What do you notice about the position of the direct and indirect objects in each pattern?

1	**Verb**	+ IO	+ DO
	Give	me	that book.
2a.	**Verb**	+ DO +	*to* + IO
	Give	that book	to me.
2b.	**Verb**	+ DO +	*for* + IO
	I bought	a book	for her.

Which of the following sentences can be converted to pattern 2a., and which to pattern 2b.? Which can't be converted to either pattern? Can you work out why? Think about the meaning of the verbs.

1 Could you get this customer a glass of water?
2 Why did you lend Jane your book?
3 Will you save us some birthday cake?
4 Doing the decorating themselves saved the Smiths a lot of money.
5 I've written my friend several letters.
6 Sir Cripps gave his youngest son all his property.
7 Let's give Maria a farewell party.
8 Your behaviour has caused your parents a great deal of trouble.
9 The soldier's bravery cost him his life.
10 We still have to buy my mother a birthday gift.
11 Spare us the embarrassment of having to say no.
12 Could you spare Peter and me some time next week?

ENGLISH IN USE 2

Exam File: Part 3, Error correction

The task below is similar to the one you did in Unit 2. You have to identify the extra words that should not be there. Remember to watch out for:

- unnecessary conjunctions (linking words).
- wrong use of prepositions.
- incorrect particles for phrasal verbs, or phrasal verbs that don't exist.

1 Read the text below quickly. What is the writer objecting to?

2 Some of the lines in the text are correct, but most have **one** extra wrong word. Tick the correct lines and underline the wrong words in the incorrect lines, as in the examples.

0 <u>by</u>
0 ✓

The Uses and Abuses of People

0 "In that case, we can't use you." This is how a young woman by working
0 in public relations ended our phone conversation when she discovered that
1 I was not being prepared to break a long-standing lecturing engagement.
2 She wanted me to do some work for her company and while I was trying
3 to be as accommodating to her as possible, despite such accommodation
4 could not include breaking up my promise to the university. Her choice
5 of words caused to me considerable distress. I don't like being used. I
6 told myself that the young woman had simply been too upset to choose her
7 words carefully. She had a difficult task and my being unavailable made
8 it even harder than for her. I thought about writing her a little note
9 pointing it out that she could offend people by saying she was using them
10 but then I decided not to bother about. Such good advice is never
11 appreciated. However, I had to revise my conclusions when, a few days
12 later, a television producer phoned to ask myself if he could meet me
13 to talk about a programme he was making up. When he arrived at my
14 flat, he said, "I want to see if I can use you in this programme." If the
15 words "can use you" have become the common phrases, it's a serious
16 matter. What's wrong with "I'd like you to take a part in this programme"?

9 Making a living

SPEAKING 1

1 Work in pairs. Choose two photographs each and answer these questions.

1 What kind of work does each job represent? Choose from these words.

seasonal work / freelance work / shift work / casual labour / teleworking / a job share / a 9—5 job

2 Which of the following could be a feature of these jobs?

- working as part of a team or on your own
- a high salary and/or high status
- working in a competitive environment
- working flexible or fixed working hours
- lots of variety or repetitive, mundane tasks
- independence or working under supervision
- travelling a lot for your job
- a good career structure
- strenuous physical work
- working under pressure to tight deadlines
- job security

Do you agree with what your partner has said?

2 Discuss these questions.

1 Which features listed in Exercise 1 would you consider drawbacks or benefits?

2 What **three** things are most important for you in a job?

READING
Part 4, Multiple matching

1 You are going to read an article about an air stewardess, a miller, an art gallery owner and a furniture maker. Before you read, think about these questions.

1 What does each job involve?
2 Which jobs could involve long or irregular hours?
3 What sort of training do these jobs require?
4 What kind of skills and personal qualities are needed for these jobs? For example:

To be a ..., you have to

... have self-control / physical strength / stamina / personality / initiative / good interpersonal skills ...

... be highly committed / extremely hard-working / shrewd / creative ...

2

1 Look at the instructions and skim the texts. Then decide which technique, from those already suggested, is the most appropriate for tackling this task. (See Units 1, 2 and 4.)

2 Match the statements in 1—16 with the person (A, B, C or D) that they refer to.

A Joanne	
B Nigel	
C Anna-Mei	
D Dennis	
This person	
has achieved a long-term ambition.	**1** ....
works irregular hours.	**2** ....
thinks of him/herself as a salesperson.	**3** ....
is highly regarded in his/her field.	**4** ....
is judged on the basis of physical appearance.	**5** ....
is dependent on personal contact for success at work.	**6** ....
does some mental preparation before arriving at work.	**7** ....
has plans for change.	**8** ....
draws inspiration from the working practices of the past.	**9** ....
has an unusually long working week.	**10** .... **11** ....
has a job that involves strenuous physical activity.	**12** ....
finds it difficult to get away from the place of work.	**13** ....
has travelled to acquire appropriate expertise.	**14** ....
has integrated traditional and modern approaches.	**15** .... **16** ....

3 There are several references to money in the texts. What do these words and expressions mean?

1 We don't pay *retainers* ... *(text C)*
2 We have a *set commission* for all our artists. *(text C)*
3 If you give *discounts* ... *(text C)*
4 Although *turnover* has risen steadily ... *(text C)*
5 [He] accepts *commissions* to recreate Korean bureaus ... *(text D)*

4 What do these expressions from the text indicate about the difficulties of each person's job and his/her attitude to it?

1 ... these briefings can be really fraught. *(text A)*
2 So much for glamour. *(text A)*
3 ... to cope with the physical challenge ... *(text B)*
4 Anybody can walk through the door. *(text C)*
5 ... he found it difficult to balance commercial success with the artistic aspects ... *(text D)*

5 Discuss these questions.

1 Who do you think is getting the most/least satisfaction out of their job? Justify your answer.

2 Which of these jobs appeals to **you** the most and the least?

Ⓐ The air stewardess

IT WAS 3 am. Joanne ate her breakfast with her eyes closed. Her flight was due to leave at 6 am. She had to be at the airport for 4.30 am.

"I've got one hour to make myself 'presentable' for work. It's a
5 wonderful word, isn't it? All things to all people — reassuring professional to the over-anxious first-time flyers, challenge and disciplinarian to the lager louts, bubbling bimbo to the old hands of the flight crew."

She opened her make-up box. "I go on automatic pilot, really. It
10 takes a good twenty-five minutes to put it all on and transform myself into the cool professional that I know I have to be. I think that if you look well-groomed, then you look as if you've got self-control and self-respect. When I'm putting my make-up on, I usually run through all the questions that are going to be asked at
15 the pre-flight briefing. You can be asked about first-aid, aspects of passenger safety care or about the technical aspects of the aircraft. Some senior cabin staff really like to stamp their authority on the briefing, to show who's boss. Consequently, these briefings can be really fraught."

20 She'd had a lot of late departures recently. There was usually no time for a meal on the stopover. She had to tidy the litter off the seats, check all the sick bags and the magazines in the backs of the seats and restock the range of toiletries laid out in the toilet. "So much for glamour," she said.

lager lout: young man who likes to get drunk and behave badly *(colloquial)*
bimbo: attractive but not very intelligent young woman *(colloquial)*

Ⓑ The miller

25 NIGEL MOON, a graduate in history and archaeology, always wanted to buy a windmill. When a chance came to buy Downfield Mill, he left his job and took a variety of part-time jobs for the five years needed to restore the building to working condition.

On milling days, he can be seen dashing frantically around the five
30 floors, tools usually in hand as he strives to keep all systems going. "Even when there is no wind and the sails are down, it is hard work because I have a set of stones powered by an electric motor. Working the mill this way is not as satisfying as when it is running on the sails, but the two systems often run in concert and the electric system helps to keep
35 production going. I'm not really in the business for the money. There must be thousands of easier ways of making a living." On the days he is not milling, he is on the road delivering his organic brown and white flour, milled oats, rye, maize and barley to warehouses, bakers and hotels.

Although it is an exhausting, seven-day-a-week occupation, Moon says
40 he would not do anything else. He has reluctantly concluded, however, that the only way to expand his business and to cope with the physical challenge of handling ten tons of machinery as a one-man operation, is to sell Downfield and buy a more efficient mill.

⊙ The art dealer

"IT IS a myth," says Anna-Mei Chadwick, "that running an art gallery is all about opening shows and bottles of wine." She regularly works ten hours a day, seven days a week. She regards herself first and foremost as a retailer.

50 "The retail trade is very tough — you need stamina and a lot of help. Dealing with the general public takes a certain strength. Anybody can walk through the door."

Initially, she approached artists she knew and found others by going to shows and competitions. She concentrates on artists with
55 promise who are not necessarily well-known.

"We don't pay retainers and we don't have exclusive contracts with our artists, so we rely on their loyalty to come back. We have a set commission for all our artists. They know we don't juggle around with the prices on the wall. If you give discounts, people
60 know that the pictures on the wall were overpriced in the first place."

Each year the gallery runs seventeen shows. Although turnover has risen steadily since the gallery opened, it was two years before she took on a full-time assistant. She still needs to be in the gallery
65 much of the time. Clients and artists expect to see her. "Running an art gallery is a very personal business — you have to be there rather than an assistant."

⊙ The furniture maker

TO DESCRIBE Dennis Young as a carpenter is unfair. For Young is a woodworking virtuoso. This American artist fashions beautiful writing desks
70 for Japanese rooms, accepts commissions to recreate Korean bureaus and sculpts from wood his own variation of the modern Windsor chair. At the same time, he voices great concern over the disappearance of traditional skills in Japan, including years of woodworking craftsmanship.

"My first experience of making furniture was in Japan. At that time in Japan
75 it was not unusual to find hand-made merchandise. But traditional-style workshops have become very, very rare."

After learning the basic skills in Japan, Young went to England and was apprenticed at a small workshop in order to master the skill of making Windsor chairs. He went back to the United States to open his own workshop,
80 and quickly established a reputation as one of the leading modern cabinet-makers. His bow-back chair, the fruit of years of effort to simplify the traditional Windsor chair to fit modern environments, has won many prizes. Some of his finest pieces have been displayed at London's Victoria and Albert Museum.

85 Young has developed some unique working techniques: he uses American machines that are more than one hundred years old to do the basic job of shaping the wood and then he switches to English and Japanese tools for the details. Three years ago, Young returned to Japan, giving up a successful business in California because he found it difficult to balance commercial
90 success with his commitment to the artistic aspects of woodworking.

ENGLISH IN USE 1
Part 1, Multiple choice cloze

1 Discuss this question.

Do you think there is a single, right job for each of us or could we all do a number of different jobs equally well?

2 Read the text below to find out how people normally choose jobs, according to the writer. Then read the text again and circle the word (A, B, C or D) that best fits each space. Look back at Unit 4 for advice on how to do this type of task.

3 Discuss these questions.

1 What has influenced you in your choice of your actual or potential career?

2 What other careers have you considered?

3 To what extent has chance or good luck played a part?

4 What jobs would you recommend for people with the following combinations of qualities?
- numerate, computer-literate, meticulous
- patient, caring, physically fit
- articulate, outgoing, persuasive

How do you choose the right job?

A few people decide early in life what they want to do and then follow a prescribed path of training to reach their (1) .... . More often, a young person takes the best job available, and that (2) .... to a lifetime in a particular field. Of course, both *who* you know and *what* you know are important. Frequently an individual finds a job through a friend, relative or other (3) .... person. However, with a university degree the minimum (4) .... for many jobs — and advanced training and qualifications a (5) .... in most professional fields — what you know can be the (6) .... to a good job.

There is probably no single 'right' job for anybody. Out of the (7) .... 20,000 types of occupations available in modern society, there are probably hundreds that you could perform well and find rewarding. Although circumstances (8) .... one's choices, there are still more possibilities than most people realise. Chance always (9) .... a part in finding a job you like, but vocational counsellors believe that a person can improve the (10) .... by analysing his or her ambitions, interests and (11) .... . One person may want to earn a lot of money. Others may (12) .... priority to being active, helping people or having a low (13) .... of becoming unemployed. Personal interests, such as love of the (14) .... or a fascination with computers, may point the (15) .... to a job a person enjoys and respects.

1	**A** plan	**B** goal	**C** end	**D** object
2	**A** leads	**B** directs	**C** conducts	**D** introduces
3	**A** valuable	**B** beneficial	**C** helpful	**D** advantageous
4	**A** necessity	**B** obligation	**C** offer	**D** requirement
5	**A** need	**B** must	**C** want	**D** demand
6	**A** ticket	**B** admission	**C** direction	**D** certificate
7	**A** expected	**B** assessed	**C** estimated	**D** calculated
8	**A** shorten	**B** press	**C** shrink	**D** narrow
9	**A** takes	**B** gives	**C** puts	**D** plays
10	**A** odds	**B** difference	**C** angles	**D** favour
11	**A** faculties	**B** aptitudes	**C** inclinations	**D** tendencies
12	**A** make	**B** set	**C** give	**D** place
13	**A** risk	**B** hazard	**C** danger	**D** uncertainty
14	**A** outwards	**B** outside	**C** outdoors	**D** outback
15	**A** course	**B** way	**C** passage	**D** progress

WRITING 1

Exam File: Part 1, Job application

Questions on the CAE Writing Paper often relate to employment, and you may be asked to reply to a job advertisement. To do this successfully, you need to:

- know the vocabulary connected with job applications.
- identify the qualities and qualifications necessary to do the job.
- highlight areas in the advertisement which you'd like more information about.
- write your letter in an appropriate register.

Read the writing task on page 119 carefully and follow the **Steps to Writing** below.

Step 1 Task interpretation
How many pieces of writing does the task require? What text types do you have to produce? Who will read them? What will be the most appropriate register for each task?

Step 2 Selecting and summarising
1 Read the job advertisements carefully. Decide which job you want to apply for and write down the reason why (e.g. more interesting, may be better paid, etc.). Make a list of the qualities and qualifications the job requires and note down any relevant experience you may have. For example:

Tour leader

Job description	Relevant experience
need two languages	speak English and Spanish
good organiser	president of college cycling club, organised club outings
interpersonal skills	worked part-time in travel agency during summer holidays

2 Remember you have to ask for extra information as well as give details about yourself. Look at the handwritten notes. Are there any other aspects you'd like to ask about? Don't forget to rephrase your questions in an appropriate register.

Step 3 Layout and organisation
You have to produce two types of writing.

1 For the note, use an informal register and informal punctuation. Don't forget to mention which job you applied for and **why**.

2 For the letter, begin and end with a formal greeting. Follow this plan.

Paragraph 1: Say who you are and why you are writing.

Paragraphs 2/3: Give reasons why you are interested in the job and why you think you are suitable for the post. Say what experience you have had and what sort of person you are.

Concluding paragraph: Ask for more information about the job.

Step 4 Write
Write the note and letter. Remember you only have about 200 words for your letter.

▶ Present perfect (page 16), Indirect questions (page 107), *be used to* (page 63)

▶ Language Bank

Step 5 Evaluate and edit
▶ Writing checklist (page 214)

Language Bank

I am writing to apply for the post/position of ...

Giving reasons

I believe that I have the necessary experience and personal qualities ...

Firstly, I am used to organising outings ...

In addition, I have already done some part-time work ...

I would appreciate the chance to ...

Asking for information

I would like to know if/whether ...

I would appreciate it if you could send me further details about ...

Concluding

I enclose a completed application form/my curriculum vitae with full details of ...

I am available for interview at any time convenient to you ...

I look forward to hearing from you ...

You have asked an English friend to send you information about jobs in England during the summer. He has sent you the two advertisements below, to which you have added your comments. Read the note from your friend and the two advertisements and then decide which job you would like to apply for.

Here's a couple of adverts for you to look at — more coming soon. They are quite different types of job. I don't know which one will appeal to you. Which one will be best for improving your English? Or maybe that isn't the most important thing for you now.

Let me know which one you choose and good luck!

Dave

what dates exactly?

STUDENT WANTED

We require a student to help out in our small, friendly hotel during the busy <u>summer months</u>. Duties include reception, serving food and cleaning rooms. Hard work and <u>long hours</u> but a friendly atmosphere. Food and accommodation provided. <u>Previous experience of hotel work desirable</u>.

Write to Mrs Turner, Mentmore Hotel, Castle Lane, St Ives, Cornwall.

which days would I have off?

is it essential?

Study Tours
INTERNATIONAL

Tour Leader

Study Tours International is looking for a tour leader to join its committed, enthusiastic and hard-working team during the <u>busy summer months</u>. It could be you! This is a temporary post but could become permanent. You will have the drive and initiative necessary to help organise <u>international study tours</u> for <u>students aged 18–25</u>. You will be able to speak <u>two languages</u> as well as English. You must thrive on working under pressure, have excellent interpersonal and organising skills, and accept the need to work <u>unsociable hours</u>. You will spend about half your time at Head Office in London and the other half <u>overseas</u>. An <u>attractive salary</u> is offered. Write and convince us that you are the person we are looking for.

Write to Clare Clairmont, Director, STI, Trelawny House, Byron Crescent, London

hectic!

which months exactly?

where to?

from where?

does it matter which ones?

how much?

what hours exactly?

which countries?

Now write:
a) a **letter** of application for the job that you would like to do. Give information about yourself and ask about any points that you are not sure of. Write about 200 words.

b) a **note** to your friend thanking him and saying which job you have applied for and why. Write about 50 words.

LISTENING 1
Part 3, Multiple choice questions

1 You are going to listen to Barbara talking about her experience of working in offices. First, think about aspects of working in an office that would make it pleasant or unpleasant. For example:

- getting on/not getting on with your boss
- having a good/bad relationship with colleagues

2 ⌨ Before the first listening, remember to read the multiple choice questions (but not the options). Turn the stems into questions and be ready to note down your answers.

Before the second listening, read the options — A, B, C and D — carefully. Choose the one closest to your own answer.

1 At the moment Barbara is
   A looking for work.
   B working as a legal assistant.
   C enjoying a vacation.
   D out of work.

2 With regard to relations among colleagues, Barbara thinks that nowadays
   A offices put more pressure on employees.
   B people have become more self-centred.
   C business is more competitive.
   D employees are less committed to their work.

3 Barbara prefers to work in places where
   A there is a reward for each person's effort.
   B goals are understood by everyone.
   C individual talent is recognised.
   D there is a shared aim.

4 Barbara works best when jobs are done
   A late in the day.
   B according to a fixed timetable.
   C early in the day.
   D by a group.

5 Barbara has had to accept
   A lack of organisation in offices.
   B the unpredictability of most working days.
   C the need to work to deadlines.
   D the requirement to keep everything in its place.

6 In Barbara's opinion, offices run smoothly when people
   A start work as early as possible.
   B give priority to important matters.
   C concentrate on mainly small matters.
   D anticipate the near future.

3 Discuss these questions.

1 Do you think the workplace is becoming more competitive? Why?

2 Do you find that you work better at a certain time of day? If so, why do you think this is?

VOCABULARY 1
Phrasal verbs with *down*

1 Identify the phrasal verbs in these extracts from Listening 1 and explain what they mean. Can you match the meanings of *down* with the definitions below?

1 Unfortunately, my last office closed down, partly I think due to the recession.
2 I'm more alert first thing in the morning, in the evening I tend to slow down …
3 … people used to be more helpful … there were fewer barriers to break down …

A stop completely
B destroy
C decrease/become less or inferior

2

1 Complete the sentences below with one of these verbs in the correct form.

tear / run / let / burn / die

1 He had let his business .... down to the point where most of the employees had to be laid off.

2 He was terribly late for work — someone had .... down the tyres on his car!

3 The fire was definitely an arson attack. The warehouse had been deliberately .... down.

4 As panic about the recession .... down, the company began to invest in new staff.

5 The steel factory where your grandfather used to work was .... down years ago.

2 Group the verbs according to the meaning of *down*.

SPEAKING 2

1 Look at the pictures and read the details below.

Imagine you have just started work for a large company together with another ten people. The Human Resources manager wants to arrange an event that will help you all get to know each other, understand each other's strengths and weaknesses, and learn how to co-operate and communicate.

You have been asked for your views on which of the activities illustrated in the pictures would best achieve these aims.

With your partner, discuss each activity and try to select the one you think will be most suitable.

2 Report your conclusions to the rest of the class. Were you able to agree on one activity?

Language Bank

Justifying and defending opinions

Personally, I'd go for ...

A course like that would offer a real challenge whereas a party ...

After all, the purpose is to learn how to co-operate.

But that kind of thing is very expensive and besides ...

I mean, don't you think we have to consider ...?

Actually, I think that ... would give us a better chance to get to know each other.

You may be right. But I still think ...

Well, what do you think of ...?

It sounds a bit dull. Still, I suppose it might be the best option, all things considered.

If you think about it, ...

1

a party

3
a social evening at a bowling alley

4

a one-day training seminar

2

a survival training course

ENGLISH IN USE 2
Part 6, Discourse cloze

1 Before you read the text below, discuss these questions.

1 What do you think is a reasonable number of hours per week to work, if you are in a full time job?

2 What pressures might force people to work very long hours?

2 Quickly read the text through, ignoring the gaps. According to the writer, why are so many people suffering from overwork? What type of problems are caused by heavy workloads?

3 Now read the text more carefully. Choose the best option from A—J below to complete the gaps. Three phrases don't fit at all. As you do the task, remember to check:

• the meaning of the sentence.
• the grammar. Does the correct structure come next?
• the punctuation.

4 Discuss these questions.

1 How does this situation compare with your country?

2 Can you suggest any solutions?

Managers under fire

James Sullivan leaves home at 7 a.m. for his office in the City of London and returns every night just after 9 p.m. He is in his early forties (0) ..J.. . He fears that if he does not work so hard he will lose his £90,000 a year job. But if he continues to put these hours in, he may lose his wife and his children. He is an unhappy and unwilling workaholic and knows that these long hours threaten a happy family life.

Experts have warned that heavy workloads are pushing marriages towards divorce (1) .... . Research has shown that British managers work an average of 55 hours a week, in blatant disregard of their contracts, which specify between 35 and 40 hours. A survey of two hundred directors last year showed that nearly half started work before 8 a.m., (2) .... . About two-thirds worked at least one weekend in four, (3) .... .

Most middle managers have taken on new tasks because layers of management have disappeared (4) .... . In many companies there are half the number of managers as before, paid twice as much (5).... . It leads to stress. When a man gets home, he feels very stressed and has little left to give. He is often too tired to talk to his wife. What makes matters worse is that more than two-thirds of managers have wives who work, (6) .... .

A and there are fewer people to do the work

B and has led to much higher profits for companies

C and the day may have been equally stressful for them

D and turning the offspring of wealthy parents into deprived children

E and a quarter were still working after 6.30 p.m.

F and more than half found that they could not take their full holidays

G and expected to be three times as productive

H and discriminates against female managers

I and there will then be more women in management

J and has three children aged eight, six and two

LANGUAGE STUDY

Writing complex sentences (Notes page 208)

1 The conjunction *and* can indicate a range of other relationships besides addition, depending on the context.

1 Decide what *and* means in the sentences below. Choose from this list of concepts.

Addition / Time sequence / Condition / Cause and effect / Contrast

1 James Sullivan leaves home at 7 a.m. ... *and* returns every night just after 9 p.m.
2 He is in his early forties *and* has three children aged eight, six and two.
3 When a man gets home, he feels very stressed *and* has little left to give.
4 [Employers] just want you to start working *and* sometimes you need to organise and see what's ahead ... *(Listening 1)*
5 He worked flat out on the project for a year *and* had a nervous breakdown.
6 Take a two-week holiday away from it all *and* you'll feel a lot better.
7 I've worked here for two years *and* I haven't had a raise.
8 My boss praised me for my report *and* I felt very pleased.
9 He got home *and* started on the report right away.
10 I'm currently on a work placement in a local company *and* I'm being trained in office skills.

2 Which sentences can you rewrite using an added link word or an adverbial clause to express the relationship between the clauses more emphatically? Use words from the list. Be careful with punctuation (see Unit 4 pages 55—56).

when / even though / despite the fact that / if / yet / whereas / with the result that / as a result / so ... that / As soon as / Immediately

Examples:
When a man gets home, he feels very stressed and, *as a result*, has little left to give.
When a man gets home, he feels *so* stressed *that* he has little left to give.

3 Which sentences can you rewrite using a present participle clause? a relative clause?

2

1 It is important that you use a range of structures in your own writing, and combine your sentences using conjunctions and link words. However, be careful not to overdo it. You should avoid:

- unnecessarily complicated sentences
- overuse of link words
- illogical use of link words
- repetition of words that are unnecessary or mean the same thing

What's wrong with this sentence? Can you improve it?

I have heard a lot about your company and that it is owned by a multi-national company from one of your employees who is a friend of mine.

You should also be careful to use the correct punctuation. What's wrong with the punctuation in this sentence?

During vacations I gained work experience in various companies, in addition I speak German fluently.

2 Can you correct and improve these sentences?

1 *I have seen your advertisement in the local paper and I am writing to apply for the job of tour leader that appeared yesterday.*
2 *At present I am a student at Melchester University and I am currently studying for a degree in Business Administration.*
3 *I am very interested in this job and in addition I believe that I have the abilities and experience needed for the job.*
4 *Although I am the President of the cycling club in my college, I have a lot of experience in organising outings as well as being experienced at leading groups of people.*
5 *I would appreciate it if you would send me more details about what the job involves, especially I would like to know about the hours of work and the salary.*

PRONUNCIATION

Weak forms

1 📼 Say these sentences aloud, then compare them with the recording. What do you notice about the pronunciation of the word *to*?

1 Two to Cambridge, please.
2 You don't have to go if you don't want to.
3 Take the road to Exeter and then drive on to Bristol.

The weak form of *to* is used except when there is a following vowel sound or when *to* is the last word before a pause. Getting this right can make a big difference to the way your English sounds.

2 📼 Now listen to these extracts from the Listening text you are going to hear in the next section. Mark the stressed forms of *to*.

1 they don't have to travel to work
2 It's also a way for the company to economise
3 usually the company will pay for the necessary connections to its own computer
4 the chance to escape from daily commuting

1 📼 Another very common weak form is *and*, which is rarely pronounced strongly. Try saying these phrases quickly. Then compare with the recording.

1 fish and chips (sounds like *fishnchips*)
2 food and drink
3 oranges and lemons
4 in and out
5 boys and girls

2 📼 Say and listen to these extracts from the Listening text you are going to hear. Notice how *and* is pronounced.

1 the idea of an office with a desk and a number of filing cabinets and a few potted plants
2 You check in ... and then you request a workstation
3 you take your possessions out of a locker and carry them to the workstation

LISTENING 2

Part 2, Note completion

1 You are going to hear a radio talk about different types of offices. Before you listen, read through the notes below and try to predict what kind of information is missing. What do you think is meant by a 'virtual office'? Do you know what 'teleworking' refers to?

2 📼 Listen and complete the notes according to the information you hear in the recording. Use one or two words in each gap. Remember that the words in the task summarise or rephrase the words in the recording. In the exam, you will hear the recording **once** only.

Changes in office work

Traditional office:
   each employee has an (1) ....
   located in a prime (2) ....
   running costs are (3) ....

Virtual office:
   on arrival staff (4) ....
   then request a (5) ....
   collect belongings from (6) ....
   popular with companies and their
   (7) ....

Teleworking:
   staff work (8) ....
   communicate by fax, telephone and
   (9) ....

3 Discuss these questions.

1 How much does the idea of working in a 'virtual office' appeal to you?
2 Can you think of any advantages for employees?

VOCABULARY 2

Idiomatic expressions to do with work

Use these idiomatic expressions to comment on the sentences below. The first one has been done as an example.

the daily grind / donkey work / slave driver / pull your weight / drive yourself too hard / work your fingers to the bone / not do a stroke of work

1 Mr Fraser makes his staff work much too hard.

   He's a slave driver!

2 The new computer will do the repetitive, mundane work so we can concentrate on the creative side of the business.

3 Sally was fed up with the same journey to work and doing exactly the same things every day.

4 Jack just sits at his desk, doing nothing at all.

5 Jenny's parents worked terribly hard for years in order to send her to an expensive school.

6 If Tony continues to work such long hours, he will make himself ill.

7 Mary doesn't work as hard as other members of her team.

WRITING 2

Part 2, Article

Read the writing task and follow the **Steps to Writing** below.

> A student magazine has asked you to contribute an **article** entitled '9—5 in the 21st century'. You have been asked to write about how working life in your country will change in the future, and the benefits and drawbacks of these changes. Write about 250 words.

Step 1 Task interpretation
What points do you have to include in your article? Who will read it? What is the most suitable register?

Step 2 Generating ideas
Think about the situation now, then imagine how working patterns may have changed in 20 years time.

Now	The future
work in offices	work at home
work 9 to 5	flexible hours
face-to-face meetings	contact via video phone

Benefits

More flexible working hours

Less pollution as fewer commuters

Working mothers/fathers can stay at home

Drawbacks

Lack of communication — people feel isolated

Less sense of working in a team

Less commitment??

Step 3 Layout and organisation
Organise your ideas into paragraphs. Decide on the number of paragraphs you will have.

Step 4 Write
Write your article, using a range of vocabulary and structures for variety.

▶ Future tenses (page 96)

Step 5 Evaluate and edit
▶ Writing checklist (page 214)

UNIT 10

Just deserts

SPEAKING 1

1 Work in pairs. Look at the photographs and discuss these questions.

1 What type of crimes are being/have been committed?

2 How serious are they?

3 Why do you think young people commit crimes like these? For example, is delinquent behaviour the result of

- peer pressure?
- lack of leisure facilities for young people?
- social disadvantage (poverty etc.)?
- violence on TV, violent computer games?
- not enough love/attention at home?
- the desire to rebel?

2 Look at these methods of dealing with young offenders. Discuss these questions.

1 Which method do you consider to be most/least appropriate for the crimes illustrated in the pictures?

- Sending them on an 'Outward Bound' course (e.g. mountain climbing, canoeing etc.).
- Making them apologise to the victim.
- Sending them to jail.
- Making their parents pay a fine.
- Making them do community service (e.g. helping to paint an old person's home).
- Giving them counselling.

2 Which approach is most appropriate for these crimes?

joy-riding / arson / mugging / murder /assault

Language Bank

Evaluating solutions

In the case of petty/serious/violent crimes such as ...

I (don't) think that making them apologise would be an effective measure because ...

A prison sentence could be counter-productive ...

A fine may be the best solution ...

It (all) depends on the circumstances. For instance, if someone commits an act of vandalism, ...

Hooligans should be made to ...

It's important to encourage a sense of responsibility.

LISTENING 1

Part 1, Note completion

1 🖭 You will hear part of a talk about why some young people commit crimes and others don't. Before you listen, read the notes below. You will need a few words or a number to complete them.

Why do youngsters become offenders?

The speaker refers to young people under the age of (1) ....
The percentage of youngsters from disadvantaged backgrounds not involved in crime: (2) ....

Key risk factors:
father's (3) ....
combined with (4) ....

Protective factors:
achievement at school
opportunity for social activities e.g. membership of (5) ....
good parenting
mother's ability to cope with (6) ....

Unexpected findings:
fewer offenders among children born (7) .... or (8) ....
link between criminality and (9) ....
at home
access to (10) .... was not a relevant factor.

2 Discuss these questions.

1 Were you surprised by any of the findings presented in the talk?

2 Can you think of possible reasons for some of the findings which the researchers hadn't expected?

3 Imagine you have been asked to present recommendations to the government on ways of reducing juvenile crime. What recommendations would you make based on the results of this research?

VOCABULARY 1

Words to do with crime

1 Number the following actions in the correct chronological sequence.

☐ commit a crime
☐ release someone on bail
☐ charge someone (with)
☐ stand trial
☐ arrest someone (for)
☐ pass sentence (on)/sentence someone (to six months)
☐ deliver/return a verdict
☐ serve time/a prison sentence
☐ release someone (from prison)
☐ convict someone (of)

2 Now match these people to the actions in Exercise 1.

the suspect / the police / the criminal / the judge / the jury / the defendant / the prison authorities

READING 1
Part 3, Multiple choice questions

1 Discuss these questions before you read the article opposite.

1 Think of a celebrity you admire: a film star, a sports personality, a rock star etc. Explain why you admire them.

2 What are some of the drawbacks of being a well-known celebrity? For example: loss of privacy.

3 How acceptable or unacceptable would you consider the following behaviour towards a celebrity?

- asking for their autograph
- taking photos without their permission
- phoning them after 10 p.m.
- following them home
- standing outside their house
- sending gifts

2

1 Read the headline and the first three paragraphs of the article to find out:

1 who are 'the obsessed' referred to in the headline?

2 what is meant by 'stalking'?

2 Skim quickly through the rest of the article to find out:

1 who is particularly concerned about stalking?

2 what has been learned about stalkers and their motivation?

3 Read the text more carefully and answer the multiple choice questions that follow. Choose the best option (A, B, C or D) according to the information in the text. Do you remember the advice on how to approach this task type?

1 Helena Bonham Carter went to court to
   A find out if the law applied in her case.
   B show an obsessed fan how displeased she was.
   C find a solution to an unpleasant situation.
   D demand punishment for a wrong-doer.

2 Parliament may introduce new laws against stalking because
   A American crime trends may spread to Britain.
   B stalking is a tough crime to control.
   C ordinary citizens need protecting.
   D there is pressure from the police to do so.

3 Hollywood is concerned about stalking and stalkers because
   A of warnings from security companies.
   B actors are constantly demanding greater protection.
   C there may be serious financial consequences.
   D ordinary fans are becoming more of a threat to stars.

4 The typical stalker is a person with
   A a reputation for violence.
   B a talent for personal relationships.
   C an unsatisfactory personal life.
   D predictable behaviour patterns.

5 The stalker that is the most difficult to track is one who has
   A fabricated a relationship.
   B been unable to give up a relationship.
   C established a superficial relationship.
   D met victims through leisure activities.

6 Detective Greg Boles of the LA Police Department believes that
   A investigating domestic stalking is a priority.
   B stalking cases are getting stranger and stranger.
   C potential victims of stalkers over-react.
   D other police departments need more training.

4 Find these words and expressions in the text. What do they mean? Which are colloquial? Can you think of neutral alternatives to replace them?

1 To date (line 16)
2 if ... are anything to go by (line 18)
3 institute (line 28)
4 pioneer (line 54)
5 intimidate (line 64)
6 a sorry business (line 67)
7 get a line on (line 73)
8 foil (line 144)

5 Discuss these questions.

1 Can you name any other celebrities who have been victims of stalking? Describe what happened.

2 If you were a famous person, what precautions could you take against stalkers?

Can laws stop the obsessed?

The British actress Helena Bonham Carter went to court last week to ask for protection from an obsessive fan.

Five years of harassment from a 27-year-old man who plagued her with unwanted telephone calls, visits and letters had driven her to act. For many celebrities and thousands of ordinary people, the problem of the over-zealous fan or unrequited lover has become much more than a matter of tiresome phone calls in the middle of the night.

To date, no British laws deal specifically with stalking, though if America's crime trends are anything to go by, Parliament may soon be forced to follow that country's lead in making it a punishable crime. Lawmakers and corporations there are both taking steps to protect not just stars but also ordinary citizens from the mad, the bad and the deluded.

In 1990, California became the first state to institute anti-stalking laws: today 31 states have such laws which guard against wilful, malicious and repeated harassing of another person and/or their families. Convicted stalkers face prison sentences ranging from 30 days to seven years, and may be fined from $750 to $10,000. But even with new laws on the books, stalking is a tough crime to control.

For those in the entertainment industry, stalking is a real and ever present danger. Apart from the personal risk, the loss of a major movie star can cost a company millions; and there is also the threat of lawsuits from actors who feel they have not been properly protected.

Driven by such fears, Hollywood has been searching for the way to sift the psychotic from the ordinary fan. International Security Management, an American firm that assesses threats for companies around the globe, has pioneered a computer program known as Threat Data Tracking System and has managed to break down stalking activity into several different categories.

The company has input more than 500 letters and photographs into its system, and noted phone calls, visits and other attempts to intimidate victims, as well as stalkers' characteristics.

Scanning through the data base is a sorry business. It is an unrelenting tale of loneliness and despair — of people pouring out their frustrations to individuals they have never met in a mixture of poetry, prose and madness.

"Once we get a line on these people, we hope to be able to predict what will trigger them to commit violent actions," says Noel Koch, ISM President. Then we can develop a more effective intervention strategy — whether that means protecting the victim or restraining the stalker."

Three basic types of stalker have been identified: those who refuse to give up real relationships that have gone wrong; those who become obsessed with a superficial relationship through work or leisure activities; and those who invent completely artificial relationships with someone, usually a celebrity, whom they have never met.

The last category of stalker, usually known as the celebrity stalker, is the most difficult to track. According to Beth Finkelstein, a senior analyst at ISM, the first letters or phone calls received by a victim might seem relatively innocuous so they don't get noted right away. Only after letters and phone calls increase do people finally take action, by which time data has been lost. Also letters or phone calls may be received by several members of a celebrity's entourage instead of the celebrities themselves, making it more difficult to co-ordinate information and assess the level of danger posed by a potential attacker.

The actress Rebecca Schaeffer was used to receiving fan mail from ardent admirers. The 21-year-old actress was a rising star with Warner Brothers. To Robert Bardo, a 17-year-old high school student from Tucson, Arizona, she represented the ideal woman. He wrote her fan letters, collected articles about her and repeatedly watched videotapes of her television show. He then attempted to visit her at a Hollywood studio, carrying a giant teddy bear and a bouquet of flowers.

Not long after being turned away, Bardo paid a private detective to find Schaeffer's home address. He called on her one morning and when she answered the door shot her once in the chest, killing her instantly. The ISM database should be able to give early warning of future Bardos.

"The people who express love are often more threatening than those who express hate or direct aggression," says Laure Lynch, a consultant at ISM who has analysed hundreds of letters sent to victims.

But while technology may make it easier for the stars to foil stalkers, it may be some time before ordinary citizens enjoy access to such sophisticated systems. Meanwhile, police departments across America are taking cues from the Los Angeles Police Department, which runs the nation's only Threat Management Unit dealing primarily with domestic stalking.

Detective Greg Boles says, "We never tell a victim, 'It's okay, nothing is going to happen to you.' We realise anything can happen in these cases. Just when we've seen the most abnormal and bizarre, something else comes along to beat it."

LANGUAGE STUDY

The passive (Notes page 209)

1 Identify the passives in these examples and answer the questions below. Look back at the text on page 129 if necessary.

a. Parliament may soon be forced to follow that country's lead in making [stalking] a punishable crime. *(line 19)*

b. ... there is also the threat of lawsuits from actors who feel they have not been properly protected. *(line 44)*

c. Three basic types of stalker have been identified: those who ... *(line 82)*

d. ... letters or phone calls may be received by several members of a celebrity's entourage instead of the celebrities themselves. *(line 104)*

e. The youngsters who did that should have been sent to jail.

f. I don't remember his name being mentioned at the trial.

g. Robert Bardo was convicted of murder.

h. John had expected to be promoted soon.

i. He felt disappointed not to have been selected for the job.

j. It was felt he had not yet acquired enough experience.

1 What is the general rule for the formation of the passive?

2 What form of the verb *be* is used to form the passive

- after a modal verb in the present?
- after a modal verb in the past?
- after a verb taking the infinitive?
- after a verb taking a gerund?
- after an adjective?

2 Try making the sentences above active. Decide why the passive was used in each case. Choose from this list.

- Because the agent or doer of the action is unimportant, unknown or obvious from the context.
- To avoid using vague informal pronouns e.g. *They* or *You* as the subject of the sentence.
- To make a statement more impersonal.
- To place special emphasis on the agent.
- To make new information the topic of the sentence.

! *make, see* and *let*

Compare these pairs of sentences and answer the questions.

1a. The judge made the vandals pay for the damage.

 b. The vandals were made to pay for the damage.

2a. We saw her leave at 5 o'clock.

 b. She was seen to leave at 5 o'clock.

3a. My parents didn't let me stay up late as a child.

 b. I wasn't allowed to stay up late as a child.

1 What form of the verb is used after *make* and *see* in the active? in the passive?

2 What verb replaces *let* in the passive? (Notes page 209)

---

2 Rewrite these sentences using the passive. Decide if the agent/doer needs to be mentioned or not.

1 Be careful! That car might have run you over!

2 Sally really wanted the director to notice her.

3 I don't like the police following me around.

4 I'd like someone to offer me the opportunity to travel round the world.

5 I am thrilled that our country's President has paid me this honour.

6 Why didn't the teachers let you all go home from school early today?

7 You can't make a child do something he/she doesn't want to.

3 The following impersonal constructions can be used with verbs of mental processes and reporting verbs to focus attention on the information in the last part of the sentence.

It is alleged/believed/feared/known/reported/ rumoured/said/thought that X ...

X is alleged/believed etc. to + present or perfect infinitive

Rewrite these sentences in two different ways.
Note: In one sentence, only one option is possible.

1 People say that movie starlet Angie Carter has been under the care of a psychiatrist recently.

2 They believe she's been feeling depressed about gaining weight.

3 There is a rumour that her husband has been seeing other young ladies.

4 In addition, there is a report that she is getting very difficult to work with on the set.

5 Some people fear that her contract may be terminated.

Reduced relative clauses (Notes page 209)

1 Look at these examples from the text on page 129. The words in italics are reduced relative clauses. They have a passive meaning. What words can be added to make them into full relative clauses?

a. ... the first letters or phone calls *received by a victim* might seem relatively innocuous. *(line 97)*

b. The last category of stalker, *usually known as the celebrity stalker*, is ... *(line 93)*

2 Can you identify the reduced relative clauses in these examples and re-insert the missing words?

1 A young man, arrested on suspicion of murder, appeared in court today.

2 The evidence presented in court suggested that the man was guilty.

3 I wouldn't like to live in a house haunted by a murdered woman.

4 The house, occupied by the Vince family for generations, now stands empty and derelict.

5 Over £1 million were stolen in the bank robbery, but the men involved were never caught.

5 Rewrite these sentences using reduced relative clauses to include the information given in brackets.

1 Mr Manners faces life imprisonment. (He was found guilty on all charges by the jury.)

2 The painting still sold for £2 million. (It is widely regarded as a fake.)

3 All the cars were impounded by the police. (They were damaged in the accident.)

4 Mr Marks is seeking compensation. (The police wrongfully arrested him.)

5 The passengers were taken to hospital. (Firefighters rescued them from the blaze.)

Vocabulary 2

Collocation

1 Some *-ed* and *-ing* participles can be used as adjectives before a noun. They often collocate with particular nouns, for example:

an unrequited lover / a convicted criminal / a contributing member of society

Complete these sentences using a verb and a noun from each list in the correct form.

help / swear / break / spoil / drive / steal / hide / rampage
enemies / child / catch / mob / hand / man / goods / glass

1 Stop behaving like a .... !

2 The police managed to recover the .... after a tip-off.

3 The two men are .... because of a dispute about land.

4 Neighbours should always be ready to lend a ....

5 He's a .... — he never stops working.

6 The peaceful crowd had turned into a ....

7 It sounds like a great offer. There must be a .... !

8 We heard the sound of .... — someone had thrown a ball through the window.

2 Write down the noun and adjective forms of these verbs. There may be more than one form of the same word class.

1 incriminate 3 obsess 5 deter
2 offend 4 accuse

3 Use appropriate forms of the words in Exercise 2 to complete these sentences.

1 The police arrested the suspect after finding .... evidence at his home.

2 A baseball bat can be used as an .... weapon.

3 Fraud is a .... offence.

4 Tough prison sentences are not effective in .... persistent ....

5 The jury was told that, as a child, the .... was .... with guns.

6 60% of boys from disadvantaged backgrounds have a .... record by the age of 18.

ENGLISH IN USE 1

Part 2, Structural cloze

1 The text below is about a man who served on a jury. Read it through, ignoring the gaps. What was the crime and the punishment? How did David Laver feel about his experience?

2 Complete the text by writing **one** word in each numbered gap. Remember:

- you need short, simple structural words.
- read the whole sentence carefully and look at the words surrounding the gap for clues.
- check that your answers make sense in the context.

'I'LL NEVER BE ABLE TO FORGET'

Sitting in a hushed courtroom, David Laver forced himself to look at the grim photographs of a murder scene. Until he was called to jury service two years (1) ...., David had never been inside a court. But (2) .... he saw and heard there has haunted him ever (3) ....

'I thought I'd be trying a drink-driving (4) .... a fraud case,' says David. 'I never dreamed I'd end (5) .... on a murder trial.'

In Britain, jury service is a public duty and (6) .... over the age of eighteen may (7) .... called upon to do it.

'When the charge was read out, I began to feel scared, but I had (8) .... warning of the emotions I was going to go (9) .... as the trial went on. I started having nightmares, but (10) .... you're not allowed to discuss what you've heard in court, I couldn't even tell my wife.'

David can still vividly remember the tape recording of the 999 call made by the victim. She was pleading for help but because she (11) .... not speak properly, the telephone operator thought it was a child messing about and didn't put the call through to the police.

'When the tape was played in court, (12) .... went so quiet you could hear people breathing. It was so awful that you didn't (13) .... look at anyone else.'

The jury returned a guilty verdict and the accused was jailed (14) .... life.

'I wanted to put the whole thing (15) .... me quickly,' David says, 'but I'll never be able to forget it.'

LISTENING 2

Exam File: Part 3, Sentence completion

The task in this section is another example of a Part 3 sentence completion task like the one in Unit 6, page 84. Remember:

- you need to understand the main ideas of the text, not just specific items of information.
- the words you need to complete the sentences aren't necessarily in the recording.
- the words you write must fit grammatically into the sentence.

1 You will hear an interviewer, Matthew Tennison, talking to Professor Edward Manners and TV researcher Anna Hill about identity parades. Identity parades are used by the police in many countries. The suspect stands in a line with a number of innocent people, and the victim or witness is asked to try and identify the wrong-doer. Before you listen, discuss these questions.

1 How reliable do you think identity parades are?
2 If you had to pick out someone in this way, would you feel confident about it?

2 🔊 Read the sentences below and make sure you understand the words. For example, what do you think 'sequential identification' is? Then listen and complete the sentences with a word or short phrase.

BANX

Identity parades

Anna Hill believes that in an identity parade, no one (1) ....

Professor Manners appeared on TV to (2) .... identity parades.

The witness believed Professor Manners had carried out an (3) ....

Professor Manners produced (4) .... to prove that he was in a television studio.

Professor Manners believes (5) .... cannot be depended on.

Anna Hill was misled about someone's (6) .... because of his (7) ....

She thinks police interview techniques have (8) ....

But she still thinks witnesses feel forced to (9) ....

Sequential identification allows witnesses to concentrate on (10) .... after another.

Professor Manners says sequential identification reduces false identification.

3 After listening to the recording, have you changed your mind about how effective identity parades are? If not, read on ...

ENGLISH IN USE 2
Part 4, Word formation

1 Read the text below, ignoring the gaps. What was the crime? How was Alfred Beck punished? Who was the real criminal?

2 Now complete the text with the correct form of words 1—8. Remember to look carefully at the grammatical context. If the gapped word is preceded by *a* or *the*, it is probably a noun or adjective. If it is used with a verb, it is probably an adverb.

A SAD (BUT TRUE) TALE OF MISTAKEN IDENTITY

In 1895 a lady was walking along a dimly-lit street in London when she recognised a man who had robbed her of some jewellery a few days before. She called the police, who arrested the man, who protested his (1) .... He said his name was Alfred Beck and he was a Norwegian businessman. The police insisted that he was John Smith, a (2) .... criminal. Ten different women picked him out at identity parades as the thief who had robbed them. In court, Beck was sentenced to seven years (3) ...., but he was still (4) .... denying that he was guilty. A year after he was released, he was arrested again following an (5) .... by three woman that he had stolen their rings. All the women (6) .... identified Beck as the thief. He was again sent to prison but at this point the police found the real John Smith, who bore an astonishing (7) .... to Beck. Beck received £5, 000 in compensation but died, a (8) .... man, in 1904.

---

(1) INNOCENT	(5) ACCUSE
(2) NOTORIETY	(6) CONFIDENCE
(3) PRISON	(7) RESEMBLE
(4) ANGER	(8) BREAK

READING 2
Part 2, Gapped text

1 You are going to read an article about the role of prisons. First, decide which of these statements you agree with. Jot down some arguments in favour of your position.

1 The best way to deter criminals from re-offending is to make prison as unpleasant as possible.
2 The best way to deter criminals from re-offending is to give them training and education while in prison.

2 The article contains a number of quite formal words relating to crime and criminals. Match these words from the text with their neutral or less formal equivalents below.

1 incarceration *(main text)*
2 remorseful *(main text)*
3 recidivism *(main text)*
4 dispassionate *(main text)*
5 felon *(main text)*
6 miscreant *(main text)*
7 travesty *(para C)*
8 penal/correctional institution *(para D)*
9 slain *(para E)*

A killed, murdered
B wrong-doer
C person who has committed a serious crime
D prison or similar place for convicted offenders
E re-offending (after being released from prison)
F very sorry (for what you have done)
G objective
H imprisonment
I mockery

3 Read the base text, ignoring the gaps, and try to follow the development of the argument. Think about these questions.

1 The first paragraph refers to a TV debate. Who are the participants in the debate? What is the debate about?
2 Which views are those of the participants? the writer of the article?

4

1 Read the base text **and** the paragraphs that have been removed and try to decide where they fit. Look for reference words, link words and any other lexical items in the base text that point to a missing section. Clues in the first two paragraphs have been italicised to help you. Note that there will always be six or seven missing paragraphs in the exam.

2 Check your answers by reading the whole article in sequence. Does it make sense?

5

1 Briefly note down the arguments presented in the article:
• in favour of harsh treatment of criminals in prison.
• in favour of providing prisoners with education and training.

What view of punishment is behind the different approaches?

2 Has your opinion about prisons and punishment changed after reading the article?

6 The text uses a lot of short sentences as well as some fragments (incomplete sentences), for example:
'And the actual amount was hardly dramatic.' *(main text)*
'Makes you sit up and think. Except that, ...' *(main text)*
Look for more examples.

What is the stylistic effect? How would you describe the register and tone of the writing: colloquial, semi-formal, formal? serious, humorous, objective, personal?

CRIMINAL REHABILITATION

Prison – revenge or rehabilitation?

One night, I turned on the television and found myself in the middle of an emotional and highly-charged debate. *On one side was a father* whose teenage son had been murdered. He was outraged that the convicted murderer, also a teenager, had applied for a special grant to pay for college courses.

(1)

On the other side was the convict, a person who had murdered a teenage boy for no reason, at least not one that I remember being mentioned. The prisoner did not claim his incarceration was unjust: he actually seemed remorseful.

(2)

His points made sense. Indeed, no one was handing him a degree. He had to study and prove his academic fitness. He had no money: without the grant he was applying for, there would be no courses. And the actual amount was hardly dramatic. It could be called a modest investment for the future.

(3)

Makes you sit up and think. Except that, as with all passionate speeches, this argument was more than a bit exaggerated. The number of prisoners who receive the grants represents a very small percentage, less than one-half of one per cent of the total. Those who complete their college education and those who go on to graduate programs — also with a government grant — have a zero recidivism rate, I am told. If true, and I have no information to prove otherwise, that's significant. But dispassionate logic wins few inflamed arguments.

(4)

Why should some rapist get a degree in psychology? Why should some drug-using armed robber get a law degree? The truth is, many people do not believe that convicted felons should receive three meals a day, the opportunity to exercise or the right to watch TV. For a while, the stories about people who, immediately after they were released from jail, lost no time committing another crime — mugging, break-ins, car theft — were oddly amusing. Now they are simply scary.

Something has to change. Since it is not possible to imprison every miscreant for life, the logical alternative is to stop warehousing prisoners and teach them to do something of value — a trade, a profession, an appreciation of art and music, a new way of life.

(5)

We cannot have it both ways. The best way to control crime is to eliminate criminals, and one way to do that is by helping people to become productive, thoughtful members of society. Grants for prisoners to study may not be a popular approach, but it is a successful one.

A Now enters a new voice, a politician who is furious. "Do you know how many boys and girls will be unable to attend college because their families haven't got the money to send them, but who don't qualify as poor enough to get such a grant? They will lose out and prisoners will take their place," he warned.

B Everyone will sympathise with this reaction from a bereaved parent, but this is hardly a sound basis for a change in a long-established and proven policy. The current prison population is aware of society's conflicting attitude to the way they are treated, but recognises the potential dangers of leaving prison with no up-to-date job skills.

C It was, *he* said, a travesty of justice. *His* son lost out on college and on life, yet his taxes were going to make possible a college education for his son's killer. It was impossible not to empathize with him. Where was the fairness, the justice?

D Prisons are hot topics these days. People are understandably resentful when confronted with what is claimed to be a luxury holiday camp for felons. Penal institutions shouldn't be luxurious.

On the other hand, correctional institutions shouldn't be medieval dungeons. There can be a middle ground. The dilemma in finding it is that we can't quite get past the desire for revenge. We want people to be punished, then reformed. Mostly, though, we want them to suffer for making others suffer.

E Nothing will ever ease the pain left by a murdered child or a slain parent. And some future success for a felon, made possible through a tax-supported scholarship in prison, will be difficult to swallow. But it is necessary for society's survival. We talk about the need for people to repay their debt to society, then we object to giving them the means to do so.

F If he could do it over again, he said, he would give up his life instead. The reality was that he couldn't exchange places, and that at some point he will complete his prison term. If he doesn't use his time in prison to educate himself, he said, how will he ever be able to be a contributing member of society?

SPEAKING 2

Exam File: Part 3, Debate; Part 4, Summarise conclusions

In Part 3, you may have to comment on one or two short written extracts. This could involve you in responding to and developing an argument.

Try to:

- present your ideas in a logical order.
- acknowledge opposing ideas.
- counter opposing ideas.
- reach a conclusion.

1 Read the extracts below about the role of prisons and discuss these questions with a partner.

1 Which of the opinions expressed do you most agree with and why? Can you think of any advantages or disadvantages to the solutions described?

2 What, in your opinion, is the purpose of prisons?

A

I don't believe prison is the answer for most crimes, except really serious ones like murder. But if we do have to put offenders in prison, then surely losing their freedom is enough of a punishment. We don't need to punish them twice for what they've done by making them live in bad conditions. Some people claim that prisons are like holiday camps, but that's just not true. It's our fault if people become criminals, so we should give them a second chance. We've got to offer them an opportunity to study or train so they can do something useful when they get out again.

B

It's currently fashionable to blame unemployment and poverty for criminal acts. But there is no denying the fact that each individual has a choice. Despite difficult circumstances, many people do not turn to crime. Those who do and are caught often re-offend. It's clear from this that attempts to reform criminals are a waste of time. For these reasons, I believe that prisons should be centres of punishment, not leisure centres or university campuses, and the only way to deter crime is to introduce tougher, longer sentences.

2 Summarise your conclusions for the class. Did you agree or did you have different opinions?

Language Bank

Acknowledging opposing ideas ...

Certainly, it can be argued that ...

While I agree/accept that ...

... and countering them

However, / Nevertheless, / On the other hand, ...

... research has shown that ...

In fact, ... / The truth is ... / The fact of the matter is ...

It follows that ... / Therefore, ... / As a result, ...

Asking for/giving clarification

I don't (quite) follow you. Do you mean ...?

What exactly do you mean by ...?

Well, you see ...

To put it another way ... / In other words, ...

Summarising, concluding

Everything points to the conclusion that ...

To sum up, I (firmly) believe ...

There is no alternative but to ...

3 Look again at the extracts you discussed in Exercise 1. Which extract sounds more like spoken English? Re-write it so that it sounds less personal and more formal. Use passives where appropriate to focus attention on key points and get rid of personal pronouns.

WRITING
Part 2, Article

Read the writing task and follow the **Steps to Writing** below.

You have seen the following announcement in a magazine for young people.

> *Society Today* invites you to send in an article entitled 'How should society deal with young offenders?' Prizes will be awarded for the best articles. First prize: an all-expenses-paid two-week trip to the USA. Second prize: £500. Third prize: £250.
>
> The competition will be judged by the editor of *Society Today*, assisted by a judge. The winning article will be published in the June edition of *Society Today*.
>
> Write an **article** for *Society Today*. Your article should include:
> - typical crimes teenagers commit and reasons why they commit them
> - the pros and cons of different punishments
>
> Write approximately 250 words.

Step 1 Task interpretation
Read the question and highlight the key points. What type of text do you have to produce? What **two** things do you need to include? What register would be appropriate? Remember, you are writing an article for experts in this area.

Step 2 Generating ideas
Note down some ideas under these headings. You can refer back to **Speaking 1** and **2** for extra ideas.

> *Types of crime*
> petty crime, e.g. vandalism, shoplifting, joy riding
> major crime, e.g. bank robbery
>
> *Reasons for offending*
> boredom, drugs, parents are offenders
>
> *Possible punishments / pros and cons*
> community service
> pro: reform + educate   con: soft option
> prison sentence
> pro: real deterrent   con: bad environment
> imposing a fine on the parents
> ....

Step 3 Layout and organisation
Your notes will have generated more ideas than you will be able to use in a 250-word article, so you must select. Which of the ideas interests you most? Which do you feel most strongly about? Which do you know most about? Think carefully about what you select and how much you will be able to say in the space available.

Organise your ideas into paragraphs. Note down what you want to include in each. Here is a possible plan.

Introduction: Outline the problem as you see it and then mention the points you are going to deal with in your article.

Paragraphs 2/3: Outline the types of crime teenagers commit and possible causes.

Put forward ways of dealing with them. Support your points with evidence based on your own knowledge if possible.

Concluding paragraph: Draw together the strands of your argument and summarise your point of view. What do you think is the most effective way of dealing with the problem?

Step 4 Write
Think about the language you are going to use. Try to demonstrate your knowledge of the vocabulary relating to law and order, crime and punishment. Make sure you use linking words and phrases to connect and develop your ideas. Write a short, punchy final sentence that makes your conclusion clear.

▶ The passive (pages 130—131)
▶ Language Bank (pages 126/136)

Step 5 Evaluate and edit
▶ Writing checklist (page 214)

Exam Practice 2

Reading

Part 2

For questions **15—20**, you must choose which of the paragraphs **A—G** fit into the numbered gaps in the following article. There is one extra paragraph, which does not fit in any of the gaps.

The War Against Crime Begins At Home

My girlfriend appeared in the kitchen, gesturing helplessly upstairs towards the hall, with a look of terror on her face. She did not need to explain: we were being robbed. We raced out on to the street just in time to see two men with a dog, disappearing down the street. One of the men was carrying a large object under his arm. Propelled by my momentum, I raced after them, only to lose them when they rounded the corner.

15	

I just could not passively accept that our house could be broken into while we were in it and we would do nothing about it. Burglary is a grudgingly accepted form of 'taxation' in many urban areas. Yet to be robbed while actually in the house was pushing it too far. And after all, the burglars must still have been within spitting distance of the house.

16	

I would like to say that I confronted them as I caught up with them walking along the road at the end of the alley. But my politeness ensured that the situation was too absurd to be a confrontation. "Have you got my girl-friend's bag there?" I asked, rather lamely. "Sorry?" one of them snarled aggressively.

17	

Do I feel brave? I might do, were it not for my knees wobbling, hands shaking and heart racing every time I think about it. If they had pulled a knife or threatened me, I would have run away.

18	

The crime at our house was cleared up. A man returned the next day with the keys that had been stolen and tried to take our car. An eagle-eyed neighbour alerted the police, who were jubilant to have 'solved' a crime.

19	

Not much of a solution, throwing him in jail, I thought the next day. The intractability of the crime problem, the difficulty of finding a solution, is one of the main reasons people feel defeated by it and fail to see how anything they do will help solve it. So they turn away from it.

20	

We must find ways for communities to work more closely with police who are genuinely local and don't spend their time whizzing around in helicopters and fast cars. But it also means re-equipping people to provide more effectively for their own security. The police cannot defend a public space within which people can move about without fear of random crime. The ultimate responsibility for defending that space rests with the people who inhabit it.

A That response is unnecessarily pessimistic. We have to find ways for people to assert themselves against crime with responses which do not leave them with an unenviable choice: either risk your life 'having a go' or feel guilty about standing by and doing nothing.

B Yet the idea of finding a solution for a crime is extremely elusive. The man they arrested lives round the corner, is rumoured to have been in and out of a psychiatric hospital and according to one police officer 'is only half there'.

C So off I went — feeling nervous — in search of them. I spotted them two streets away, as they crossed the road. I parked the car and watched them walk down an alley towards a housing estate. To have turned back then would have been to admit defeat, so I followed on foot, without the slightest clue what I would do when I caught up with them.

D I returned to my distraught girlfriend, telephoned the police and reported the loss of her briefcase and handbag as well as one set of keys to both house and car. It was at around 10.30 p.m. I am not really sure what made me then grab my own car keys and explain in a matter of fact tone that I was 'going after them'. Anger was certainly one reason but it was not the main one.

E The trouble was that, by this stage, they had dropped the bag, although one of them had her cheque-book in her hand. I turned round and found both the handbag and the briefcase in some nearby bushes. Then I ran after the robbers, who disappeared into the estate. So I lost them again.

F Do I feel proud? Not really, for that implies I should have felt ashamed if I had not chased them. But it would have been a perfectly natural and entirely sensible approach not to chase them.

G Even so, the decision to 'have a go' is a mix of emotion and tactical calculation of the chances of success rather than a moral imperative.

ENGLISH IN USE

Part 3

In **most** lines of the following text, there is **one** unnecessary word. It is either grammatically incorrect or does not fit in with the sense of the text. For each numbered line **31—46**, find this word and write it next to the number. Some lines are correct. Indicate these with a tick (✓). The exercise begins with two examples **(0)**.

Example:

0	him
0	✓

AN INTERESTING MEETING

0	....	Last Saturday I met someone who I had been at university with him
0	....	several years ago. Fortunately, it was someone that I could recognise
31	....	immediately and whose name I could remember it. He told me he had
32	....	set up an adventure travel company with some of money that his father
33	....	had left by him and which had expanded over the years into quite a
34	....	large company. I remembered him as if someone who was always getting
35	....	up to dangerous things at university and he hadn't changed much.
36	....	The holidays that he told me about them sounded pretty scary to me. They
37	....	were obviously designed for people who have a great sense of adventure.
38	....	They weren't really the kind of holidays that I would like to go on myself.
39	....	However, he was very persuasive in the way so that he described these
40	....	holidays and said that many of his customers took at the least two a year
41	....	and were incredibly enthusiastic about them. They could hardly wait for
42	....	to go on the next, or so he claimed. I must be admit that he succeeded in
43	....	persuading me that perhaps I should try something bit different from my
44	....	normal holiday. Also, because that I was an old friend, although we hadn't
45	....	met for a while he offered to me a very large discount on a holiday. In fact,
46	....	it was such a generous discount that I have decided to take up his offer.

ENGLISH IN USE

Part 4

For questions **47—61**, read the following two texts. Use the words in the boxes to form **one** word that fits in the same numbered space in the text. The exercise begins with an example **(0)**.

Example: | **0** | **simultaneously** |

LETTER OF ADVICE

Vegetarianism is a great weapon for teenage children as it **(0)** .... gives them a sense of **(1)** .... and moral superiority while at the same time making their parents feel small and **(2)** .... . Not **(3)** ...., most of the militant teenage vegetarians I've known have, a few years later, resorted first to eating fish, then chicken and then, with some **(4)** ...., to meat. **(5)** ...., if you're a factory-farmed animal at least, vegetarianism is often no more than a phase in teenagers and it's important to realise that vegetarianism is more to do with teenage **(6)** .... than a real moral stand. I often think it's a soft — and rather **(7)** .... — middle-class rebellion option that is used by kids who are too well-behaved to use drugs or come home drunk with rings in their noses.

(0) SIMULTANEOUS
(47) INDIVIDUAL
(48) GUILT
(49) SURPRISE
(50) EMBARRASS
(51) FORTUNE
(52) REBEL
(53) ADMIRE

EXTRACT FROM A MAGAZINE ARTICLE

NO TIME OFF

John Roberts asked for time off work to be with his wife when she gave **(8)** .... to their first child. His boss said no, but Mr Roberts did not accept this **(9)** .... . He took time off anyway and was then told not to bother to come back to work. He thought he had been **(10)** ..... dismissed and took his case to an **(11)** .... tribunal. The court agreed with him and awarded him £6,000 damages, which his boss must now pay him in **(12)** .... . His boss, Martin Smith said, "It's a totally **(13)** .... decision. When my wife had a baby, I was too busy to have time off. Mr Roberts still has to go to work, **(14)** .... of what is happening in his private life. I can't run my company according to when the wives of my **(15)** .... are having babies."

(54) BEAR
(55) REFUSE
(56) FAIR
(57) INDUSTRY
(58) COMPENSATE
(59) REASON
(60) REGARD
(61) EMPLOY

A sense of belonging

SPEAKING 1

1 Work in pairs. Choose two photographs each. Take turns to compare and contrast the different lifestyles shown. Comment on:

- what people are wearing/doing.
- their surroundings.
- their day-to-day life.

Say which lifestyle would appeal to you most/least.

Do you agree with what your partner said?

3

4

1

2

2 Discuss these questions.

1 How attractive do you find the idea of moving to another town or emigrating to another country?

2 If you had to move, what things would you miss, or not miss, about your present lifestyle?

Language Bank

be constantly on the move
scrape a living / be self-sufficient
isolated / cut off / in the middle of nowhere
lonely / monotonous / a hard life
a real community spirit / a sense of belonging/ tradition
lively / bustling / anonymous
an opportunity to start afresh

ENGLISH IN USE 1
Part 3, Error correction

1 After the Second World War, a million Britons emigrated to Australia, under a Government-subsidised £10 passage scheme launched in 1947. Many, like the Turner family in the article below, had no idea what they were letting themselves in for. Read the text quickly and answer these questions.

1 What part of Australia did the Turners go to?
2 What difficulties did they face?
3 How did they overcome them? What personal qualities helped them?
4 What does the title of the article mean? What was the 'dream'? Who 'sold' it to the Turners?

2 Can you explain the meaning of these idiomatic expressions from the text?

1 on (their) last legs
2 make a go of something
3 against the odds

3 Some of the lines in the text are correct but most have one extra wrong word. Tick the correct lines and underline the extra wrong word as in the examples. Remember to check:

• the sense of the text.
• the underlying grammar.

0 ✓
0 <u>it</u>

'We were sold a dream ...'

0 Gasping in horror, Doreen Turner gazed at the tiny black-painted shack.
0 Jumping down from the truck that it had brought her to the deserted farm, she
1 screamed in fear. The earth seemed to be moving. 'Look at, mum,' she yelled.
2 'The earth's alive!' 'No, love,' her mum was sighed, 'It's just rabbits — just
3 hundreds of huge rabbits.' It was 1949 and Doreen, then by nineteen, had
4 arrived at their new home in the Australian outback with her parents and eight
5 brothers and sisters who had been emigrated to Australia. 'We were so naive,'
6 recalls Doreen, who now lives in Perth, Western Australia. 'We were sold a
7 dream. What we found was beyond our worst of nightmares.' Her father had sold
8 a thriving business and thought he was buying a good farm but the cattle were on
9 their last legs and the grass also was being eaten by huge rabbits. 'As it turned
10 out, we were grateful for them,' says Doreen. 'We were too poor to afford the
11 meat, so we ate rabbit every day for a year. The family had left a comfortable
12 home in England for having a two-room wooden shack with no running water or
13 electricity. But the family were determined to make such a go of their new lives.
14 'Our generation just accepted all things,' says Doreen. 'We weren't afraid of hard
15 work and we weren't whingers. There are now more over a hundred of us
16 Turners in Australia. We've all done ourselves well, mainly in farming.'

Not all the million or so British emigrants were so fortunate. Many hadn't a clue what they were letting themselves in for and felt cheated. The people for whom it worked, like the Turners, all had resilience and determination and stuck with it against the odds.

whinger: someone who complains about everything *(colloquial)*

READING 1
Part 1, Multiple matching

1 Read the headline and sub-heading of the article opposite. *Welfare* refers to state benefits for the unemployed. What associations do the words *wagon-train* and *wild west* have?

2 Skim the article to find out

1 the main reasons why these families are moving west.
2 the benefits to the local community.
3 the benefits to the families themselves.

1 Now look at the multiple matching task. Scan the text and highlight the names of the six people listed A—F. Identify who each person is:

Antony Boland – head of the Boland family, which has moved west from the city

Jim Connolly – ...

2 Now answer questions 1—15 by choosing from the names A—F. Remember, highlighting key words in each question first can help you identify the type of information you are looking for.

A Antony Boland	**D** Rebecca Boland
B Jim Connolly	**E** Noeleen Boland
C Paul Murphy	**F** Mary Roche

Which person

had to withstand criticism from a parent?	1 ....
is doing a completely different kind of work?	2 .... 3 ....
has an accent that has changed?	4 ....
has responded to fears voiced by local people?	5 ....
has recently been joined by a new colleague?	6 ....
is still without a job?	7 ....
wanted to attract people back to the community?	8 ....
has written a history of his/her new home?	9 ....
thought living in the countryside was dangerous?	10 ....
provided a scheme giving practical help?	11 ....
was alarmed by something a child said?	12 ....
has used the family's experiences for artistic purposes?	13 ....
ran the risk of being made redundant	14 ....
is now much fitter physically?	15 ....

3 Discuss these questions.

1 If you were a member of one of the families described in the article, what aspects of life in Loop Head would you find most difficult to cope with? Do you think you would be tempted to return to the city?

2 Is rural depopulation an issue in your country? If so, what has caused it? What problems have resulted, if any?

4 Replace the words in italics with a phrasal verb. Then look back at the text to check your answers.

1 Connolly *founded* Rural Resettlement ...
2 ... their plans to rent a house *failed*.
3 [Rebecca and her brothers and sisters] *increase* the number to 24 ...
4 ... the building that *faces* the Atlantic.
5 emigrants ... want to return home and *raise* their children ...
6 ... another teacher ... has been *hired*.
7 ... the act of moving helps people *go* in new directions.

Welfare wagon-train to the west

One Sunday last June, Antony Boland read an article in an Irish newspaper about a man called Jim Connolly. A sculptor who grew up on the wild, windswept peninsula of Loop Head in County Clare in the west of Ireland, Connolly looked around his village one day thinking something was missing and then realised what it was: the people had gone. So what Connolly did was start up Rural Resettlement from his front room, offering city families like the Bolands a chance to move to the country. It is a harsh landscape. A pitiless north-west wind bends the telegraph poles and for four months last winter it did not stop raining.

In 1990, Connolly went on Irish radio with a message: go west and I'll help you find a house and a plot of land. One hundred and thirty-eight families have been resettled through the scheme and so far only nine have given up and returned home.

Paul Murphy, a former Dublin bus driver, has become Connolly's second-in-command and spends his time looking for empty houses — of which there are many. Now there are 2,300 families on their waiting list. The filing cabinet is stuffed with applications from Dublin, Glasgow and London — the waves of emigrants who have left the land since the Fifties and who now want to return home and bring up their children. And there are city-dwellers who fear that the humble dream of a house, a family and, most of all, a job, might never be fulfilled.

Nine-year-old Rebecca Boland is already beginning to sound like a country girl from Clare. Rebecca and her brothers and sisters go to Doonaha school at the bottom of the road, where they make the numbers up to 24 in the stone building that looks out onto the Atlantic.

The Bolands have no car and the shopping is brought home on a tractor from Kilrush, 10 miles away. Noeleen Boland, 30, misses going to the shops herself. What Antony Boland misses are chicken curries from his favourite take-away in Dublin. Other than that, they look at each other across the table and agree that there's nothing they really miss.

Many Irish families are packing up and moving to small farms in the wild west, rejuvenating rural communities ravaged by generations of emigration.

Antony's mother told him he was mad to be leaving Dublin. Now she tells him he's looking like a Californian surfer, with his blond hair bleached by the sun and his shoulders made broad and muscular by digging the land. When the Bolands first came to Clare, their plans to rent a house fell through. They left their second house after four months. They had no phone and lived miles from their nearest neighbour. Once, Rebecca was choking on a piece of meat and there was no way of getting medical help. Noeleen said they had to go back to Dublin. She would not risk her children's lives again.

Their return was short. Youths kept ramming their garden wall with stolen cars on the way through to waste land near their home. Sometimes the car thieves did not make it and Antony remembers a Ford Fiesta that came into his garden. "I was watching my son talking to his pal. The mate was saying to him. 'Did you see the Fiesta last night. Wasn't it great?' 'Yep,' said my son, 'fab.' What worried me was that he would start doing the same thing when he got older. Now he's out in the fields with me saying, 'How long does it take to be a vet?' He wants to be a vet or a farmer — not a thief."

In Dublin, Antony Boland was just another figure on the unemployment register. "I was watching him get more and more depressed," Noeleen says. The Bolands, like many of those living along the western seaboard, depend on welfare to survive. Antony hopes to find work as a farm labourer. Local people's worries about "blow-ins" (new arrivals) taking what few jobs are left in the area have been largely calmed. Paul Murphy's standard response is that for generations the people of the west have been going to cities; now the trend has reversed.

The arrival of 260 extra children has also meant that local teachers have kept their jobs. Mary Roche watched the numbers at her school dwindle from 65 in 1974 to only 16 in 1994. Without the arrival of the settlement children, she would have lost her job. Now she has been made principal and another teacher, who is married to a local farmer, has been taken on.

The process of integration has been slow but the "blow-ins" seem committed. Three of the Gaelic football team are resettled children and their father trains the team. A "jackeen" (Dubliner) arranges the music for the choir, and Paul Murphy's history of Loop Head has sold more than 700 copies and raised IR£2,000 for the local community. Murphy has bigger plans. He has written a film script about his family's odyssey from the city to the west coast. *What Do You Think Of The Wind?* is with an agent.

Murphy thinks that he is a romantic and that anyone who makes it in the west has to be. For many, it's the children that are the chief motivation and the act of moving helps people strike out in new directions. "It is like joining a wagon-train," Connolly says. "By taking a brave step, you can boost your spirit and your sense of enterprise."

---

fab: short for *fabulous (colloquial)*

PRONUNCIATION

Assimilation

1 Assimilation refers to the way in which some sounds are affected by following sounds in fast and fluent speech. The same thing happens in many other languages besides English.

🔲 Say these phrases, then listen to the recording. What do you notice about the pronunciation?

1 He's a good boy. ('goob boy')
2 She's a good girl. ('goog girl')
3 It's made of fine gold. ('fi — ng gold')
4 The car was stuck in mud. ('im mud')
5 A dozen people were there. ('dozem people')

2 🔲 Now listen to the different ways in which *can* is pronounced in these two extracts from the Listening text in the next section. What difference in sound do you hear?

1 In warm weather these activities can be a pleasure ...
2 No strangers can come amongst us ...

3 Say these phrases aloud, using assimilation. Identify the sounds which are affected.

1 It's a good bonus.
2 It cost ten million pounds.
3 She looks after ten cats.
4 He got dressed, then made a cup of coffee.
5 Take an umbrella in case it rains.

Understanding how assimilation occurs will help you to work out what you're hearing when you're doing listening comprehension tasks.

LISTENING

Part 3, Multiple choice questions

1 Nomads are people who move from place to place. In pre-industrial societies, they move to find fresh grazing for the animals on which they depend for their livelihood. You will hear an interview with Nicola, who is a 'traveller' — a latter-day nomad. Before you listen, discuss these questions.

1 What difficulties might you face if you tried to live a nomadic life in a modern industrial state? Think about people's attitudes to travellers, as well as physical difficulties.

2 Why do you think some people choose to take up nomadism as a way of life today? Think of at least two reasons.

2 🔲 Listen to the interview with Nicola. For questions 1—7, choose the best option (A, B, C or D). See Unit 4, page 52 for advice on how to approach this type of task.

1 The police regard Nicola as a
   A teacher.
   B hippy.
   C traveller.
   D mother.

2 When Nicola left Birmingham, she and her husband
   A had somewhere particular to go to.
   B had a clear idea of how they would live.
   C wanted to return to nature.
   D wanted to escape city life.

3 When Nicola started travelling, what did she have in common with the people she met?
   A profession
   B means of transport
   C skills
   D aspirations

4 What would be likely to shock a visitor to a travellers' camp?
   A the old-fashioned way of life
   B the range of ages
   C the variety of activities
   D the amount of noise

5 According to Nicola, being in such a community means
   A sharing the chores.
   B having help with the children.
   C mutual support.
   D developing new skills.

6 What protection is there in the camp against intruders?
   A animals give warning
   B one person keeps a look-out
   C everyone is suspicious
   D guns are on hand for use

7 Nicola believes that her lifestyle
   A would be enjoyed by others.
   B has benefits for the land.
   C produces little rubbish.
   D encourages respect for nature.

3 Discuss these questions.

1 Do you think Nicola's way of life is acceptable in today's society?

2 How attracted are **you** by the way of life she describes?

LANGUAGE STUDY

Creating emphasis through grammar

Cleft sentences: *wh-* type

1 There are various grammatical devices in English that enable us to emphasise the part of a sentence we want to draw particular attention to.

1 In these examples, the second sentence in each pair uses a 'cleft' construction to place special emphasis on the object or complement.

1 a. Antony Boland misses chicken curries from his favourite take-away in Dublin.
 b. *What* Antony Boland misses *are* chicken curries from his favourite take-away in Dublin.
 (text page 145)

2 a. We wanted a place where we wouldn't be afraid of walking in the streets ...
 b. *What* we wanted *was* a place where we wouldn't be afraid of walking in the streets ... *(Listening 1)*

3 a. I am really the mother of three young children ...
 b. *What* I really am *is* the mother of three young children ... *(Listening 1)*

The *wh-* clause can precede or follow the verb *be* (though initial position is more common), as in the example below. Try switching the examples above in the same way.

4 a. They want a better life.
 b. *What* they want *is* a better life.
 c. A better life *is what* they want.

2 Compare these examples with the ones above. What element of the sentence is emphasised here?

5 a. So Connolly started up Rural Resettlement from his front room ...
 b. So *what* Connolly *did* was (to) start up Rural Resettlement from his front room ...
 (text page 145)

6 a. Antony hopes to get work as a farm labourer.
 b. *What* Antony hopes *to do* is (to) get work as a farm labourer. *(text page 145)*

What is used in the *wh-* clause as a substitute for the main verb?

2 Rewrite the second sentence in each pair, using a cleft construction for emphasis. Make any other changes necessary.

1 Most of the settlers like their new home. No one looks forward to the long, cold winters though. *(Move the adverbial.)*

2 Visitors to Ireland always comment on the beauty of the landscape. But they are particularly impressed by how friendly the people are. *(Make the sentence active.)*

3 The Tourist Information office has sent us lots of information. But they've forgotten to send us the train timetable we asked for. *(Two options: focus on the object or verb.)*

4 If you're short of time, you can miss the Art Gallery. You really mustn't miss the medieval castle.

5 You warned us about the bad weather. You didn't warn us about the terrible roads!

6 We're not sure what we're going to do for our holidays this year. I thought we might book a Mediterranean cruise.

3 Complete these exchanges in your own way and practise them in pairs.

1 A: What would you like for your birthday?
 B: What I'd really like is ...

2 A: What will you do when you've finished your studies?
 B: What I'm hoping to do is ...

3 A: What do you like and dislike about ...?
 B: What I particularly like ...

4 A: Are you in favour of ...?
 B: No, I'm not in favour of ... . What I **am** in favour of is ...

5 A: You didn't come here to tell me about ...
 B: No, what I really wanted to tell you was ...

Cleft sentences: *It + be*

4 Another type of cleft sentence construction starting with *It + be* enables us to emphasise almost any element of a sentence by bringing it to the front and placing it in topic position.

Look at these examples. Notice that the cleft construction often implies a contrast with something else.

1 a. The countryside in County Clare is harsh. The prospect of work lures people.
   b. The countryside ... It is *the prospect of work* that lures people. (*Focus is on subject.*)

2 a. For many, the chief motivation is *the children*.
   b. For many, it is *the children* that/who are the main motivation. (*Focus is on complement.*)

3 a. Millions of Britons emigrated to Australia in the 1940s in the hope of a better life.
   b. It was *to Australia* that many Britons emigrated ...
   c. It was *in the hope of a better life* that many Britons emigrated ...
      (*Focus is on adverbial*)

5 Rewrite the second sentence in each pair in the same way.

1 Mary enjoyed games at school. Her teacher first spotted her potential as a runner.

2 The weather is bad and the restaurants are nothing to write home about. You will remember the friendliness of the people for the rest of your life.

3 I would never have come here if it hadn't been for my friend John. John introduced me to the place.

4 The town isn't very attractive. The surrounding countryside and the good ski slopes attract people to the area, rather than the town itself.

5 Up until the last part of the century the chief industry in Castleton was coal. The high-tech companies didn't move here until the early 1980s. (*Which verb needs to be negative?*)

6 I didn't take the job for the money. I accepted it because I love working with animals.

ENGLISH IN USE 2
Part 3, Error correction

Spelling and punctuation (Notes page 212/213)

1 In Unit 7 you looked at a variety of spelling mistakes typically tested in this Paper 3 task type. The following exercises focus on some more typical errors, which are all to do with words ending in -*y*.

1 Plural forms
What's the plural of these words?

monkey / journey / variety / odyssey / library / century / company / city

What's the rule for making the plural of words ending in -*y*?

2 Adding -*ing*
What happens when you add -*ing* to these words, which are often spelt wrongly?

study / pay / say / cry / lie / die

3 Suffixes
What happens when we add suffixes -*er*, -*ful*, -*ly*, -*ness*, -*ous* to these words?

happy + -*ness* =
easy + -*ly* =
beauty + -*ful* =
pretty + -*er* =
glory + -*ous* =

4 Past participles
How do you spell the past participle of these words?

say / pay / lay

2 Complete these sentences with the correct spelling of the word in brackets.

1 He isn't .... (study) any more. He has finished his .... (study).

2 He is .... (pay) a lot of money as director of many .... (company).

3 Make three .... (copy). The others have already been .... (copy).

4 I think this plant is .... (die) or maybe it's already .... (die).

3 In the following text some lines are correct but most have a spelling or punctuation mistake.

Read the headline and sub-heading. Turn the sub-heading into a question. Then read the text straight through, ignoring the mistakes, to find the answer to the question.

The Good Old Days

How living in the Iron Age helped one man succeed in the computer age

0	John Rossetti typifys the successful modern company boss. The computer
0	software company he began in 1982 has twenty-five staff and an annual turnover
1	of £2.5 million, but its a far cry from the life he once led. For, some years ago,
2	he lived in a prehistoric hut and scraped a living with ancient iron tools. In 1977,
3	he and his wife Kate took part in a unique television project in which they and
4	five other young familys spent a year on a reconstruction of a two-thousand-year-
5	old Iron Age farm in a wood in Dorset in the west of England. Cut of from the
6	twentieth century, the twelve volunteers had to build their own comunal
7	roundhouse and then survive as self-sufficient farmers useing Iron Age tools.
8	Cameras filmed their strugle to grow crops and rear ancient breeds of animals.
9	It was stressful," says John. "Especially when we had to kill the animals." It took
10	two months to build the roundhouse. "We had little privacy inside," recalls John.
11	"We took turns bathing in a tub of muddy water once a week" The group found it
12	difficult to work as a team. Personalities clashed. Rows flared over food — a dull
13	diet of mostly bread and meat — and when to harvest. There bean crop was wiped
14	out by a storm and in winter the farm was a mud bath But John learned how to
15	get along with others be confident and self-reliant. He believes these character-
16	building experiences are what helped him sucseed in business.

4 Read the text again. Tick the correct lines. When you find a spelling error, write out the correct spelling of the word. When you find a punctuation error, write the correct punctuation mark and the two words either side of it. Study the examples.

0 *typifies*

0 ✓

5 Discuss these questions.

1 Would you like to have an experience like this? Give reasons why you would/wouldn't.

2 What, for you, would be the most difficult aspect of living life as people did in the Iron Age?

READING 2
Part 2, Gapped text

1 You are going to read an article in which Liz McColgan, an internationally-famous athlete, talks about her home town. Before you read, discuss and compare your attitudes to your own home town.

1 Do you feel you belong there?
2 What are its good features?
3 Are there any things about it that you would like to change?

2 Now look at the article. Five paragraphs have been removed. You must choose which of the paragraphs A—F match the numbered gaps 1—5. There is one extra paragraph that does not belong in any of the gaps.

Read the base text and highlight names of people and places, and time references. This will help you to follow the sequence. Answer these questions about the events in Liz McColgan's life.

1 Where was Liz born?
2 What was her maiden name?
3 How old was she when she left school?
4 What did she do after leaving school?
5 When and where was she offered a scholarship?
6 Where did she meet her husband?
7 Where does Liz live now?

3

1 Now read the base text **and** the missing paragraphs. Decide where the missing paragraphs fit. Look for reference words, link words and lexical connections to help you. For example:

The first paragraph mentions Liz's married name, McColgan. The paragraph after gap 1 talks about 'the *Lynch* household'. Which of the paragraphs that have been removed mentions her maiden name?

2 Check your answers by reading the whole article in sequence. Does it make sense?

Running for home

LIZ McCOLGAN has run tens of thousands of miles in training and competition. But Britain's champion long-distance runner has never, in the old-fashioned sense, run away from home. Her feet remain firmly on the ground, around Dundee on the east coast of Scotland. Born in the city 31 years ago, and brought up in a succession of council houses, she has always seen Dundee as her centre of gravity.

(1)

Money was tight in the Lynch household. Her father, Martin, was a labourer who was not always in work. Her mother, Betty, a barmaid, spent all her savings on her two sons and daughters. The money once went on a table-tennis set badly wanted by Liz, the youngest. There was no table to play on, so Martin unscrewed a cupboard door and the future athlete demonstrated her will to win.

(2)

Bennett, a former Scottish 800-metre champion, made training fun. "It seemed more of a friendly gathering," McColgan says, "with lots of bunny jumps, leaping and bounding and zigzagging up the hills to strengthen our muscles, as well as cross-country runs. The club was the centre of my social life. When I left school at 16, he told me I had great ability and could make the Commonwealth Games at the women's 10,000-metres. I got a job and went running and exercising with Harry in my lunch hour and after work."

(3)

Just before her eighteenth birthday, a phone call came offering her a scholarship to train at a college in Idaho, USA. "It was the first time I had been away from Scotland. I was homesick for Dundee, the people at Hawkhill Harriers and things like banoffee [a local banana, toffee and cream pie]. But after three months I met Peter, my husband and coach, and that made things better.

(4)

Her sport takes her to many other distant parts of the world, but she is always at her happiest running around Dundee.

(5)

The city drops from the Law Hill and spreads out along the Tay waterfront. Its housing estates may be grim, but it is well-endowed with green parks. Approached by night over the two-mile road bridge from Fife, it sparkles like a Riviera resort. There's an old joke about Dundee, that it's a good place to come from, rather than a good place to go. Not true, says McColgan, whose sister, brothers, parents and childhood friends all live within a few miles. "It's a good place to belong. I'll never leave."

---

council houses: low cost homes built by the local council and rented to low-income families

A Working in Dundee, Scotland's fourth city, means being involved with one of the three Js — jute, jam and journalism — and McColgan's first job was in a jute factory in the Perth Road. She began as a "quality control assistant and cream bun fetcher," clocking in at 5.30am. Dundee Royal Infirmary was full of patients with lung problems caused by jute dust, and she was living with her parents, both getting through three packets of cigarettes a day.

B "When I've been away for a few weeks' training in the sunshine, that first run back home beats it all, even if it's freezing cold, pouring with rain and the wind is howling in from the North Sea. A 20-mile run along the lower coast road, through Barry, with a loop round Dawson Park before coming home again, blows away the cobwebs."

C McColgan, née Lynch, now lives in a 14-roomed mansion in the countryside nearby, with her parents installed in a cottage in its grounds. Athletics has been good to her. "But money doesn't buy respect. Dundee folk would soon let you know if they thought you were getting big-headed," she says.

D There was never any doubt about the talent after that, but finding sufficient funds for training was a problem in the early years. This was where Phil Kearns came in.

E It was Phil Kearns, her PE teacher at St Saviour's High School and a keen marathon runner, who spotted his pupil's potential. He sent her to the local athletics club, the Hawkhill Harriers, where Harry Bennett coached the 11-year old until his death eight years later.

F As Bennett predicted, McColgan won the women's 10, 000-metres in front of a home crowd at the Commonwealth Games in Edinburgh and retained the title in Auckland four years later, with an Olympic silver over the same distance in between. In what was described as "the greatest performance by a male or female British athlete in the history of long-distance running", she won the 10,000-metres at the World Championship in Tokyo, less than 12 months after the birth of her daughter, Eilish.

née: French word for *born*; used to refer to maiden (unmarried) name

PE: short for *Physical Education* lessons

VOCABULARY

Describing places: creating atmosphere

1 The articles *Welfare wagon-train to the west* (page 145) and *Running for home* both use a number of descriptive words and expressions to help create an impression of place. Look back at both articles and make a list of words and expressions that can be used to describe these aspects of a place.

- landscape features
- weather conditions (wind, rain, temperature)
- buildings

For example, in the article about Liz McColgan, what words are used to describe the following?

very cold weather / heavy rain / a strong wind

Can you add more expressions? How would you describe the place where you come from?

Expressions to do with living somewhere

2 Complete the sentences with the words and phrases below, in the correct form, which are all to do with living somewhere.

sleep rough / set up house / unfit to live in / feel at home / settle down / a roof over your head

1 It's not a particularly nice flat, but at least you've got ....

2 After losing his house and his job, Mike was living on the streets, ...

3 This house is in a terrible state — it's completely ....

4 The people in the village were so friendly that Simon immediately .... there.

5 After they got married, they .... in Devon but moved to Spain a year later.

6 At the age of thirty, Tom decided it was time he ....

WRITING

Exam File: Part 2, Tourist brochure

In Paper 2, Part 2 you may be asked to write a tourist brochure or contribute to a guidebook for visitors to your town or country. A tourist brochure or guidebook aims both to inform and attract visitors. Follow this advice.

- Think about who the brochure is aimed at and include information that will interest the target group.
- Choose a layout and organisation that will present the information as clearly as possible and make it easy for the reader to find what he/she wants to know. It's a good idea to divide the text up into short sections with clear headings.
- Use words and expressions that will make your descriptions interesting and attractive, but don't go overboard, or you won't sound natural.

1 Look at the brochure extract and answer these questions.

1 What particular aspects of the town are highlighted in the introductory section?

2 What other information is included?

3 Is the brochure aimed at the general visitor or a particular group?

2 Highlight words and expressions which are used to make this place sound particularly attractive to tourists. Which words could you use in a brochure about your own town?

3 Read the writing task and follow the **Steps to Writing**.

Your town is about to host an important international sports competition for students from many different countries. The competition will last for two weeks. You have been asked to write the **tourist brochure** which will be part of the visitors' Welcome Pack. You have been asked to give some background information about your town and recommend places to visit and things to do as well as giving practical information about prices and opening times.

Write your brochure, using about 250 words.

ROYAL TUNBRIDGE WELLS

*L*ying at the heart of one of the most beautiful stretches of countryside in England, Royal Tunbridge Wells is the ideal location for a short break or a leisurely tour of the Kent countryside. In the 18th and 19th centuries, royalty and the gentry left city life behind to relax in the peaceful country atmosphere of 'the Wells'. Daniel Defoe, the author, and Samuel Pepys, the diarist, were visitors, and Queen Victoria often came to the town as a child. Today, you will still find many traces of those bygone times, particularly on the famous colonnaded shopping street known as the Pantiles, with its elegant shops and tearooms.

THE TOWN

MUSEUMS & MONUMENTS

*The **Tunbridge Wells Museum & Art Gallery** offers a richly varied display of exhibits, including locally made handicrafts. At **Cranbrook Museum**, you can find out more about local history, trades and industry.*

ENTERTAINMENT

The Assembly Hall, Trinity Theatre & Arts Centre and Broomhill Arts offer a wide range of entertainment. In early August, mingle with characters during an annual Georgian Festival of singing, dancing and dramatic events. You can also enjoy all sorts of event at venues in the surrounding area. Ask for a copy of the 'Events Leaflet' from the Tourist Information Centre.

Georgian Festivities

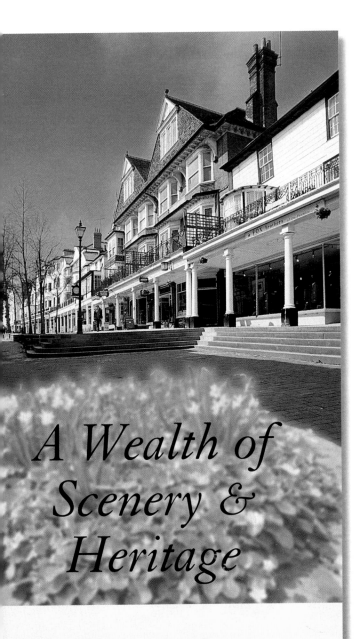

SPORT
If you fancy a bit of exercise during your stay, the Sports and Y Centre has a swimming pool and a large 4-court indoor tennis centre. There are numerous golf courses nearby open to visitors.

FOOD & DRINK
You'll find an excellent choice of restaurants and pubs for lunches, snacks and evening meals. Ask for the 'Eating Out' leaflet.

SHOPPING
Speciality shops, including antiques, can be found in and around the Pantiles, Mount Ephraim and St Johns Road. Ask for the 'See and Shop' leaflet.

A Wealth of Scenery & Heritage

Step 1 Task interpretation
Read the question carefully. Who will read the brochure? What tone and register will be suitable? What three things does the task ask you to do?

Step 2 Generating ideas
Jot down some ideas for each of the areas you have to include in your brochure. Think about your reader. What is likely to interest young people coming to take part in a sports competition?

Step 3 Layout and organisation
Your notes will have generated more ideas than you can use in a 250-word entry. Select the areas which you think would be most interesting. Organise your information into sections and provide headings.

Step 4 Write
Write your brochure. Don't forget to include practical details such as the entrance fee for students and opening times where relevant.

Step 5 Evaluate and edit
▶ Writing checklist (page 214)

Language Bank

Background information
Situated/located in … / Built on the banks of …
X has a history that can be traced back to …
X is a dynamic cultural centre/thriving industrial city/port …

Things to see and do
… is a fine/impressive/striking example of …
… offers a wide variety of activities to suit every taste.
… is the biggest leisure centre in the region, offering …
If you want to find out about …
For those of you who enjoy … /who'd like to …
You can while away an afternoon *-ing*
Especially popular with young people is/are …
Also worth seeing is/are …
No visit is complete without a trip to …

Giving practical information
With a student pass, it costs … to get in.
It's open from 9 to 5, Mondays to Fridays.
(open daily)/(closed Sundays and Mondays)

SPEAKING 2
Part 3, Select and plan; Part 4, Report decisions

1 In Part 3 of the Speaking Test, you may be shown some visual prompts to help you carry out a specific task. Look at the photographs and read the details below.

Imagine that the Tourist Office of your town has decided to organise a festival this summer to attract more visitors. The students at your place of study have been asked to contribute in some way. Discuss what contribution you could make, and the kind of planning and preparation it will require. These photos of various events may help to give you ideas.

2 Report your decisions to the class.

3 Discuss these questions.
1 What kind of organised events do you particularly enjoy?
2 Does your town have regular events aimed at attracting visitors? Describe them.
3 What problems can be caused by large numbers of visitors at a particular time?

4 If you like, you can write another leaflet for visitors, giving details of the event you have decided to organise!

Language Bank

Evaluating options

We need to do something that will appeal to a wide range of people.

We have to take into consideration things like cost, how much time it will take to organise …

We could … / I think we should …

Organising a parade might be difficult. I mean, just think about …

Well, in that case, it might be better to …

How about …

ENGLISH IN USE 3
Part 5, Register cloze

1 Read the advertising brochure opposite, to find out what it's about. Answer these questions.

1 What is a 'time ownership home'?
2 What kind of clientele is the brochure written for?
3 Highlight words and expressions in the brochure that help to give the impression of luxury and privilege. For example:

'exclusive leisure retreats'

2 Now read the letter from someone who has spent a week there. Use the information in the brochure to complete the gaps in the letter. Use no more than one or two words for each gap. You should use simpler, more straight-forward expressions than those in the brochure.

ADVERTISING BROCHURE

THESE exclusive leisure retreats are more than mere holiday homes. They are time ownership homes, exclusively reserved for those individuals who have bought the weeks they want to use, at a fraction of the cost of purchasing the whole property.

Your **PERSONAL TOUR** *of the* **EXCLUSIVE LODGES**

The weeks are their property in perpetuity. To enjoy, rent to friends, sell or even pass on to future generations.

FROM its spacious terrace each lodge has its own unique perspective over the sparkling blue waters and unruffled surface of Loch Lomond. In the supremely spacious living room, you will discover inviting leather sofas adorned with colourful scatter cushions. Even the Bang and Olufsen stereo and CD player are skilfully and discreetly housed in an elegant oak unit.

IN the stylish Allmilmo kitchen there is everything you need from microwave and food processor to exclusive Gaggenau appliances. Discover too, the irresistible opulence of the master bedroom. The elegance of gold-plated fittings and marble

THE CHARM *and* **ELEGANCE** *of a* **LUXURIOUS** *country* **HOUSE**

surrounds in the bathroom. The indulgence of whirlpool bath and impulse shower. The sheer pleasure of your own private sauna.

WHEN you consider the superb attention to detail lavished on these exceptional lodges, you might expect such luxury to be outside the price range of all but a fortunate few. Yet prices start from a not excessive £3,250 up to £22,950 per week, according to your selection. A small price indeed when you consider the pleasure of owning a share in one of the world's most exclusive country resorts. For eternity ...

EXTRACT FROM LETTER TO A FRIEND

We've been in Scotland for a week at our timeshare lodge — it's not (0) .....just...... a holiday cottage. It was (1) .... to buy a week than we thought and we can rent it to other people since we own our week (2) .... In fact we can even leave it to our (3) .... Our lodge has a (4) .... over the lake, which is very blue and (5) .... at this time of year. The living room is surprisingly (6) .... and as soon as I see the sofa I want to (7) .... The stereo system is good and fitted so that you can't (8) .... In the kitchen, there is nothing (9) .... and it is good-quality stuff. You wouldn't believe how (10) .... the bedroom is and we really enjoyed having our own sauna. You might think these lodges are beyond the reach of (11) .... but the prices range from about £3,000 to £23,000 per week depending on (12) .... of week, which is (13) ...., don't you think? I'm enclosing the brochure for you to have a look at.

Calamities and mishaps

SPEAKING

1 Work in pairs. Choose two pictures each and take it in turns to describe what has happened. Answer these questions.

1 How do you think these unfortunate situations have come about?

2 What precautions can you take to avoid getting into situations like these?

2 With your partner, choose one of the situations in the pictures and imagine you are the people involved. Decide what is the best course of action to take to deal with the problem. Then compare your ideas with other students. Who has the best solution?

Language Bank

a pickpocket

be robbed / have your money/wallet stolen

be in the wrong place at the wrong time

report the incident/the loss of ... to the police/the consulate

cancel your credit cards

capsize

a life-threatening situation

call the emergency services

have an accident / break down / run out of petrol

pitch a tent

trample on

be stranded (in the middle of nowhere)

It's best to be prepared for emergencies.

LISTENING 1
Part 4, Multiple matching

1 📼 You will hear five short extracts in which people talk about unfortunate situations they have been in. For questions 1—5, match the extracts as you hear them with the situations, listed A—H. Note that there are three options that don't go with any of the extracts. Before you listen, remember to read the options and highlight key words in the questions, for example, *asleep* in F. This will indicate what to listen out for.

This occurred

A near the sea.   1 ....

B because the speaker was unhappy.

C when the speaker was tired.   2 ....

D without the speaker noticing.

E following an unexpected meeting. 3 ....

F when the speaker was asleep.

G through not following advice.   4 ....

H when the speaker was in a busy street. 5 ....

2 📼 Now listen again. For questions 6—10, match the extracts as you hear them with the speakers' reactions to each situation, listed A—H.

The speaker

A was surprised at how people responded. 6 ....

B took action to help others.

C contacted a family member for help. 7 ....

D had expected this event to occur.

E accepted a friend's advice.   8 ....

F reacted in the same way as others.

G struggled to stay calm.   9 ....

H contacted government agencies.   10 ....

3 Discuss this question.

Summarise how each speaker coped with each situation. Would you have reacted in the same way?

ENGLISH IN USE 1
Part 4, Word formation

1 Read the text below, ignoring the gaps. How old are the children? How did they manage to survive?

2 Now complete the text with the correct form of the words given. Remember to:

* think about prefixes, suffixes and internal changes to the word.
* read the complete sentence carefully to find out if the target word has to be plural or negative.

Two tots found safe after 16-day mountain ordeal

Exhausted, (1) .... and thirsty, four-year-old Romina and her six-year-old brother Daniel were found by (2) .... today after wandering for 16 days in a mountain (3) .... in the north of Argentina.

They had left their home to look for their parents, who were rounding up cattle, and could not find their way home.

'We survived by eating apples, which were very (4) ....,' said Daniel.

They were (5) .... to get lost but fortunate not to be attacked by the pumas that inhabit the mountains.

Both children are now in hospital, suffering from exposure and (6) .... They also have (7) .... to their feet because they were walking barefoot. However, doctors are confident that they will make a full (8) ....

---

(1) HUNGER	**(5)** LUCK
(2) RESCUE	**(6)** NUTRITION
(3) WILD	**(7)** INJURE
(4) TASTE	**(8)** RECOVER

3 Do you know any other tales of survival against the odds? If so, tell the class.

READING 1

Part 3, Multiple choice questions

1 Read the headline and first paragraph only of the article opposite, and answer these questions.

1 What do these words mean: *alms, pauper, hobo, pose as someone* ? *(Look for synonyms or explanations in the text.)*

2 What does the word *this* refer to in line 2? *(Read the rest of the sentence to find out.)*

3 What experiment did the writer carry out?

4 What did he want to find out?

2 What do you predict will be the result of the experiment?

3 Read the article quickly to the end to check your prediction. Don't read for detailed understanding at this point.

2 Find these words and phrases in the text and try to work out what they mean from the context. Then check your ideas by matching them with their definitions below.

1 deceit *(line 3)*
2 there and then *(line 34)*
3 predatory *(line 68)*
4 progressive (opinions) *(line 83)*
5 con trick (short for *confidence trick*) *(line 119)*
6 be in a fix *(line 126)*
7 be the case *(line 152)*
8 substantial *(line 153)*

A a dishonest way of getting people to give money
B be true
C immediately
D liberal, modern
E behaviour intended to make people believe something that isn't true
F important, real
G behaviour that exploits someone's weakness
H be in a difficult situation

3 Answer the multiple choice questions that follow by choosing the best option (A, B, C or D) according to the information in the text.

1 When he decided to carry out the experiment, the writer
   A had no idea how people would react.
   B adopted a new approach.

   C felt uneasy about what he had to do.
   D wished he could refuse.

2 His first negative experience was when
   A he was overcharged for a service.
   B people looked at him with suspicion.
   C he went to collect his belongings.
   D an employee treated him differently from others.

3 The writer's initial attempts at begging were unsuccessful because
   A he showed how rejected he felt.
   B people felt threatened by his behaviour.
   C he should have asked a different question.
   D people were surprised by what he said.

4 The people who helped the writer when he was badly-dressed were
   A in a similar position to him.
   B of various types.
   C eager to talk to someone.
   D confused by his request.

5 When he had put on his suit and tie, the writer
   A used a different story about his situation.
   B decided to approach a different set of people.
   C showed the embarrassment he was suffering.
   D looked extremely optimistic about his prospects.

6 The writer concluded that
   A successful begging is a con trick.
   B beggars receive the treatment they deserve.
   C the greater the need, the more money is given.
   D people will give if someone is dressed in a suitable way.

4 Look at the use of the verb *dig* in this extract from the text.

'Old ladies happily dug in their purses ...'

What is the literal meaning of *dig*? What is the effect of using it metaphorically here? How is it different from 'put their hands in their pockets'?

Can you explain the literal and metaphorical meaning of the italicised words in these extracts?

1 '... you start to *sift* the crowds ...'
2 '... two other men in the same sort of *mould* ...'

5 How far do you agree with the conclusions the journalist draws in the last paragraph?

Alms for the rich but not for the poor

Is a man in a suit more deserving of aid than a pauper in rags?

I AM NOT sure about the ethics of this — its basic method is deceit — but one day last week I carried out an experiment at Charing Cross Station in London. It was a repeat of something done in the 1950s by an American sociologist. For an hour he stood begging in Grand Central Station in New York, dressed as what he called a 'hobo' and for the following hour he did the same thing, but posing as a businessman, dressed in a suit and tie. What, he asked, would be the difference in response?

To do this is quite difficult, even if it is only an act. It is a conscious stripping away of one's own dignity. I arrived at the station at about midday, wearing old jeans, several layers of T-shirts and jerseys and an anorak. I was unshaven. I took my bag with the other clothes to the left-luggage office. Other people deposited their luggage and received a ticket. They handed over no money. They would pay on collection. When I reached the head of the queue, the woman made me pay the £2 there and then and insisted on going through everything in the bag before accepting it. I felt dirty and resentful.

The usual anonymity of the station had disappeared. Even standing there, doing nothing, I had somehow become abnormal, the object of a cold, evaluating stare from the other passengers, barely suppressed expressions of contempt on their faces, perhaps in the expectation of a bad smell. What I was planning to do was an offence. I didn't want to be arrested, so I moved out of the station. I stood by the corner of a café and started to beg. The shame of it made me start out with the wrong phrase, inviting an answer in the negative. "Excuse me, you haven't got any change, have you?" "No," they said, not breaking step or in a tight, confused silence. So I turned to the affirmative. "Could you give me some change, please? Have you got some money you could give me?"

With rejection after rejection, the humiliation does not diminish. The sense of one's own uselessness is cumulative. From the inside, begging does not feel predatory, exploitative or threatening, but quite quickly, out of pure self-interest, you start to sift the crowd, to try and pick out the most likely candidates. Self-made people, who have worked to remove themselves from poverty, are useless. Heavily made-up women make no response at all. Old people on day trips to London are taken aback when I approach them, shock and muddle on their faces. What you are looking for, I realise, is educated middle-class people with progressive opinions.

A DELICATE, curly-haired man in his 40s, wearing a white mac, came up in the street, reading a book as he walked. Did he have any change? He looked me carefully in the eye. "What's the problem?" he said. "Just short of cash, really," I said. "Mm," he said, and gave me a pound. Two other men in the same sort of mould gave me 50p each, jangling the change in their pockets as they searched for the right-shaped coin. My hour was nearly up. A man who looked like a builder but said he used to be "on the beg" himself insisted on giving me 21 pence even though I told him to keep it.

"Go on," he said fiercely, "take it."

In the Charing Cross gents, I changed into my suit and tie, had a shave and then went upstairs to ask the people in the station for money. I had arrived there, stupidly, I explained, without any money, cheque book, credit cards, anything, and I needed a ticket to get down to Sussex. Could they, did they think, just give me 50 pence towards it? Really stupid, so embarrassing. I could see myself making a sort of grin of apology. This con trick worked a dream. Within twenty minutes I had £3.50. Old ladies happily dug into their purses for me. One of them said, "I must say, you're a very optimistic young man." A charming man explained how he'd been in the same fix himself once. A man from Sussex got change from a bookstall so he could help me out.

Out of every three people I asked, one gave me money. It was a matter for conversation and sympathy. I was taking money at the rate of £10.50 an hour. But it felt like theft and after twenty minutes I stopped. The point had been made. It was the same result as the sociologist had found in the 1950s.

What can one conclude? Most importantly, that people are not mean. They are prepared, on the whole, to give to a stranger. The natural sense of charity is alive. But, strangely, that readiness to give is not related to the need. The need of the homeless person is infinitely more urgent than that of the man without a ticket but people respond as if the opposite were the case. The only substantial difference between them is in what they look like.

LISTENING 2

Part 1, Sentence completion

1 You will hear Rebecca talking about a theft. First, complete these extracts from the recording with an appropriate preposition or particle from the list, and work out what each verb means.

by / off / out / out of / up / with

1 I had to *pick* someone .... at the airport.

2 Someone had just been *passing* ....
— an opportunist thief.

3 I *rushed* .... [to the funeral] in a great panic.

4 I'll just *pick* .... the messages on the answerphone.

5 I *tipped* all this stuff .... the plastic bag onto the counter.

6 I was anxious to *clear* the car .... so I had plenty of space.

7 They weren't old enough to *cope* .... getting money from a machine.

2 Listen to the recording and complete the sentences using up to four words. You will hear the recording twice.

The missing bag

Rebecca went home early to change in order to
(1) ....

She had to go to the airport afterwards to
(2) ....

She put her handbag in the car but forgot
(3) ....

At first she thought the bag was still (4) ....
....

She experienced practical difficulties because of the theft of her (5) ....

She had a surprise when she listened to
(6) ....

A girl had found items from the bag while
(7) ....

Rebecca had to work out what was missing by a (8) ....

She believed the theft was done by (9) ....

The most important thing she got back was
(10) ....

3 Discuss this question.

What precautions should Rebecca have taken to prevent the theft from taking place?

LANGUAGE STUDY 1

Uses of *get* (Notes page 210)

1

1 These extracts from Listening 1 and 2 all contain *get*, one of the commonest verbs in English. Can you re-express the sentences without using *get*?

1 There was a spring near us and we usually got water from there.
... we usually fetched water from there.

2 I got my passport back eventually.
My passport was returned eventually.

3 I got my bag stolen once.

4 This is the phone call you hoped you'd never get.

5 a young man ... got his heel caught in some lady's bag ...

6 a dreadful situation I got myself into ...

7 There didn't seem to be any difficulty getting shops to give you a credit account.

8 A friend advised me to get help.

9 Things have got better.

10 and then mum got stuck (in the mud) ...

11 I'd got my brother coming to stay that night ...

12 by the time I'd got myself organised ...

2 In which sentences is *get* used in the following patterns:

- *get* + object + infinitive
- *get* + object + past participle

Match the examples to these meanings:

A cause something to happen/be done by someone else

B manage to do or achieve something yourself

C experience something (usually undesirable)

2 Rewrite these sentences using an appropriate form of *get*.

1 I have to stay at home today. The plumber is coming round to mend the boiler.
2 By the time I was ready, the race had already started.
3 We've asked a building firm to build an extension for us.
4 Make sure you arrive on time.
5 Fortunately, my answer was correct.
6 I must finish this report by tomorrow.
7 It was my fault I was in debt.
8 Persuading John to come with me was quite easy.
9 Everything is going from bad to worse.

Linking ideas: condition

3 Look at the example. In the second sentence, the link word *Otherwise* imposes a condition that must be met.

You must prove that you took all the necessary precautions. *Otherwise* the insurance company won't pay compensation.

The same idea can be expressed in a number of ways. Can you complete these sentences so that they mean the same as the example? Which sentences are more formal? more colloquial?

1 If you can't ...
2 Unless you ...
3 ... on condition that ...
4 As long as ...
5 ... provided/providing that ...
6 ... only ... if

4 Re-express these sentences using appropriate link words from Exercise 3. How many different ways can you think of?

1 You haven't kept your receipt, so you can't get a refund.
2 You can borrow my car, but you must return it this evening.
3 You are not wearing a shirt and tie. You may not enter the club.
4 You must wear a helmet. Otherwise you can't take part in the cycle race.

5 Answer the questions, using appropriate link words from Exercise 3.

In your country, what conditions must be met if

1 you want your insurance company to pay for repairs following a burglary?

2 you want to go to the best restaurant in town?
3 you want to study at university?
4 you want to become a teacher?
5 you want to get a driver's licence?

Linking expressions in spoken English

6 Read these extracts from Listening 1 and 2. Highlight the phrases used to:

- begin a story
- add a point
- change topic
- emphasise or reinforce a point
- signal the end of (that part of) the story
- give an explanation
- avoid being precise
- introduce a repeated point

Listening 1

1 Well, I woke up around 5.45 because the room started shaking ...
2 ... about six weeks or something like that ...
3 It was actually pretty late at night.
4 And that was that until the next day.
5 Well, to cut a long story short ...

Listening 2

6 Well, I came back from work that day and I was in a tearing hurry ...
7 and of course ... as I said, I was late for the funeral ...
8 I didn't have any means of contacting the police or anybody else for that matter ...
9 And in fact (the girl) lived maybe three or four hundred yards away ...
10 ... worked out by a process of elimination what was missing. I mean, my bag is very large.
11 It had been completely scattered over this bush ... Anyway, inevitably, the cash was missing.

7 Work in groups. Describe a mishap that you have experienced, using some of the language you have looked at in this section. The other students in your group should encourage you to include as much detail as possible.

READING 2
Part 2, Gapped text

1 Do you play any sports or do any sort of regular exercise such as jogging, aerobics or cycling? What are your main reasons for doing so?

- to keep fit and healthy
- social reasons
- other

2 You are going to read an article about sports injuries, especially related to cycling. Before you read ...

1 Can you identify these parts of the body?

skull / shin / calf / thigh / knee / jaw / ribs / collar-bone / spine / wrist

2 Can you explain the function of these parts of a bicyle?

handlebars / pedals / saddle / gears

3 Now look at the article. Six paragraphs have been removed. You must choose which of the paragraphs A—G match the numbered gaps 1—6. There is one extra paragraph that does not belong in any of the gaps.

Read the main part of the article first and find out why cycling has been declared a health hazard.

Downhill all the way – to casualty

FIRST it was aerobics. Then it was jogging. Now cycling has been declared a health hazard. Jogging was never particularly good for you, so doctors said: its jarring action could damage the knees and the back. But if cycling your way to health was ever an alternative, it may not be now.

(1)

Dr Robert Kronisch, a sports medicine consultant in San Jose who recently completed a study of serious mountain biking injuries, discovered an incidence of damage far higher than for jogging or most other sports. Interviewing 265 riders, he found that more than twenty per cent had suffered injuries serious enough to require medical attention in the last year.

(2)

Many of his interviewees for the *Clinical Journal of Sports Medicine* were from US mountain bike clubs, which suggests that they were advanced riders, possibly more likely to take their machines over the most difficult routes than novices. Most beginners, like Britain's four and a half million mountain bikers, are happy to cycle in parks or on simple country paths.

(3)

Dr Kronisch is not alone in his concerns. Ron Phiffer, who lectures in cycling medicine, spoke at a conference on "The Role of Medicine and Science" in Colorado this summer. He said that mountain biking should definitely not be taken up as a means of getting fit. Beginners should get fit first, and then buy an appropriate bike. "It is important to select exactly the right bike for you," he said.

(4)

Dr Ed Burke is a physician at the Colorado Springs base of the US Olympic cycling team. He says that most mountain bikes are never used on difficult terrain, but that the roads of London or New York can be just as rough as some of the tracks in the Rocky Mountains.

(5)

Ron Phiffer, who used to race for one of mountain biking's top teams, also has some advice for beginners to take the sport slowly for the first few months and to get a full medical if in doubt about fitness. "People take a while to learn to do it properly," he said. "It is while they are learning that they are most susceptible to injuring wrists and collar bones because they can't fall properly."

(6)

Dr Burke makes no bones about recommending them. "They are a very important form of protection. Wherever you go, cycling is only a low impact activity until you crash."

A On the other hand, these advanced riders, as members of a club, are most likely to be experienced and to know their limits. Beginners may be more at risk of injury.

B He advises that people who want to get fit on a bike must cycle systematically, whether they are doing it on city roads or mountain tracks. "It is only a good way to get fit if you do it regularly, at least four times a week, and get your cardiovascular activity up for at least twenty minutes at a time."

C It is interesting to compare the cycling injuries with what happens to joggers. A number of studies show a similar incidence of knee and calf injuries.

D This is because American doctors have just put a question mark against mountain biking. Almost all cyclists interviewed by one Californian doctor had suffered at least one injury in the past twelve months, so cycling might not be as healthy as you thought.

E Getting healthy on a mountain bike is one thing: staying so another. In America last year, more than a thousand cyclists died from head injuries. The 'beer cooler' styrofoam helmet is now mandatory in many North American cities.

F Most of the injuries were fractures, lacerations and shoulder injuries, he reported. Almost all the cyclists questioned had suffered some injury in the past year.

G For novices it is crucial that the bike fits properly. One of the most common injuries is patellis tendinitis, which causes painful and inflamed knees. This happens when too high a gear is used (meaning more effort is required to push the pedals round) and when the saddle is too low. Back pain and saddle sores are other common ailments. These happen when the bike is not the right size for the rider.

cardiovascular activity: a form of exercise that increases the rate at which your heart beats.

4

1 Now read the base text **and** the missing paragraphs. Decide where the missing paragraphs fit. Look for:

• the development of an idea or argument.
For example:
The first paragraph of the main text ends: 'But if cycling your way to health was ever an alternative, it may not be now.'
The next paragraph will probably give an **explanation** why.

• lexical links. For example:
The paragraph after gap (1) refers to 'interviewing 265 riders.' Are there references to interviews in paragraphs A—G?

• extra details and elaboration. For example:
The same paragraph mentions 'injuries'. Where can we find more details of these injuries?

• reference pronouns. For example:
The final paragraph of the text says 'recommending *them*'. What does *them* refer to?

2 Check your answers by reading the whole article in sequence. Does it make sense?

5 You may like to refer back to Unit 6, Language Study 1 page 84, before doing this exercise.

1 What does *so* refer to in these extracts from the text?

1 Jogging was never particularly good for you, *so* doctors said.
2 Getting healthy on a mountain bike is one thing: staying *so* another.

2 What words have been deliberately omitted in these extracts?

1 But if cycling your way to health was ever an alternative, it may not be now.
2 Ron Phiffer has some advice for beginners to get a full medical if in doubt about fitness.

6

1 Read through the article again and make a list of injuries and ailments suffered a) by joggers b) by cyclists.

2 What advice would you give to someone thinking of taking up cycling?

7 Work in groups. Have you ever had an accident or injury while playing sport? Tell your group what happened and how you dealt with it. The other students should show interest and encourage you to give as many details as possible.

ENGLISH IN USE 2
Part 1, Multiple choice cloze

1 The article below is about another sport that can be bad for your health — yachting! Before you read, check you understand these words for parts of a ship.

deck / hull / stern / bow / mast

2 Read the article quickly to find out where the writer is and how he feels. Then read the text again more carefully. Choose the word that best fits each space (A, B, C or D).

3 Discuss these questions.

1 What is your reaction to the text? Does it put you off sailing for ever, or not?

2 Have you had any experience of sailing? Would you recommend it to others? Why (not)?

Michael Nicholson, who followed the progress of the yacht Time & Tide on the third leg of the BT Global Challenge race from Wellington, New Zealand, to Sidney, Australia, wrote this dispatch from the Tasman Sea.

Strapped to my bunk, I am suffering and in despair at the (1) .... ahead. In the bunk above me, my cameraman is groaning with the agony of a stomach that can (2) .... no more. The (3) .... is dreadful and moans fill the cabin.

I move deeper into my sleeping bag, trying to (4) .... out the sound of sea-sickness sufferers. But I cannot ignore the fury of the storm that seems to be (5) .... us. I cannot find a way of bracing myself to (6) .... the shock of being pushed hard against the hull every time we smash into a wave.

The anticipation of (7).... for the next one doubles my heartbeat as the bow (8) .... and for seconds I am suspended in mid-air between the hull and the deck. Then comes the (9) .... of impact. The whole yacht shudders to a stop as if it has been driven at full-power into a brick wall. We (10) .... the storm at dusk and there is still no (11) .... of it losing force.

I am on watch until 6am. (12) .... I must get up on deck. The yacht is (13) .... over at such an angle that I appear to be standing on the ceiling.

The cooker is jammed almost upside down against the mast and is (14) .... cold soup onto our heads.

I search for my sea boots. They have slid back towards the stern and it takes five minutes to crawl to them and another five minutes to pull them on. Then begins the dangerous (15) .... out onto deck to face the sea.

1	**A**	prospect	**B**	future	**C**	possibility	**D** view
2	**A**	sick	**B**	choke	**C**	throw	**D** vomit
3	**A**	aroma	**B**	stink	**C**	fragrance	**D** smell
4	**A**	close	**B**	shut	**C**	put	**D** lock
5	**A**	drowning	**B**	swallowing	**C**	sinking	**D** overpowering
6	**A**	withstand	**B**	support	**C**	oppose	**D** fight
7	**A**	staying	**B**	waiting	**C**	stopping	**D** pausing
8	**A**	rises	**B**	mounts	**C**	raises	**D** ascends
9	**A**	break	**B**	burst	**C**	smash	**D** explosion
10	**A**	blew	**B**	reached	**C**	found	**D** hit
11	**A**	hint	**B**	clue	**C**	mark	**D** sign
12	**A**	Anyhow	**B**	Somehow	**C**	However	**D** Anyway
13	**A**	bending	**B**	leaning	**C**	inclining	**D** bowing
14	**A**	flooding	**B**	flowing	**C**	dripping	**D** pouring
15	**A**	cruise	**B**	voyage	**C**	progress	**D** journey

LANGUAGE STUDY 2

Emphasising parts of a sentence: inversion

(Notes pages 210—211)

1

1 Read these examples from the text *In the eye of the storm*. What do you notice about the position of subject and verb? Why do you think the writer has done this?

a. ... for seconds I am suspended in mid-air ... Then *comes the smash* of impact.

b. Then *begins the dangerous journey* out onto deck to face the sea.

Starting the sentence with an adverbial and inverting the subject and verb makes the sentence more dramatic.

2 Now rewrite these sentences in the same way to make them more emphatic.

1 Suddenly this man came up and demanded to see our passports.
2 The boy rushed off, clutching the letter.
3 A £20 note lay on the pavement.
4 Our train is coming. (Start: *Here ...*)
5 The matter of money is not to be overlooked.
6 The question of how to convince people is equally important.

2

1 Compare these examples. They have a similar meaning, but b. is more dramatic. Why?

a. I got out of the car and a thief grabbed my briefcase.

b. Just as I got out of the car, a thief grabbed my briefcase.

The same kind of emphasis can be achieved by starting with a negative adverbial and using inversion.

c. *Hardly* had I got out of the car *when* a thief grabbed my briefcase.

d. *No sooner* had I sat down *than* the doorbell rang.

2 Use the patterns given to combine these ideas.

1 The football match began. It began to rain.
2 We sat down. There was a knock on the door.
3 I picked up the phone to call him. He walked in the door.
4 The aircraft landed. It took off again.

3 Inversion is also used after other negative adverbials and conjunctions for dramatic effect. Compare these pairs of examples.

1 a. You must on no account ride that bike.
  b. On no account must you ride that bike.
2 a. I didn't speak to the judge at any time.
  b. At no time did I speak to the judge.
3 a. We only realised we had forgotten our tickets when we got to the theatre.
  b. Only when we got to the theatre did we realise ...
  c. Not until we got to the theatre did we realise ...
4 a. I had to look after the children and do the housework too.
  b. Not only did I have to look after the children, I had to do the housework too.

When you use inversion, what do you have to insert if there is no auxiliary verb?

4 Rewrite these sentences using an appropriate introductory expression to make them more emphatic.

1 I haven't had such a wonderful holiday since I was a child. (Not since)

2 I have never felt so frightened in my life.

3 You seldom come across such a promising first novel.

4 We didn't hear until later that our team had won an award for bravery.

5 You only get that kind of thrill from sailing.

6 The thief stole my wallet and my jacket as well!

7 We weren't allowed to stay up late and we weren't allowed to watch TV on week nights either.

5 A combination of ellipsis (omission) and inversion can be used with conditional sentences. This is normally used only in writing.

1 a. If you (should) need any more information, please do not hesitate to contact me.
  b. Should you need any more information, ...
2 a. If this information had been made public, there would have been an outcry.
  b. Had this information been made public, ...

Rewrite these sentences in the same way.

1 If we were to accept their demands, we would be setting a dangerous precedent.

2 The disaster would not have occurred if the government had acted promptly.

3 If you require assistance, phone this emergency number.

WRITING

Part 1, Report writing

Read the writing task on page 167 carefully. Then follow the **Steps to Writing** below.

Step 1 Task interpretation

Think about who you are writing for. What register will be most suitable? What **three** things does the report ask you to include?

Step 2 Selecting and summarising

You need to include a description of the course and advice to future participants. Read the article and leaflet on page 167 and complete the lists below.

What the course offers

chance to develop practical skills

develops ability to deal with difficult situations

good social life

specialist facilities

Advice for future participants

must be fit

must have experience of chosen activity

safety precautions: do's and don'ts

what to bring

Step 3 Layout and organisation

Look at the notes you made in **Step 2**. Use these headings to help you plan your report.

Introduction
Explain the purpose of the report.

What the course offers
Point out the aims of the course and describe the facilities available.

Advice for future participants
Include advice about safety, as well as practical advice about what to bring etc.

Recommendation
Say whether you would recommend the course to other students and why/why not.

Step 4 Write

Write your report. Remember that you have to paraphrase the information given, which may involve a change of register. Avoid lifting whole sentences from the texts.

Step 5 Evaluate and edit

▶ Writing checklist (page 214)

Language Bank

Introduction

This report describes …

The aim of this report is to describe/advise/recommend …

Describing

The course offers/comprises …

As well as providing excellent facilities for students' preferred activities …, the centre also has …

The course develops students' ability to deal with difficult situations.

Giving Advice

Students must be experienced in their chosen activity.

No matter how experienced a participant may feel, they mustn't …

Other points participants should consider are …

Recommendation

Despite/Because of the unfortunate incident this year, I would recommend …

The college should consider …

As long as/Provided basic safety precautions are observed, …

You have recently supervised a group of students from your college on a sailing course at Herrington Adventure Centre. Using the information in the newspaper report and information leaflet, write a **report** for the Principal of your college giving information about the Centre and advice for future course participants. You have been asked if you would recommend a similar course to other students next year.

Your report should be about 250 words.

HERRINGTON
ADVENTURE CENTRE

This leaflet provides advice and guidance to course participants. Please read this information carefully before registering for any course.

- **ACCOMMODATION**
  Course participants sleep in single-sex dormitory-style accommodation. Bedding is provided, but participants must bring their own sleeping bags for camping trips away from the centre. Breakfast and dinner are served in the centre's canteen.

- **CLOTHING**
  All participants must bring suitable clothing and footwear. We recommend lightweight adventure clothing, waterproofs and at least one warm sweater. Specialist equipment is available from the centre. Casual clothing is recommended for evening and social activities.

- **ABILTY AND FITNESS**
  We offer courses in sailing, hang gliding, rock climbing and orienteering. The courses are aimed at those who have had experience of similar activities. The aim is to build on the skills you already have, so you need to be in good physical shape. Our courses are challenging from Day 1!

  The centre boasts a gymnasium which may be enjoyed while participants are resident at the centre. There is no swimming pool, but swimming is possible in Herrington Bay, weather permitting.

- **SOCIAL ACTIVITIES**
  The emphasis at Herrington is on developing the ability to cope with testing situations, but there is a discotheque from 9 p.m. to 11 p.m. every other evening for those with sufficient energy left to dance! Video films are shown each evening.

Dramatic rescue in bay

FIVE teenagers from Herrington Adventure Centre were airlifted by helicopters from Herrington Bay yesterday and are now recovering in hospital.

MASSIVE WAVES!

'We're lucky to be alive!' said Jake Wetherall. 'The sea was really rough and the waves were huge. It was so exciting. We weren't scared till we realised the canoes were full of water. But then the helicopter came. The people at the centre were pretty annoyed though.'

STORM WARNING

A spokesman for the adventure centre stated that only experienced canoeists were allowed into the bay. He said that the group had left on their own initiative and taken the canoes without permission. Because of storm warnings, the group wouldn't have been allowed out yesterday.

ENGLISH IN USE 3
Part 2, Structural cloze

1 The article opposite is about sport. Before you read it, discuss these statements in pairs. Which statements do you agree or disagree with? Support your opinions with reasons and examples.

1 Sportspeople are good role models for teenagers.

2 Sports build character and encourage team spirit.

3 These days, sport is just about winning and making money.

2 Now read the text for the main ideas, ignoring the gaps. Does the information confirm or contradict the ideas you discussed in Exercise 1?

3 Complete the text by writing **one** word in each numbered gap. Remember:

- the words you need are short, simple structural words.
- look at the words surrounding the gaps for clues.
- make sure the word you write is grammatically correct and makes sense in the context.

4 Discuss this question.

Are you surprised by the findings of the research described in the article? Does your own experience and knowledge bear out these findings or not?

Sport and delinquency

The popular belief that organised games build character and moral values in young people is a myth, and teenagers who are keen on sport are (1) ………… , rather than less, likely to be delinquent, according (2) ………… the latest research.

Scientists in New Zealand found that fifteen-year-olds who did a lot of sport were almost (3) ………… as likely as their less sporty counterparts to be delinquent at the age of eighteen. The finding was stronger for girls than for boys.

"Our study (4) ………… not support the view that involvement in sporting activity is a panacea (5) ………… delinquent behaviour. (6) ………… anything, it may exacerbate the problem," they say.

The researchers (7) ………… been monitoring around one thousand people from birth and examined sporting participation and anti-social tendencies at the ages of fifteen and eighteen.

It (8) ………… to be thought that "sports build character", and that (9) ………… participating in organised sport young people would (10) ………… exposed to strong conforming influences and would therefore become good citizens. It (11) ………… assumed that young people's aggression could be safely channelled through sport.

The alternative view, the New Zealand researchers now point (12) ………… , is that involvement in sport encourages aggressiveness and even cheating, (13) ………… can be successful in games.

They conclude that Outward Bound-type activities, (14) ………… as hill-walking, canoeing, rock-climbing and sailing, which provide individual challenges, are likely to be more effective (15) ………… helping young delinquents than organised games.

UNIT 13 The natural world

SPEAKING 1

1 Work in pairs. Look at the photographs and discuss these questions.

1 Where and when are you likely to see these animals?
2 Which are thriving and which are endangered species?
3 What might be the reasons why these species are doing well or are in danger of extinction today?

2 Are any animal species endangered in your country? Explain why this is so.

3 How can endangered species be protected? With a partner, rank the following suggestions in order of their effectiveness, in your view.

- by encouraging and supporting captive breeding programmes in zoos
- by passing legislation protecting the animal
- by relocating the animal to a safer environment
- by educating the public through wildlife documentaries and films
- by employing rangers to keep the species under surveillance and protect them from poachers

Can you add any more suggestions?

Language Bank

Describing

a bird of prey / a game bird

They're found in ... / native to [country]

You can see them hovering in the air over fields. / at dawn or dusk.

be nocturnal / only come out at night

become urbanised

scavenge / a scavenger

be (considered) a pest (by farmers/landowners)

be persecuted

Speculating

They could be endangered because of/due to persecution/loss of habitat/intensive farming/deforestation.

READING 1
Part 2, Gapped text

1 You are going to read an article about the filming of a rare and elusive wild animal for a TV wildlife documentary series. Before you read, discuss these questions.

1 Are wildlife programmes popular in your country? Why (not)?
2 Have you seen any documentary or feature films about wild animals? Describe briefly what they were about.
3 What do you think are the difficulties of filming wild animals?

2 Now look at the article. Six paragraphs have been removed. You must choose which of the paragraphs A—G match the numbered gaps 1—6. There is one extra paragraph that does not belong in any of the gaps.

1 Quickly read the base text to find the main ideas.

2 Read the base text **and** the missing paragraphs. Decide where the missing paragraphs fit.

3 Check your answers by reading the whole article in sequence. Does it make sense?

WILD THING

It might look like an over-sized tabby but the wildcat is no pussycat purring by the fireside! It took two years to capture this rare, elusive beast on film.

Every morning in the half-light of dawn, Michael Richards would haul supplies and heavy equipment to the top of a scaffolding tower.

(1)

His kit of thermal underwear, layer upon layer of woollen jumpers and socks, plus a balaclava over his head, helped the hunter withstand the cold, damp atmosphere. Occasionally, he would spot the beast and quickly, calmly capture it — on film!

(2)

Over a period of two years the film-maker stalked the wildcat and eventually his patience paid off and he struck lucky. Michael perched in his hide eight metres above the ground on a specially-built tower so he could film unnoticed above the heads of the wildcats. 'The result is a rare look into the life of one of the rarest animals in Britain. It's really amazing stuff,' says series producer Keith Scholey.

(3)

The British wildcat looks much like a tabby cat but is much bigger and has a broad, black-ringed tail. Until the last century, it used to roam the whole of Britain, along with the wolf and the bear, and is a survivor of the ice ages. It was much feared in ancient times because of associations with the devil and witchcraft and was killed if spotted.

(4)

Then in the last century it became a favourite target of gamekeepers who shot it almost to extinction to protect game birds. No one knows for sure how many wildcats are left, perhaps only a few hundred, and now it has full legal protection.The stars of the film documentary are a female and her four kittens. Says Keith, 'The kittens are just a few weeks old and adorable, with bright blue eyes. Real cuties, you think.' But they are not as sweet as they look!

(5)

Because the Scottish summer is short the kittens born in spring are grown-up by autumn, when they leave mum to survive alone.

(6)

'In one wonderful scene, we see one of the kittens at about twelve weeks old in a brook catching a small trout,' says Keith.
The wildcats live mainly on small mammals like mice, and rabbits, but they are quite partial to fish and occasionally birds. But this is one of the coldest and windiest parts of Britain, and starvation is a threat to them, as are birds of prey, such as eagles, who take kittens.
'Life is tough for the wildcats,' says Keith. 'They probably only live for four years. Another great danger is that they might mate with domestic cats and gradually become extinct as a separate species.'

balaclava: a woollen hat that covers the whole head, with holes for eyes and mouth

A To add to its problems, the deforestation of Britain over the centuries took away the wildcat's natural environment. Slowly, it was forced to move further and further north to the Highlands of Scotland.

B There, in his hiding place, he would perch in silence for at least twelve hours at a time. Peering through the mist or staring through the rain, he would strain to capture a glimpse of his prey.

C A further complication arose during extremely cold weather. That was the time when both mother and young showed greater awareness of the camera.

D 'When Mum brings them a dead rabbit which they quickly skin and devour, you realise there is no getting away from the fact that they are wild!'

E This is how wildlife cameraman, Michael spent many uncomfortable days in Inverness, Scotland, collecting footage of the rare and elusive British wildcat for a TV documentary series.

F 'Mum feeds them herself in their den at first. But they must quickly learn about hunting for themselves.'

G And the footage taken, especially of the wildcats out hunting their prey, has excited scientists too. They have never been able to observe this before.

Vocabulary 1

Idiomatic expressions

1 Find these colloquial words and expressions in the text. Can you think of a more formal way of saying the same thing?

1 pay off *(main text)*
2 strike lucky *(main text)*
3 amazing stuff *(main text)*
4 along with *(main text)*
5 for sure *(main text)*
6 cutie *(main text)*

2 Use a dictionary to help you answer these questions.

1 What other things can 'pay off'?
2 What other things can you 'strike'?

Choosing the best word

1 Read this sentence from the article.

'Michael Richards would *haul* supplies and heavy equipment to the top of a scaffolding tower.'

The verb *haul* has the general meaning of *pull*. Why has it been used in this context?

2 Complete these sentences with the correct form of one of these verbs, which all have the general meaning of *pull*.

draw / tug / tow / wrench / pluck

1 When the car broke down, a lorry .... it to the nearest garage.

2 The princess travelled in a horse-.......... carriage.

3 The pheasants had to be .... before the chef could cook them.

4 The police attacked the door with such force that it was .... off its hinges.

5 The child .... so hard at the door knob that it came off in his hand.

3

1 Look at this sentence from the article.

'*Peering* through the mist or *staring* through the rain, he would strain to catch a *glimpse* of his prey.'

The words in italics all have the general meaning of *look*. What does the context tell you about the differences in meaning?

2 Complete these sentences with the correct form of one of these words.

blink / gaze / peep / wink / view

1 The archaeologists .... in awe at the piles of gold and diamonds in the tomb.

2 We .... in the bright sunlight as we came out of the church.

3 Anne didn't seem to be around, so I took a quick .... inside her room.

4 Mary realised that Jack's comment had been meant as a joke when he .... at her.

5 The public may .... the paintings on the day before the auction.

LISTENING 1

Part 2, Note completion

1 You are going to hear part of a radio programme about coral reefs. Coral reefs have an important role in the marine ecosystem. How much do you know about this subject? Try this quiz.

1 Coral reefs are found in
  A the Pacific Ocean.   **B** the Atlantic Ocean.

2 They are formed from
  A the skeletons of tiny animals.
  B lava rock thrown up by volcanic eruptions.

3 For a coral reef to develop, it takes
  A just a few years.
  B hundreds of years.

4 Coral reefs are covered in a film of mucus which
  A deters fish and other marine life from eating the coral.
  B helps protect them from infection.

5 The percentage of coral reefs already damaged is
  A over 85%.   **B** over 50%.

2 Listen and complete the notes according to the information you hear on the recording, using up to three words. Remember that, although you will hear this type of recording only once in the exam, the information is repeated in different ways.

Coral reefs

Features of coral reefs:
    slow (1) ....
    great biodiversity
    very vulnerable to (2) ....
Human damage caused by:
    snorkelling and scuba-diving
    (3) ....
    (4) growing .... in reef curios
Reefs damaged by breakage or just by
(5) ....
(6) .... affected by
reduction in number of species
Action already taken at international level to
increase (7) ....
Action needed at local level, especially by
organisations that depend on (8) ....

3 Discuss this question.

On the basis of what you have heard, what do you think governments and the tourist industry need to do to deal with the problem of destruction of coral reefs?

SPEAKING 2

Part 2, Describe, comment and hypothesise

1 Work in pairs. Choose one photograph each, and take turns to talk about your picture. Answer these questions.

1 How has the area been developed for tourism?
2 What impact do you think this development has had on the local environment, the people and the wildlife?

2 Comment on what your partner has said. Do you agree or disagree? Say which development you think is less likely to cause damage to the environment.

Part 3, Discuss and plan; Part 4, Report decisions

2 Look at the picture, which shows an undeveloped area of coastline. Imagine that you have been asked to draw up plans to develop this area for tourism. The aim is to improve the standard of living of the local people by providing them with more opportunities for work, while causing as little damage as possible to the environment. Work out your proposal, taking into account the following points.

- the type of tourists you want to attract
- the facilities that will need to be provided
- the effect on the existing environment and the local wildlife
- possible pollution problems
- the economic viability of any development

3 Report your decisions to the class.

4 Discuss these questions.

1 Do you think mass tourism has generally been a beneficial or a negative development?

2 Do you think the interests of people and the environment will always conflict? Mention some examples of this conflict in your own country, other than tourism.

Language Bank

Describing

This is an example of sympathetic/environmentally friendly development

Commenting and hypothesising

have a negative/beneficial impact on the environment/local culture

increase living standards/provide employment opportunities

Making proposals

We propose to ...

This will have the effect of ...

In order to avoid ... / cause the least damage to ...

make the most of

promote/encourage sustainable tourism

READING 2
Part 3, Multiple choice questions

1 Discuss these questions before you read the article opposite.

1 Mention some species of wildlife that are found in towns and cities.
2 How do you think wild animals find food and a place to live in towns?

2 Now scan and skim the article to answer these questions.

1 What does the title of the article refer to?
2 What species are mentioned in the article? *(Scan the whole text.)*
3 What two different groups of urban wildlife does the writer identify?
4 Which animals have been most successful in adapting to the urban environment?
5 Which animals have not adapted well?

3 Read the text more carefully and answer the multiple choice questions that follow. Choose the best option (A, B, C or D) according to the information in the text. (For advice on how to approach this type of task, look back at Unit 3.)

1 In cities, the species that originally lived in the area
 A have no problems adapting.
 B find alternative food sources.
 C move to other areas.
 D are unable to thrive.
2 In what ways are pigeons typical of town life?
 A They are fed by visitors.
 B They exist in large numbers.
 C They take food from other birds.
 D They are regarded as pests.
3 What makes a city attractive to species from abroad?
 A the type of vegetation
 B the similarity of environment
 C the grassy landscape
 D the presence of similar species
4 What features of the suburbs appeal to foxes?
 A the comfort of the homes
 B the parks and gardens
 C the availability of food
 D the lack of competing species

5 Which creatures have been adversely affected by increased construction?
 A cat fleas
 B reptiles
 C starlings
 D frogs

4

1 Find these words in the article and use the context to work out what they mean.

1 domesticated *(line 31)*
2 biomass *(line 51)*
3 exotics *(line 74)*
4 frequent *(line 90)*
5 roost *(line 113)*
6 creepy-crawlies *(line 126)*

2 Now find five more words from the text that you would like to remember and use.

5 Find these extracts in the article. What do they tell you about the tone of the article? Is it serious, humorous, ironic?

1 'Then it soon hit the streets ... Cold chips are not the pigeons' sole food ... .' *(line 33)*
2 '... in the House of Commons there is a ... spider ... which seems to thrive on the hot air produced by politicians.' *(line 78)*

6 Think of a wild animal that you consider a) to be in need of protection because it is endangered or b) to be a pest. Describe its appearance, its behaviour and its habitat. Discuss the way human beings treat it and/or its impact on human society. Make recommendations on how to deal with it.

Your neighbours are ANIMALS

On safari in the urban jungle

Pigeons making their home in town? No big deal. And it's no surprise to see a fox trotting away from your bin bags. But the urban
5 jungle is being populated by a lot more than these. Despite our efforts to keep our habitat human only, falcons hover overhead and hedgehogs amble around suburban
10 gardens, safer than they would be in the rolling fields of the countryside.

Ecologists accept that the urban environment is a habitat in its own
15 right and that urban wildlife is here to stay. There are two types of urban animal: those that live in towns in spite of us and those that do so because of us. The former are
20 generally native species. Often towns simply imprison them as buildings surround their existing habitat. These species tend to be on the decline as their home is
25 slowly destroyed by human activity. The latter thrive in town.

The biggest success of all, the urban pigeon, originally lived on the coast. There it's known as the
30 rock dove, but centuries ago it became domesticated when it began to nest in specially-built wooden dovecotes. Then it soon hit the streets and began to
35 scavenge for food thrown away by humans. Cold chips are not the pigeon's sole food: the city provides a warm place to sleep at night, but during the day thousands head out
40 to surrounding farmland to feed on crops.

Pigeons truly epitomise town wildlife. "There are very few resident bird species in places like
45 central London," says George Barker, of the conservation agency English Nature, "but those which are there are there in huge volumes. It's a city wildlife
50 characteristic — low biodiversity, high biomass."

Invasions of foreigners

Much of the most fascinating wildlife comes from abroad. Species from abroad end up in our
55 cities in a variety of ways, but for a single reason. From a wildlife point of view, a city is a city. The vegetation of, say, Moscow, is more similar to that of London or Paris
60 than to the Russian countryside. At least forty per cent of the plants in an average city are "introduced" — non-native species — and therefore similar in cities separated by vast
65 distance. A foreign, city-dwelling species falling from a passing aircraft has a good chance of finding a habitat similar to its home territory.
70 Cities also offer warmer climates than the surrounding countryside. Warmer houses provide an excellent breeding ground for exotics. "Urban spiders are
75 definitely on the increase," says Paul Hillyard of the Natural History Museum, "and many are from abroad." For example, in the House of Commons there is a
80 large, wall-living spider — *Sepestria Florentina* — normally found in Spain — which seems to thrive on the hot air produced by politicians.

Suburban slaughter

Where town and countryside merge, in the suburbs, some
85 species do exceptionally well. The fox favours the appetising dustbins and compost heaps of the wealthy and middle-class, and is far less
90 likely to frequent poorer parts of the city. But numbers are declining of late because mange — doubtless encouraged by a junk food diet — has killed thousands. The
95 hedgehog does better. Hedgehogs live in higher populations in the suburbs, with parks and gardens and cemeteries, than they do in the countryside.

Winners and losers

100 Large bats have always done badly in urban areas, where large insects are scarce. On the other hand, when the going is good, bats can move into towns quickly. Recently,
105 a parti-coloured bat was discovered roosting in a block of flats in Ilford, Essex. The short-sighted visitor had mistaken the flats for its usual desolate Siberian cliff roost.

Dusk is the time birds, like bats,
110 really get around town. Millions of starlings choose this time to leave the countryside, preferring to roost in the relative safety and warmth of
115 the city. It's interesting to note that city starlings are declining not because towns are difficult places for them to live in, but because intensive agriculture is destroying
120 their feeding grounds.

Reptiles are doing badly in towns because derelict ground is disappearing. Frogs, on the other hand, are abundant — there has
125 been an increase in the number of garden ponds. Creepy-crawlies are thriving in most towns and suburbs, many of them having arrived on aircraft from warmer
130 countries.

Not all insects are thriving. The human flea is close to extinction because our houses are too warm and dry. Instead we have got the
135 rapidly spreading cat flea and carpet beetle, which are fond of warm, centrally-heated homes. A nice thought to curl up with.

VOCABULARY 2

Words to do with animal behaviour

1 Complete the following sentences with these words that describe animal behaviour and movement, in the correct form.

perch / roam / spin / trot / slither / roost / wheel / crawl / hop / swoop / fly

1 Bears and wolves used to .... widely over the whole of Europe.

2 Many species of bats .... in caves at night.

3 Starlings .... in huge flocks over the fields before coming to .... in a tree for the night.

4 Falcons .... down on their prey and carry them off in their talons.

5 Spiders, cockroaches and other .... insects are thriving in our cities.

6 The female spider .... a web of silk to catch .... insects.

7 Roofs, window ledges, bridges all provide a useful .... for pigeons.

8 If disturbed, a snake is more likely to .... away as fast as possible than attack you.

9 It's not unusual to see a fox .... along the road in city suburbs.

10 Some species of frogs run rather than ....

More animal expressions

2 We often use verbs formed from animal names to describe human behaviour. Complete the following sentences with one of the animal words listed, in the correct form.

fox / rabbit / duck / dog / fish / wolf / badger

1 My son keeps .... me to buy him a computer.

2 The criminals left no clues at the crime-scene. The police were completely ....

3 John never stops talking! He's still .... on about his trip to France.

4 Mary was dressed to kill and, as usual, was .... for compliments.

5 Throughout his life, he was .... by bad luck.

6 If I hadn't .... in time, I would have been hit on the head by a flying golf ball.

7 He was so hungry that he .... his food down in ten seconds flat.

LANGUAGE STUDY

Present and perfect participle clauses
(Notes page 211)

1 Read these examples and identify the participle clauses. Then answer the questions below.

a. Peering through the mist or staring through the rain, he would strain to catch a glimpse of his prey. *(text page 170)*

b. The Scottish summer being very short, the wildcats have to learn to hunt very quickly.

c. Creepy-crawlies are thriving in most towns and suburbs, many of them having arrived on aircraft from warmer countries. *(text page 175)*

d. Putting its paw in the stream, the kitten scooped out a trout.

e. The number of garden ponds having increased, frogs are now more abundant.

1 In which sentences is the subject of the participle clause a) the same as the main clause?
   b) different from the main clause?

2 In which example(s) does the participle clause

• describe an event close in time to the action described in the main clause?

• describe an event that finished well before the action in the main clause?

• give a reason for the action in the main clause?

2 Answer the same questions about these examples, which all express negative ideas.

f. Hardly feeling the pain from his injury, Edward continued his climb.

g. The group leader clearly not being very sure of himself, I decided not to ask any questions.

h. Never having been scuba-diving before, I felt rather nervous.

2 These sentences aren't quite right. Can you explain why and correct them?

1 Reading and enjoying the book, I lent it to a friend.

2 Having been hungry, I ate twice as much as usual at lunch.

3 Being an elusive creature, Michael Richards had to be very patient when filming the wildcat.

4 After persecuting it for hundreds of years, the wildcat now has legal protection.

5 By touching the coral reef, the mucus which protects it can be damaged.

6 Having introduced central heating, our homes now provide a good breeding ground for exotic insects.

3 Combine these pairs of sentences into one, using a present or perfect participle.

1 Jack parked his car in the lay-by. He set off across the fields.
2 He had walked that path many times before. He didn't need to consult the map.
3 He reached his destination. He unpacked his bag.
4 He settled himself comfortably. He scanned the horizon for sight of his prey.
5 By late afternoon he decided to go back. He had waited for six hours without success.
6 He heard a sudden noise. He spun round and saw a magnificent stag close by.
7 He had packed his equipment away. He was unable to shoot.

> **! Spelling reminder**
>
> Look at these sets of words. What spelling changes are necessary when we add -ing?
>
> A sit – sitting, hop – hopping, drop – dropping
> B make – making, take – taking, shake – shaking
> C sleep – sleeping, study – studying, talk – talking, see – seeing
> D open – opening, iron – ironing, happen – happening
> E forget – forgetting, begin – beginning, occur – occurring
>
> (Notes page 213)

Past participle clauses (Notes page 211)

4 Identify the present, perfect and past participle clauses in these examples.

a. Rescue workers have found three young climbers missing since last night.
b. Trapped by high winds on a ledge, the youngsters had clung to the side of the mountain, too terrified to move, until found by the rescue team.
c. Exhausted by their ordeal, and suffering from exposure, they have been taken to hospital.
d. Their job finished, the rescuers are enjoying a well-deserved pint in the pub!

Using participle clauses enables you to express yourself very economically. Without participle clauses, we would have to use more words, or write shorter sentences, for example:

Rescue workers have found three young climbers *who have been* missing since last night.

The youngsters were trapped by high winds on a ledge. *They were* too terrified to move, so they had clung ... until *they were* found ... .

How would you re-express examples c. and d. without using participle clauses?

5 Improve this story, using present, perfect or past participle clauses to combine the ideas where possible.

Sarah had lost her compass and didn't know which way to go. She looked up into the night sky and searched for the Pole star to find out which way north was. She was tired out as she had been walking all day. She decided to stop for a short rest. After a few minutes she felt better. She picked up her rucksack and set off again. She had not expected to get lost so she had not taken much food. She felt very hungry but she kept on going. She walked for two hours. Then she saw the lights of the Youth Hostel. She felt very relieved and quickened her pace.

6 Give a short account of something interesting that happened to you once, for example: a difficult journey, an unusual incident in the street, a memorable holiday. Include as many participles as you can.

LISTENING 2

Exam File: Part 4, Multiple choice

In Part 4, you may have to listen to five short extracts and answer three-option multiple choice questions. For this type of task you may have to identify the topic, the context and the opinion of the speaker. You should read the stem and all the options before listening, and hold the ideas in your head while you listen.

1 📼 You will hear five short extracts in which different people are talking about adventurous activities that they have experienced. Listen to the recording once. Which texts are about:

- camping?   - climbing?   - cycling?

2 📼 Now listen again. For questions 1—10, choose the correct option A, B or C. Before you listen, quickly read the questions and options.

1 On the mountain, the first speaker
  A couldn't see anything.
  B had to make sure his family were safe.
  C had to keep moving.

2 Unlike the first speaker, the second speaker
  A kept to his timetable.
  B did not feel cold.
  C stayed on the summit for a while.

3 What does the second speaker complain about?
  A feeling tired
  B noise
  C a long walk

4 What do the mountain-climbers have in common?
  A They reached the top.
  B They were surprised by something.
  C They were climbing in the dark.

5 As for wild animals, the third speaker
  A wanted to shoot them.
  B felt slightly anxious.
  C didn't see any.

6 Why didn't the third speaker take a radio?
  A She wanted to get away from people.
  B She had arranged for the pilot to return.
  C She thought it was too heavy to carry.

7 The fourth speaker
  A ate something he'd never eaten before.
  B saw something he'd never seen before.

C visited a cave he'd never been to before.

8 The fifth speaker is
  A giving advice on how to travel.
  B describing her journeys.
  C explaining how to save money.

9 Which speaker refers to a failure to do something?
  A the first
  B the third
  C the fourth

10 All the speakers mention
  A the weather.
  B tiredness.
  C feeling afraid.

3 After hearing what happened to the people in the recording, discuss which of these adventurous activities you would like/not like to do. Justify your answer.

WRITING
Part 1, Leaflet and note

Read the writing task and follow the **Steps to Writing** below.

> You are leader of your local youth group and you are about to take a group of students (aged 16—24) on a walking trip during winter. You have been asked to prepare a leaflet for the members of your group informing them what they should do when out in the mountains in sub-zero weather.
>
> Read the information in the news item and article extract. Use the information to write:
>
> a) a **leaflet** of about 200 words. Outline what kind of clothing should be worn on the trip. Give advice on what should be done if walkers find themselves getting cold.
>
> b) a brief **note** to the secretary of your organisation confirming what you have done. Write about 50 words.

Step 1 Task interpretation
How many pieces of writing do you have to produce? Who will read them? What is your purpose in writing? What register is most suitable?

Step 2 Selecting and summarising

Decide what information you need to include in your leaflet. Select only relevant information — a lot of the material in the input texts won't be useful. Underline or highlight important points. Remember, the leaflet is specifically for your target audience, not a general article, so you will have to express the same points in a different way.

Step 3 Layout and organisation

1 Think about how to organise and present the information. You are giving important information and advice, so your leaflet should be clear and easily accessible.

Think of an eye-catching title. Use subheadings and bullet points to divide up information. Some headings could be questions, followed by information and advice, for example:

Where will we be walking?

What should I wear?

What should I do if ...?

2 Your note needs to be clear and to the point. It should be a paragraph in length.

Step 4 Write

Write the leaflet and the note. Choose an appropriate style for your target audience. They must read and understand your leaflet, so keep the sentences short and punchy. Try using exclamation marks or capital letters for emphasis. Don't forget that the style of your leaflet will be different from the style of the texts.

▶ Conditionals (page 35)

▶ Language Bank

Step 5 Evaluate and edit

▶ Writing checklist (page 214)

Missing climber walks to safety

Missing in the icy, windswept wilderness of Scotland's mountains, Andrew Wilson walked into a local police station early this morning. He had survived for three days in Arctic conditions, and been given up for dead.

Andrew was cold, tired and hungry but otherwise unscathed by his ordeal. Trapped by savage winds and deep snow, he had been unable to descend.

'I knew that I had to get out of the wind and conserve body heat, so I dug a hole in the snow and stayed there. I ate the sandwiches and chocolate that I had brought with me and I had a flask of coffee. As soon as the storm died down, I walked off the mountain,' said Andrew.

'Andrew has a lot of experience and knew exactly what to do,' commented Richard Frobisher, leader of the local mountain rescue team. 'He knew that hypothermia, a severe drop in the body's core temperature, can cause death within two hours. It is crucial to prevent this. Andrew may well have survived because of the sandwiches and chocolate and hot drink he had brought with him to maintain his energy levels.

'Wind chill can be a real killer. People can get so tired they just lose consciousness. Andrew knew he had to protect himself against the wind.'

Richard added, 'Andrew was lucky not to get frostbite — your fingers and toes can go numb before you even notice — but he was well wrapped up.'

How to wrap up warm

The easiest way to prevent heat loss is to wear the right clothes. Wool and down are excellent insulators but tend to absorb moisture. This is a disadvantage since heat loss is 250 times greater through wet clothes than dry. Polyester and acrylic fabrics, which do not retain water, are a better bet. A cotton layer such as a T-shirt, which absorbs water like a sponge should be avoided at all costs. Over these goes a windproof layer. Feet and hands need special attention, since blood flow to them is restricted in cold temperatures. You can use up to three layers of gloves, and spares are useful too as gloves often get wet. The head, for which sixty per cent of our metabolism is reserved to keep the brain supplied with blood, is a major escape route for heat, and ears are especially sensitive to frostbite so a good hat is essential.

Language Bank

Always take ...

Make sure you have plenty of ...

If you start to feel cold ...

This will help conserve body heat.

Just a quick note to let you know ...

Let me know if there's anything missing/anything you want me to add.

Hope you approve!

ENGLISH IN USE
Part 6, Discourse cloze

1 Can you answer these questions?

1 What is the difference between: a dormant volcano/an extinct volcano/an active volcano?

2 What happens when a volcano erupts?

3 What are the destructive effects of volcanic eruptions?

Read through the article opposite, ignoring the gaps, to check your answers.

2 Choose the best phrase from A—J below to complete the gaps. Some answers don't fit at all. Many of the phrases will fit grammatically, so it's important to check the overall meaning of the sentence.

A definitely be big enough to swallow London

B occur twice every 100,000 years

C be more frequent and death tolls will rise

D last much longer

E even be at a volcano thought to be extinct

F provide early warning of impending disaster

G cause unusual animal behaviour

H have been the trigger that plunged the Earth into the last ice age

I prevent solar radiation reaching the surface

J threaten the lives of millions of people.

The next dormant volcano to erupt could be the biggest anyone has ever seen.

The fire next time

Many of the world's dormant volcanoes are showing signs of renewed life. Some of them are close to cities where eruptions would (0) ..J. . We can be virtually certain that the next catastrophic eruption will occur where we least expect it. It will probably occur at a volcano that has not erupted for several hundred years, and could (1) .... .

Modern civilisation has still never experienced a really big eruption. One of the biggest recently was Mount St Helens in 1984 but the eruption of Tambora, Indonesia, in 1815 was 100 times more powerful and created a hole 15 kilometres wide.

Such explosions can influence the entire planet through their effect on the global climate. The dust and ash they throw into the atmosphere can (2) .... . This leads to dramatic falls in temperature.

Even Tambora is insignificant compared with Toba, Sumatra, 73,000 years ago. This created a hole 50 kilometres across and 1000 meters deep, which would (3) .... . Temperatures plummeted and the Earth entered a volcanic winter comparable to the conditions scientists predict would follow a full-scale nuclear war. It seems that Toba may (4) .... .

An eruption as big as that would devastate the global economy. Although a return to normal climate might be expected within a few years, the social and economic effects would (5) .... .

It is not a matter of *if* we experience another Toba but *when*. Evidence from the geological record suggests that such eruptions should (6) .... . We are living on borrowed time.

14 Human behaviour

Speaking 1

Read these dilemmas. In pairs, discuss what you would do, and circle the appropriate option. Then compare your answers with the class.

1 **You are standing in a queue for the cinema. There's a limited number of seats left for the film, and you don't know if you'll get a ticket. Suddenly an old man rudely pushes in front of you. Do you:**

A say nothing? He's an old man, after all.
B tell him to go to the back of the queue?
C complain loudly to the person next to you?

2 **You are a young man sitting on a crowded bus. Standing in the aisle is a woman in, you think, her early fifties. Do you:**

A get up and offer her your seat?
B open your newspaper, deciding that to offer her your seat would imply, offensively, that she was 'elderly'?
C get up without saying anything and leave the seat and the dilemma to her?

3 **You are at a party talking to someone you don't know very well. You are joined by a third person whose name you can't remember. Do you:**

A introduce the second person by name and then hope the third person will say his/her name?
B pretend not to notice the third person?
C apologise to the third person for forgetting his/her name?

4 **You are sitting in a café having a conversation with a friend. Several times your friend's mobile phone rings and she answers it every time. Do you:**

A ask her to switch it off?
B say nothing?
C call her on your own mobile phone?

5 **You buy two books in a bookshop and pay for them. Outside the shop, you realise that the shop-assistant has accidentally put a third book in your bag. Do you:**

A keep the book?
B take the book back?
C keep the book if it interests you and return it if it doesn't?

6 **You are a couple enjoying a romantic evening in a busy restaurant. At the next table a man is smoking like a chimney. Do you:**

A say nothing?
B politely ask him to stop smoking, even though it is permitted in the restaurant?
C call the manager and ask him to do something?

READING

Part 4, Multiple matching

1 Here are the titles of the four articles opposite. Can you predict what each article is about?

Call me mother

Totally fobbed off

Restaurant shells out for oyster surfeit

The dockyard thief

2 Now skim the texts and match the correct title to each article.

Match the statements in 1—17 with the text (A, B, C or D) that they refer to. As each section refers to one topic, use the process of elimination technique introduced in Unit 2 (page 22).

Text **A** Text **B** Text **C** Text **D**	
A person avoided paying for what was consumed.	**1** ....
Someone was a victim of another's anger.	**2** ....
There was an insistence on the literal meaning of a description.	**3** ....
An unlikely object was stolen.	**4** ....
Selfish behaviour affected other consumers.	**5** ....
People were victims of a con trick.	**6** ....
The weather increased frustration.	**7** ....
Initial attempts at investigation were unsuccessful.	**8** ....
The manager was required to provide an explanation.	**9** .... **10** ....
A financial penalty was incurred.	**11** ....
There was a mechanical failure.	**12** ....
People's sympathies were exploited.	**13** ....
A long-established business method was put to the test.	**14** ....
Offensive language was used.	**15** ....
A business man put forward an argument that failed during the incident.	**16** ....
Persistent efforts revealed that a crime had been committed.	**17** ....

3 Can you explain the puns in the titles of texts A and D? Use these clues to help you.

1 Oysters are a type of shellfish.
2 A fob is a small object fixed to a key ring for decoration.

AMERICAN restaurateurs have always felt fairly confident that an "all-you-can-eat" menu is a good way of luring customers from the nation's thriving junkyard of hamburger joints, milk bars and hot-dog stands. Alan Wald has made them think again.

When Mr Wald paid $15.95 for an "all-you-can-eat" menu at the Moonraker restaurant in Pacifica, a seaside town near San Francisco, he was left with the clear impression that he could eat as much as he liked. So he downed one plateload of oysters, then another, and another, and another ...

It was only after the management reckoned he had polished off more than six dozen (he put the number at forty) that they called a halt. "The man had piled up the oysters like a pyramid," said Ken Albrecht, the manager. "He had taken all the oysters and another customer was complaining."

Mr Wald was not pleased. Arguing that "all-you-can-eat" should mean exactly that, he sued the restaurant for "pain and humiliation" suffered by his guzzling being questioned. "I was discriminated against, and my rights were violated," Mr Wald told a judge at San Mateo County Small Claims Court.

The Moonraker's owner, John Scheider, was not pleased either. "In this day and age, people will sue you for anything. If you ate a hundred oysters and got sick, you'd probably sue us." He countered by studying etiquette books, which were presented to the judge, highlighting extracts that said that good manners require customers to show some restraint and not "eat like a pig."

The judge failed to swallow the argument. Mr Wald left the court with a $125 award.

B

A FRIEND of a friend and her new husband were enjoying a romantic evening at a top restaurant. Staring mistily into each other's eyes, they noticed an elderly lady sitting all alone and looking in their direction. They smiled back politely and the old dear made her way to their table. "I'm sorry to trouble you," she began, stifling a tear, "but you look so like my daughter. She was killed last year and I do miss her terribly. I wonder if you would do me an enormous favour?" The couple nodded compassionately.

"It would give me such a thrill if, as I am leaving, you would say 'Goodbye, mum,' and wave me off."

"Certainly," the couple replied. How could they possibly refuse? A few minutes later the old lady gathered her belongings and stood up to leave, and the two diners cheerily waved and said goodbye as "mum" tottered out.

Feeling good about themselves, the couple asked for their bill. But after checking, they called over the manager, demanding to have the total explained.

"It includes the charge for the lady's meal," the manager revealed. "She said that her daughter would pay."

D

A FRIEND of a friend was stuck slap-bang in the middle of the infamous Friday-night drag across Sydney Harbour suspension bridge. Cars were nose to tail as far as the eye could see. The multi-lane highway was completely jammed with frustrated commuters crawling home at a snail's pace. To make matters worse, it was the height of the sweltering Aussie summer. Tempers were fraying.

Apparently, a classic automobile from the golden age of motoring (a knackered old banger) stalled as the traffic lurched forward. Immediately, a medallion man in a flash new Ferrari started honking his horn and giving the unlucky driver all kinds of grief.

When the traffic started to inch forward again, Mr Macho in the swanky new motor quadrupled his aggressive behaviour, pumping his klaxon and giving the stranded motorist the benefit of his colourful vocabulary.

Suddenly, the driver of the jalopy got out of his chariot, sauntered coolly up to the open-top mean machine, reached in and plucked the keys from the ignition. Then he strolled between the grid-locked cars, tossed the keys over the side of the bridge, ambled back to his own vehicle, cranked her up and cruised off into the sunset.

crank up: start a car by turning the crankshaft of the engine manually with a starting handle

C

A FRIEND of mine was a docker during the 1940s, and recalls the time a workmate fell under suspicion. Every evening, he strolled up to the dock gate on his way home, pushing a wheelbarrow with a large oilcloth draped over it. This was a time of hardship and shortages, and it was feared that the bloke was half-inching some of the essential supplies.

Every night the dock police stopped him and checked under the cloth. But the handcart was always empty. Undaunted, the puzzled coppers continued with the inspection every night for weeks. But each time they lifted the cloth, the barrow was bare, and the shifty docker resumed his journey home.

Apparently, one enterprising bobby then followed the docker home and watched him trundle up his back alley, open his gate and wheel in the barrow. When the suspect had gone indoors, the PC scrambled over the wall — and found 57 stolen wheelbarrows stacked inside!

half-inching: Cockney rhyming slang for 'pinching' (stealing).

VOCABULARY 1

Adding drama and colour

The four texts on pages 182—183 are all anecdotes — short, amusing stories about real people and events. To make them more interesting, the writers have:

1 used precise and colourful words.
2 avoided repetition by using synonyms and paraphrase.
3 used metaphor to evoke specific images.
4 used euphemism to describe unpleasant things in a pleasant way.
5 used emphatic devices such as intensifying adverbs.

1 In these extracts from Text A, the italicised words are used to describe the action of eating. What exactly does each word mean? What image does it convey?

1 ... he *downed* one plateload of oysters, then another ...
2 It was only after he had *polished off* more than six dozen ...
3 ... he sued the restaurant for "pain and humiliation" suffered by his *guzzling* being questioned.

2 In Text B, find words that have the following general meanings. Decide what precise meanings the words used convey.

1 came over to their table
2 walked
3 asked
4 told them

 To avoid repetition, the same idea is often expressed using different words. For example, 'honking his horn' *(text D)* is the same action as 'pumping his klaxon.'

Answer these questions.

Text B
1 How many different ways is the old lady referred to?

Text C
2 How many different ways is the writer's friend referred to?

3 How many different words for 'policeman' can you find? Which ones are colloquial?

Text D
4 How many different ways are these referred to?
• the car that stalled   • its driver
• the driver of the Ferrari   • the Ferrari

5 How many different words for walking can you find? What do they suggest about the driver?

1 In Text A, it says, 'The judge failed to *swallow* the argument,' meaning he didn't accept it. When do we usually use the verb *swallow*? Why is this an appropriate metaphor to use in this story?

2 Now look at these extracts from Text D. Can you explain the literal and metaphorical meanings of the italicised words?

1 The multi-lane highway was completely jammed with frustrated commuters *crawling* home at a snail's pace.
2 Tempers were *fraying*.

4 In Text D, 'Mr Macho' is described as 'giving the stranded motorist the benefit of his colourful vocabulary.' *Colourful vocabulary* is a euphemism for 'using obscene words'. The writer is humorously describing an unpleasant thing in a pleasant way.

Identify the euphemisms in the following sentences. What not-so-pleasant meaning is being expressed in the nicest possible way?

1 We've had to have our dog put down.
2 'I can't go out with you tonight, Charles. I'm washing my hair,' said Miranda.
3 The company has been engaging in a large downsizing operation.
4 'It's time for you to look for further opportunities to develop your career, John,' said the manager.

5

1 Look at these extracts from Text D, which illustrate ways of adding emphasis to a statement or description.

1 ... they noticed an elderly lady sitting *all* alone.
2 "... you look *so* like my daughter."
3 "I wonder if you would do me an *enormous* favour?"
4 "It would give me *such* a thrill ..."
5 How could they *possibly* refuse?

2 Identify the emphatic devices used in these sentences. Which words could be removed to soften them?

1 The plot of the film was highly implausible.
2 She's very nice, but she does talk a lot.
3 The situation was far worse than we had imagined.
4 I insisted on seeing the manager himself.
5 Why ever did you do that?
6 What on earth has happened?
7 He came to see me the very next day.

6 Read this anecdote. Use some of the above techniques to make it more dramatic.

This is a true story. It's about a man who bought a £6,000 engagement ring for his girlfriend. One evening he went round to her house and said, 'Are you ready to go out? It's a special evening tonight.'
'Is it?' she said. 'What's special about it?'
'It's my birthday!' said the man, who was annoyed that she had forgotten.

He got more annoyed when he noticed that she wasn't wearing his ring. Losing his temper, he found her jewellery box and took the ring out of it. Then he got into his car and drove to the sea shore where he stood on a cliff and threw the ring into the sea 50 metres below.

By this time, the woman had called the police and he was arrested on the cliff-top, still angry. Police divers searched for the ring but without success.

The girlfriend charged him with theft and a few months later he appeared in court. When the judge heard that the man was still paying the shop for the ring, at £200 per month, he decided to let him off. He left the court a free, but wiser and sadder, man.

SPEAKING 2
Part 2, Describe, comment and hypothesise

1 Work in pairs. Choose one photograph each, and take it in turns to talk about your picture. Answer these questions.

1 What type of problem is illustrated?
2 How serious is this problem? What impact does it have on the environment and the people who live in the area?

Do you agree or disagree with your partner? Say which problem you think is the most serious for the local community.

Part 3, Suggest solutions to a problem; Part 4, Report conclusions

2 Imagine that you are members of a committee of local people. You have been asked to give your opinion about the ways in which the appearance of your town is being spoilt and to suggest solutions. Think about:

• pedestrianising certain parts of the town
• providing better public transport
• organising a 'Clean up our town' campaign
• imposing fines

3 Report the problems and solutions you agreed on to the rest of the class.

Language Bank

Commenting
We really **do** need to do something about it.
It's getting to be quite a serious problem.
I detest that kind of behaviour.
In my opinion, it's highly irresponsible to ...
That sort of thing doesn't bother me all that much.
It's just a lot of fuss about nothing if you ask me.

Suggesting solutions
One way of dealing with this would be to ...
Wouldn't it be much better to ...?

LISTENING 1
Part 4, Multiple matching

1 You will hear five short extracts in which different people are talking about their neighbours. Before you listen, discuss these questions.

1 What are the advantages and disadvantages of living close to other people? Think about privacy, noise, safety, feeling part of a community etc.
2 How would you describe your relationship with your neighbours? Have you ever experienced any problems with them?

2 You will hear the expressions in italics in the recording. With a partner, discuss what they mean. Which statements are true for you?

1 Our neighbours tend to *keep themselves to themselves*.
2 My neighbours and I have what I call *neighbourly* rapport.
3 I think you should *live and let live*.

3 🎙 For questions 1—5, match the extracts as you hear them with the neighbour referred to in A—H. Note that there are three options that don't go with any of the extracts.

Which speaker refers to a neighbour who

A work/s unusual hours?	1 ....
B provide/s practical help?	
C is/are out of work?	2 ....
D does/does not come into the house?	
E used to stay at home?	3 ....
F made false accusations?	
G showed anger towards family members?	4 ....
H has/have borne a long-standing grudge?	5 ....

4 🎙 Listen again. For questions 6—10, match the extracts as you hear them with what the speakers say.

Which speaker

A compares the current situation with the past?	6 ....
B talks about conflict between children?	7 ....
C complains about problems with noise?	
D outlines future building plans?	8 ....
E provides a reason for bad feeling?	
F outlines a friendship between children?	9 ....
G wishes neighbours were less familiar?	
H describes a relationship with an older person?	10 ....

5 Read this extract from Speaker 3. Would you say this was true of the situation where **you** live, or not?

'It was different when I was a kid — you **did** know your neighbours, everyone knew each other ... and now when everybody is rushing around ... you don't get to know the people.'

VOCABULARY 2
Expressions with *get*

Complete these sentences with the correct form of *get*, adding any other words necessary. You heard all these expressions in the recording.

1 A: Do you have a good relationship with your neighbours?
   B: Yes, we *get* .... really well.

2 A: Did she make you angry?
   B: She certainly did. I .... very .... with her.

3 A: Do you think I should join him in his business venture?
   B: No, don't .... with him. He's bound to let you down.

4 A: Are you able to spend a lot of time with your children?
   B: Well, I work late every evening so I don't .... them much.

5 A: Have you made friends with your new neighbours?
   B: Well, they've only just moved in, so I haven't had time to .... them.

ENGLISH IN USE 1
Part 1, Multiple choice cloze

1 Quickly read the letter and reply below and answer these questions.

1 What is the problem?
2 What is the advice?
3 Can you explain the pun in the title?

2 Now read the texts more carefully. Choose which word best fits each space (A, B, C or D).

3 Discuss these questions.

1 What is your opinion of the advice given?
2 If you had the same problem, what would **you** do?

Noise annoys

Problem:

I live on the first (1) .... of a house that has been (2) .... into three flats. Five months ago, a couple moved into the flat (3) .... and since then my life has been a nightmare. They get up at 6 a.m. and make a terrific noise. They listen to the radio at top (4) ...., talk loudly and stamp on the floor. In the evening they play the same record on their stereo over and over again. It's beginning to (5) .... me mad. I've tried turning my own stereo up to (6) .... out the noise but I like (7) .... and quiet and find loud music stressful. I have tried talking to them but it hasn't done any (8) .... . I realise I should live and (9) .... live, but I have begun to have quite irrational revenge fantasies about them — like switching off their electricity or deliberately making a lot of noise late at night when I know they are asleep. What on earth can I do?

Advice:

I understand your problem (10) .... too well. Like you, I do not (11) .... loud music and shouting at 3 a.m., frequent occurrences in the (12) .... of flats where I live. I, too, have found that direct requests get (13) .... . I contacted the environmental health officers at the Town Hall, who were very helpful. I would (14) .... advise you to do the same. The officers took action on my (15) .... and were able to solve the problem without going to court.

1	**A** floor	**B** stage	**C** story	**D** landing
2	**A** changed	**B** converted	**C** adapted	**D** remade
3	**A** over	**B** higher	**C** up	**D** above
4	**A** power	**B** volume	**C** pitch	**D** intensity
5	**A** drive	**B** force	**C** turn	**D** put
6	**A** wipe	**B** sound	**C** deafen	**D** drown
7	**A** harmony	**B** peace	**C** calm	**D** silence
8	**A** benefit	**B** point	**C** more	**D** good
9	**A** let	**B** make	**C** have	**D** be
10	**A** wholly	**B** only	**C** merely	**D** except
11	**A** agree	**B** admire	**C** appreciate	**D** acknowledge
12	**A** area	**B** block	**C** house	**D** building
13	**A** nowhere	**B** somewhere	**C** everywhere	**D** anywhere
14	**A** mainly	**B** hardly	**C** strongly	**D** powerfully
15	**A** favour	**B** support	**C** interest	**D** behalf

LISTENING 2
Part 1, Note completion

1 You will hear part of a radio talk about attitudes to sleep. First, discuss these questions.

1 How much sleep do you get each night?
2 How much do you need?
3 How do you feel if you don't get a good night's sleep?
4 What sort of things prevent you from getting a good night's sleep?

2 Check that you understand the following words and phrases relating to sleep.

1 doze off   3 have a siesta
2 take a nap   4 be deprived of sleep

3 📼 Read the notes below and try to predict the missing information. Then listen to the recording and complete the notes with a few words or a number.

Consequences of lack of sleep:

People become bad-tempered:

they cannot (1) ....

they talk in clichés

higher production of (2) ....

greater occurrence of accidents

Sleep patterns:

sleeping at night typical of (3) ....

....

research shows natural sleep lasts for

(4) ....

average time spent sleeping now (5) ....

average in 1910 (6) ....

Thomas Edison:

caused change in sleeping patterns with

(7) ....

while at work often (8) ....

Correct attitudes to sleep:

admiration for those who (9) ....

....

time spent sleeping considered (10) ....

4 Discuss this question.

If the electric light bulb had never been invented, how would our sleep patterns be different from what they are today?

ENGLISH IN USE 2
Part 2, Structural cloze

1 Shakespeare was a keen observer of human behaviour, which is illustrated in the rich and varied language he used to describe it. Test your knowledge of Shakespeare and the English language. Read these statements and decide which are true and which are false.

1 Before Shakespeare's time, many English writers preferred to write in Latin.
2 Shakespeare introduced over 600 new words to English.
3 New English words were usually taken from Latin or French.
4 Many titles of films and novels are taken from Shakespeare.
5 We rarely use expressions from Shakespeare's plays in everyday language today.

2 Quickly read the text below, ignoring the gaps. How many of your answers were correct?

3 Complete the text by writing one word in each numbered gap.

4 Here are some more expressions taken from Shakespeare. They are all used in modern English. Discuss what you think they mean. In what type of situations would you use them?

1 He's a tower of strength.
2 There's method in his madness.
3 He's more sinned against than sinning.
4 It's neither here nor there.
5 He loved not wisely but too well.
6 If music be the food of love, play on.

Shakespeare had a word for it

Many of Shakespeare's phrases have passed into our everyday language. When you have a sleepless night (0) ..and.. complain that you did not sleep a wink, you can console (1) .... that even in your exhausted state you are using Shakespeare's words. "I have not slept one wink" is from the play *Cymbeline*, (2) .... Shakespeare wrote in 1610. Even (3) .... it is not a popular play, we are using his line in (4) .... daily lives four hundred years later.

When a guest devours absolutely (5) .... in your kitchen cupboard, you (6) .... complain that you "have been eaten out of house and home". It is Shakespeare again. "He hath eaten me out of house and home" comes from Henry V.

Lines from Shakespeare crop (7) .... in all kinds of places, (8) .... titles of films and novels. Shakespeare was writing when it had (9) .... fashionable for authors to give up Latin in favour of English (10) .... the language of literature. But there were not enough English words to express all their ideas, (11) .... writers began making words up. Shakespeare introduced about 600 new words into English. These include many that we could hardly imagine

(12) .... without: *admirable, educate, generous,* and *tranquil*. He also made up compounds such as *lack-lustre* and *sharp-toothed*.

Words were usually made up from Latin, but writers also turned (13) .... French. This is (14) .... we have so many words to describe almost the same thing, and in nearly all of (15) .... there is a slight difference of feeling. For example, we have the English word *end*, the French-derived *finish* and the Latin-derived *conclude*.

I have not slept one wink

LANGUAGE REVIEW

This section reviews the main grammar points that you have studied in this course. You may find it useful to refer to the Grammar Notes for each unit at the back of the book.

1 Choose from options A—C to complete the following sentences. There may be one or two correct answers for each question.

Modal verbs (Unit 1)

1 I .... told him the truth, but I decided not to.
  A would have
  B could have
  C should have

2 All sports equipment was provided, so .... our own. We travelled light.
  A we needn't have taken
  B we didn't need to take
  C there was no need to take

Relative clauses (Unit 2)

3 Jack lent me a book ....
  A he had just read.
  B what he had just read.
  C which he had just read it.

4 The person .... has disappeared.
  A from who I bought the car
  B who I bought the car from
  C that I bought the car from

Tenses (Units 1, 2 & 7)

5 When we arrived on the island, it ....
  A had been raining for seven days.
  B was raining for seven days.
  C rained for seven days.

6 By the time they finish the bridge next year, they .... for twenty years.
  A will have been working
  B will have worked
  C will work

7 I'll phone you ....
  A as soon as I get back.
  B when I will get back.
  C when I've got back.

Tenses in hypothetical situations (Units 3 & 7)

8 If I'd given you that information last week, ...
  A it wouldn't have helped you.
  B you will be able to use it.
  C you would be in a better position now.

9 I wish ....
  A you wouldn't have done that.
  B I would have a better car.
  C I didn't have to write this letter.

10 It's high time ....
  A you go home.
  B you went home.
  C you were going home.

Verb patterns (Units 4 & 6)

11 The escaped prisoner avoided ....
  A to be captured.
  B being captured.
  C capture.

12 Jenny advised ....
  A that we should buy our tickets in advance.
  B to buy our tickets in advance.
  C everyone to buy their tickets in advance.

Link words, conjunctions (Units 6, 9 & 12)

13 The actor managed to perform ....
  A despite his sore throat.
  B even though he had a sore throat.
  C if only he had a sore throat.

14 Tom was quite badly injured, ... he continued to race.
  A nevertheless
  B however
  C but

15 You can join the expedition .... you have your own equipment.
  A providing
  B unless
  C as long as

Passive (Units 10 & 12)

16 We expected the project ....
  A to have been completed by now.
  B would have been completed by now.
  C had been completed by now.

17 I got my friend .... the car from the garage for me.
  A picking up
  B to pick up
  C picked up

Participle clauses (Units 5 & 13)

18 We decided to continue our journey ....
  A despite having hardly any food left.
  B despite not having much food left.
  C despite we didn't have much food left.

2 Identify the sentences that contain mistakes and correct them.

1 As a graduate in Business Administration, I have good knowledge of accountancy.

2 I was told you could help me with the project I was working on for the last two months.

3 The people I have invited have all agreed to come.

4 We decided to catch the train was leaving at 10 a.m.

5 I don't remember to have met this person before.

6 This restaurant is considered as one of the best in our town.

7 If you are planning to visit America, I recommend this book, which offers very good advice.

8 Why should I be blamed for this fault, which was made by someone else?

9 I understand you need someone to look out for your home while you will be abroad.

10 It's possible to have a wonderful time here without spending nothing.

11 I wonder if you could give to me some information about how are coral reefs formed.

12 It was my friend's advise that made me to change my mind about going.

13 What I wanted to ask you was whether you could help me with my homework.

14 If you want to exercise yourself, you can get a good discount at the gym with a student card.

15 We didn't succeed to persuade our friends to come out with us.

16 A private detective was called in to investigate the mystery.

WRITING

Exam File: Selecting a Part 2 task

In Part 2 of Paper 2, you have to choose **one** task from a choice of **four**. When deciding which topic to write about, it's important to consider:

• your knowledge of the subject.

• your ability to use language appropriate to that subject.

• your knowledge of the layout and style required.

1 Look at the writing tasks below. Follow these steps to help you select the right task for you.

1 Highlight the key words in each task that indicate the subject, the format and the target audience.

2 Now consider the language you will need for each task. Is any specialised knowledge and vocabulary required?

3 Finally, think about how you would prepare for each question. Remember what you have learned in previous writing sections. List the **Steps to Writing**. What is the first step? What is the final step?

2 Now choose one task and write your answer. Remember to write about 250 words.

1 As part of the services to newcomers to your college, you have been asked to write an **article** introducing your town for the student magazine. The article should explain any unusual, amusing or puzzling aspects of life in your town that would interest visitors from overseas. Write the article, selecting three aspects.

2 Young people who visit your town and don't have much money often ask which restaurants are the best to eat at. In your student newsletter, write a **review** on eating out, including information about at least three establishments, and providing details of type of cooking, standard of service and cost.

3 The local council has plans to provide 100 low-cost homes in the centre of your town. However, they plan to build on a park with trees and flowers where people of all ages go to relax and which also provides a home for urban wildlife. Write a **letter** to a local newspaper arguing against the plan.

4 You have just returned from two weeks spent on a work-placement scheme arranged by your college. You have to submit a **report** to the principal of your college, giving information about your experience and saying whether you would recommend a similar placement to other students next year.

ENGLISH IN USE 3
Part 3, Error correction

1 Read the article below to find out what it's about.

2 Read the article again carefully. In most lines, there is either a spelling or a punctuation error. When you find an error, write out the correctly spelt word or the correct punctuation. Indicate the correct lines with a tick. Study the examples. Remember, it's a good idea to read each line backwards the second time, to stop your eye skipping over mistakes.

0 *£5. I*
0 ✓
0 *faintly*

Spelling Quiz

3 🖭 A recent survey of British people's spelling ability revealed which common words were the most difficult to spell correctly. Listen to the recording and see if you can write the twelve words down correctly in your notebook.

Diary Of A Nobody

0	The other day, in a junk shop, I bought a man's life for £5 I had
0	already bought his cupboard, which was pale green and smelt
0	feintly of soap powder. For £5, I could take with it a set of
1	pencil-written diaries, bound in brown lether. They had been
2	found in the cupboards drawer and they ran from 1928 to 1993. I
3	saw that a page of personal details had been filled in: hight, hat
4	size, name — I'll call him John Cooper. The shopowner told me the
5	cupboard came from a house clearence. She had tried to trace
6	Mr Cooper, but had failed I took the books home and read page after
7	page year after year. I read about university, work, retirement — there
8	were no blank days. I discovered, amazingly nothing. Mr Cooper
9	had nothing to say and yet he had an irrepressible desire to say it. On
10	12 July, 1928, he writes: "Hot day. Played tennis." Jumping fourty
11	years to 30 June, 1966, he writes: "Day at office. Evening at home."
12	He goes to the office, has a meeting of some kind goes to the cinema
13	but does not name the film. He hears orchestras but does not say what
14	was played there is not the slightest emotion or judgement. There is no
15	detail. I found only one referance to a world beyond his. On 3 September,
16	1939: "War!" he wrote, useing the only exclamation mark in the entire diary, and then added: "Walk in afternoon".

Exam Practice 3

ENGLISH IN USE

Part 5

For questions **62—74**, read the following informal note about a trip to Canada and use the information to complete the numbered gaps in the formal letter. **Use no more than two words** in each gap. The words you need **do not** occur in the note. The exercise begins with an example **(0)**.

Example: | **0** | **regret to**

INFORMAL NOTE

Jack,

I'm sorry to give you this bad news, but I thought you'd like to know straightaway. Our trip to Canada is off. It seems that the travel agency which had the job of putting it together has closed down. No one has a clue where the owner is and there's nothing left in their bank account! I had a word with the local police — they're trying hard to find him so that he can answer a few of their questions. They told me that if the agency has already handed over any money to airlines or hotels we may be able to get it back, some of it at least, but don't raise your hopes too high — it looks like we've lost the lot.

Our insurance policy doesn't cover this sort of thing — it's tough luck. If you want to know any more details, give me a ring. I'm sending an official letter to all our members.

Peter

FORMAL LETTER

Dear ...

I **(0)** .... inform you that the study tour to Canada arranged by the Geographical Society can no longer **(62)** .... We have discovered that the travel agency **(63)** .... the organisation of this tour is no longer **(64)** .... It is **(65)** .... where the owner of the agency, Mr Michael Daly, is at this moment but it seems that large sums of money **(66)** ....

In my role as secretary of the Geographical Society, I have been in **(67)** .... the police, who are making **(68)** .... to establish his whereabouts so that he can help them with **(69)** .... It seems that if any money was paid **(70)** .... to airlines or hotels by the agency, we may be able to obtain a **(71)** .... However, it must be said that this is extremely **(72)** .... We must accept the fact that, almost certainly, we have lost **(73)**......... money. Regrettably, our insurance policy does not **(74)** .... in these circumstances.

If you require more information, please do not hesitate to contact me.

Yours faithfully

Richard Hakluyt

Richard Hakluyt
Secretary, Geographical Society

READING

Part 3

Read the following article and answer questions **21 — 25** that follow. Write the letter **A, B, C** or **D** against the number of each question **21 — 25**. Give only one answer to each question.

DO MEN AND WOMEN SPEAK THE SAME LANGUAGE?

Do men and women understand the same things from the spoken word? Judging by the misinterpretation, misunderstanding and general mystification that can arise from a single simple sentence, there are grave reasons for doubt. In fact, I would put it even stronger. Do we even speak the same language?

First — and contrary to the general impression — men use language more. "Like everyone else, I used to believe that women were the talkative sex," says Dale Spender, a sociolinguist. "But when I analysed the results of over one hundred and forty recorded conversations between men and women, the result was quite the opposite. Whether we're talking about social gatherings or business meetings, one element never changes: in any conversation with a man, a woman who talks more than a third of the time is seen as talking too much.

Nowhere is this more obvious than on radio or TV talkshows. One host, Robert Robinson, once said, "It's difficult to find the right kind of woman to participate in my programme. Most of them can't stand up to me and so stay silent. They also find interrupting a bit tricky." On one occasion, a well-known female thinker became so cross and unhappy at being what she regarded as "shouted down" that she remained silent for the last fifteen minutes of the programme. Even those women who are perfectly capable of holding their own are notably less talkative than their male counterparts.

Another female characteristic is the belief that conversation should be a reciprocal exchange rather than an attempt to dominate the other person. According to sociologist Jennifer Coates, "When a woman in a group raises a topic, the others will encourage, sympathise or elaborate. The next female speaker may enlarge on some point, add a personal anecdote, or simply make 'Go on' interjections. But one thing she won't do is flatly contradict the previous speaker and abruptly change the subject. But men in a group with women often get bored with what they see as the slow build-up of a topic." The tried and tested method of avoiding this hazard is by doing what most women hate: interrupting.

"The effect constant interruption has on women is that they become silent," says Dr Coates. It isn't solely that men regard conversation as a contest; there is also a clash of styles. "We all think we know

what a question is. But with men and women it triggers different reactions. Men think questions are requests for information, whereas women think they are part of the way in which a co-operative conversation works. If a woman asks a man a question, she's trying to keep the conversation going, while the man thinks this is a request for information, so he gives her a lecture." In social situations, this different view of the polite enquiry can often cause bad feelings. "The woman thinks, 'What is he on about? I didn't want a run-down on company accountancy,' and the man thinks, 'Why is she looking so cross? If she didn't want to know, why did she ask?' "

Although women have much greater sensitivity to what the other person is feeling, it is equally true that, in situations where power is concerned, the male cut-and-thrust style is the norm. "Male language allows them to have clear goals, stick to decisions, answer directly without fudging and assert themselves," says Natasha Josefowitz, author of *Paths to Power*. "Women say 'I *think* I can', where men say, 'I can'. And though the woman may be right — who knows if she can carry out a particular task until she is doing it? — what employers go for is confidence." In female conversation, this general tentativeness emerges in the use of 'soft' phrases such as 'I wonder if I might ...?', and 'Perhaps this isn't the moment to disturb you but ...' instead of the simpler expressions 'Please may I ...?' or 'Can I come in?'.

Dr Coates believes female politeness involves other factors as well. "Partly it is a recognition that other people may not be imposed on. If I go next door, I say, 'I hope you don't mind, but could you possibly lend me a pint of milk, please?' not 'Can I have some milk?', which allows my neighbour the freedom to say 'Yes, of course' or 'I'm sorry, I haven't got one.' What it is doing is giving the other person a chance to get out of an obligation without losing face. Partly, too, it is a question of giving what Dr Coates calls 'positive face', which means reassuring others about their own value.

The reason for such discrepancies is something that frequently makes male English a rather different language from the female version of English: most men use language to conceal their feelings whereas women see it as means of revealing their emotions.

21 Before Dale Spender undertook her research, she
    A intended to show what made women aggressive.
    B thought she knew what the outcome would be.
    C realised men tended to speak more than women.
    D wanted to discover the situations where women spoke most.

22 When women appeared on his chat show, Robert Robinson
    A was delighted they had agreed to appear.
    B provided special support.
    C found their behaviour inappropriate.
    D thought they were impolite.

23 According to Dr Coates, in a mixed group of speakers
    A men tend to contradict.
    B women concentrate on talking about themselves.
    C women discuss boring topics.
    D men experience feelings of frustration.

24 Dr Coates considers that questions can cause bad feeling if
    A the reason behind the question is misunderstood.
    B a sensitive subject has been raised.
    C there is a desire to hide the truth.
    D an uninteresting topic has been introduced.

25 Dr Coates thinks that the politeness of female language
    A works against women.
    B is helpful to other people.
    C could easily be modified.
    D allows others to be assertive.

ENGLISH IN USE

Part 6

For questions **75−80**, read through the following text and then choose from the list **A−J** the best phrase given below it to fill each of the spaces. Write one letter **(A−J)** in each gap. **Some of the suggested answers do not fit at all.** The exercise begins with an example **(0)**.

Example: | **0** | J |

DOES CORRECT SPELLING MATTER?

In a recent experiment, school teachers were asked to spell the words *satellite*, *harass* and *embarrassment*. The result was a dreadful failure, according to some. But there were others **(0)** .... . For surely spelling is the least important aspect of anyone's language? Are not those **(75)** .... ? People mention great historical figures **(76)** .... . Shakespeare, it seems, couldn't even spell his own name.

I should like to argue that spelling is important. I speak as one **(77)** .... . I do not share the view of one of my colleagues **(78)** .... . She "does not accept that mistakes are possible in a native user of a language". Of course, some of the people who say that spelling does not matter spell adequately themselves. English is not an easy language to master, either in spoken or written form. There are many native speakers **(79)** .... . It would be best for us all to recognise this, but there is considerable resistance to accepting it, since many people assume that language is a natural and easy acquisition, and is expressive of the spontaneous self. For many years, educationalists have been divided between those **(80)** .... . Of course, language changes but I see no virtue in language changing because of carelessness or ignorance.

A   who if they were forced to take the tests administered to foreign learners would fail
B   who did not consult a dictionary
C   who wish to accept this view and those who wish to challenge it
D   who told me she never corrects the mistakes of her students
E   who have spent hours at school doing spelling tests
F   who couldn't spell
G   who never use electronic spell checkers
H   who believes that good spelling is a necessity
I   who worry about spelling mere pedants, anxious to inflict petty rules on students

J   who thought it was completely insignificant

UNIT 1

Modal verbs (pages 12–13)

Degrees of likelihood: *could, may, might, must, will, can't, should/ought to*

1 *could, may* and *might* can all express **possibility** in the present/future.

*He **may** be in a meeting, I'm not certain.*

May/might + not expresses negative possibility. We use *can't* or *couldn't* to express impossibility.

We usually use *can* for possibility only in questions, or with a negative adverbial.

Can that be John over there?
It can hardly be right to punish an innocent man.

2 We use *must* and *will* for **assumptions** and **deductions** based on evidence. They indicate greater certainty on the part of the speaker than *could, may* or *might*.

The opposite of *must* is expressed with *can't* or *couldn't* and **not** with *mustn't*.

*That **must/will** be George knocking at the door.*
*No, it **can't/couldn't** be – he just phoned.*

3 By contrast with *must* or *will*, *should* and *ought to* for assumptions tend to assume only positive or desirable things.

I shouldn't have any difficulty finishing in time.

4 *must, could, may* or *might* + perfect infinitive are used to express degrees of likelihood in the past.

*We **must have sent** it to the wrong address.*
*No, we **can't/couldn't have made** a mistake.*

Ability: *can, could*

1 We use *can* or *be able to/will be able to* to express present/future ability.

2 We use *could* for past ability when we talk about **general** ability or something which happened more than once. Compare:

*I **could** read well by the time I was five.*
(this refers to general ability, so is correct.)

By staying up until 2 a.m., I **could read the report in time for the meeting.*
(This refers to one particular occasion, so is incorrect.)

Instead of using *could* in the second sentence, you should say:
- *was able to read.*
- *managed to read* (if you want to emphasise the difficulty).
- *succeeded in reading* (if you want to emphasise achievement).

Permission: *can, may, could, will/would*

1 We can use *can* or *may* to ask or give permission in the present. *May* is more polite than *can*.

2 *could* and *was/were allowed to* can be used to talk about **general** past permission.

*When we were children we **could/were allowed to** stay up late.*

3 We also use *was/were allowed to* (but not *could*) to talk about permission resulting in a **specific** action.

*On my seventeenth birthday, I **was allowed to** drive my father's car.*

Note: For perfect and continuous tenses and passives, *allowed to* must be used.

4 In question forms, *will* and *would* can be used to make requests.

Will you type this letter for me?

Obligation: *must, have to, should/ought to*

1 *Must* and *have to* are usually used for rules and regulations or to express strong advice. *Should/ought to* can also be used to express strong advice in the present.

2 In the **positive** form *must/have to* are very similar in meaning, although *have to* expresses the authority of the third person and *must* the authority of the speaker.

*We **have to** hand in our essays by Friday.*
*The fridge isn't working properly. I **must** get someone to fix it.*

3 When used in the **negative** form, *have to* and *must* have quite different meanings.

*You **must not** go there.*
(This is an order not to do something – the speaker is prohibiting you from going there.)
*You **don't have to** go there.*
(It's not necessary to go there – you can probably choose whether to go or not.)

Lack of necessity: *need*

1 We use *needn't have done* to talk about something we did that wasn't necessary.

They **needn't have** bought so much food.
(They did buy the food but it wasn't needed. They didn't know, when they bought the food, that it was unnecessary.)

2 We use *didn't need to* to talk about something which we didn't do because it wasn't necessary. The meaning is similar to *didn't have to*.

She **didn't need to** say thank you but it was very kind of her to do so.
(She knew it was not necessary but she did it.)

would/used to

Would can describe a regular or repeated activity in the past, like *used to*. The difference is that *used to* can refer to states **and** actions, whereas *would,* with this meaning, can only refer to actions and not to states.

He **used to be** a postman. (state)
We **used to play** a lot of football. (action)

Present perfect simple and continuous tenses (page 16)

Present perfect simple vs. past simple

1 We use the **present perfect simple** to express:
- states and single or repeated actions that have occurred at an unspecified time in a past period extending up to now. In this sense it is often used with *ever/never/always*, which indicate an extended time period.

I've never been to Paris.

- single actions in the recent past with a present result, often with *just/already/yet/recently*.

I don't want to see that film, I've already seen it.

- states and actions in a period of time which is still continuing, often with phrases such as *all my life, this week/month/year, so far*.

For is used for periods of time starting at a definite point in the past. *Since* is used for a length of time.

I've lived here for a year.
I've lived here since 1998/since I left university.

2 The **past simple** refers to states, single and repeated actions and habits that occurred in a period of time which is finished. Time markers used with the past simple include: *ago, yesterday, last year, in 1980, when I was a child* etc. These are not normally used with the present perfect tense.

Present perfect simple vs. continuous

1 In some contexts both the present perfect simple and continuous are possible, for example when the verb refers to a state that lasts for some time, e.g. *live, stay, work, study, wait*.

I've lived here/been living here for 10 years.

The use of the continuous here puts the emphasis on the **duration** of the state.

2 The continuous differs from the simple tense in the following ways. The use of the continuous form:
- implies **recent** activity if no time adverbial is used to indicate otherwise. The activity can be continuous, often with a result in the present:

'You're covered in mud! What have you been doing?'
'I've been playing football.'
or involve a number of repeated actions:
They've been winning a lot of games (this season).

- suggests an incomplete action.

He's been reading his book this morning. (This implies he hasn't finished the book.)

By comparison, the simple form indicates completed action/achievement.

He's read his book this morning. (This implies he has finished it.)

Notes:

1 To express a series of completed, consecutive actions we use the simple, not the continuous form. Compare:

He's read three books this week. (one after the other)
He's been reading three books. (This implies he's been reading them simultaneously.)

2 Expressions such as *twice/several times*, which indicate the number of actions, cannot be used with the continuous form.

I've visited my home town **twice** since I left.
Not
*I've been visiting ...

Stative verbs

1 Verbs that describe continuous states do not usually occur in continuous tenses. These include:
be, believe, belong, exist, hate, know, mean, own, understand

2 A number of verbs have two different meanings, one referring to a state and another referring to an action. When referring to an action, they may appear in the continuous form. These verbs include:
appear, feel, have, look, see, smell, think, taste

Compare these sentences:
I haven't seen you for ages. (= with my eyes)
I've been seeing a lot of David recently. (= go out with)

We have a small car. (= own)
We're having a party on Saturday. (= hold)

He appears to be rather depressed. (= seem)
He's appearing in a play. (= act)

UNIT 2

Relative clauses (page 25)

Defining relative clauses

1 These give us essential information about the preceding noun.

*The girl **who/that had won the race** was very pleased with herself.*
*The painting **which/that was damaged** has now been repaired.*

The information in the relative clauses helps us to identify which girl and which painting are being referred to.

2 In these clauses:
- there are no commas.
- *who* and *which* can be replaced by *that*.
- we can omit the relative pronoun in object clauses.

*That's the man **(whom/that/who)** I told you about.*
*Here's the radio **(which/that)** I have repaired.*

When the words in brackets are omitted, these are called **contact clauses**.

Note: *Whom* is traditionally used in object clauses but it is common to see *who* as well. If you use a contact clause you don't have to use either word.

Non-defining relative clauses

1 These give us extra information about a preceding noun which has already been clearly defined or identified.

*Mr Taylor, **who gave a talk here last month,** will be here again on Wednesday.*
*A painting by Picasso, **which was thought to have been lost for ever**, has recently been discovered.*

2 In these clauses:
- commas are needed around the clause.
- *that* cannot be used as an alternative to *who* or *which*.
- there are **no** contact clauses.

Note: The relative pronoun in a relative clause **replaces** the subject or object to which it refers. The following sentences are therefore **incorrect**:
* The girl who ~~she~~ had won the race was pleased with herself.*
* Here's the radio that I have repaired ~~it~~.*

The words *she* in sentence 1 and *it* in sentence 2 are unnecessary.

Whose

We can use *whose* to replace possessive words such as *his*, *her* and *their* in both defining and non-defining clauses.

That's the boy. His story won first prize.
*That's the boy **whose** story won first prize.*
Janet Smith will be off work for a month. Her leg is broken.
*Janet Smith, **whose** leg is broken, will be off work for a month.*

Reduced relative clauses

Where the verb in a defining or non-defining relative clause is in the passive, the auxiliary verb *be* and the relative pronoun may both be omitted.

*A BASE jump **(which is)** done for the entertainment of millions cannot be acceptable ...*

▶ For more information about reduced relative clauses see **Unit 10, page 209**.

Prepositions in relative clauses

1 In formal English, the preposition is placed before the relative pronoun. In informal English, the preposition moves to the end of the sentence.

*That's the man **to whom** I lent my book.*
*That's the man **who** I lent my book **to**.*

2 In relative clauses defining place or time, we can use *in which* and *on which* instead of *where* and *when*.

*Tuesday's the day **on which** we decided to meet.*
*Tuesday's the day **when** we decided to meet.*

Sentence relatives (page 31)

A relative clause may refer not only to the noun immediately preceding it, but to the whole of the preceding clause.

*She did badly in the exam, **which** surprised her teacher.*

Here the relative pronoun *which* refers to the fact that the girl did badly. Relative clauses of this type are always introduced by *which*, and separated off by a comma.

Narrative tenses (page 27)

Past simple

We use the past simple for events in the past that we regard as finished and complete, often with a clear past time reference. The past simple can be used to describe a series of actions in the past.

*I **left** England in 1989 and **emigrated** to Australia, where I **got** a job in a bank.*

Past continuous

We use the past continuous tense to describe past events which go on for some time, and when the starting point and finishing point do not matter. This tense can describe the background to another event.

*We **were living** in France at the time of the election.*
*I **was waiting** for the bus when the accident happened.*
or
*When the accident happened, I **was waiting** for the bus.*

Past perfect

1 We use the past perfect tense when we look back on an event in the past from a point in the past. Therefore, it is important to know what the point in the past is. We can indicate this point in the past by:
• using the past simple in the same sentence.

*We **ate** the food that they **had left** in the fridge.*

• using the past simple in a preceding sentence.

*Sally **walked** towards the house. She **had parked** her car out of sight.*

• using a time word or phrase.

***By 4 p.m.**, we **had finished** all our work.*

2 The past perfect cannot be used for a series of consecutive actions. The past simple must be used instead.

*Martin **picked up** his briefcase, **locked** the door and **hurried** to the station.*

3 When a time conjunction such as *before*, *after*, *as soon as* makes the sequence of events clear, we can use two past simple tenses or a past perfect and a past simple.

*I **wrote** several letters **before** my guests arrived.*
*I **had written** several letters **before** my guests arrived.*

But compare:

*Jack left **when** Bob arrived.*
(Jack left at the same time.)

*Jack had left **when** Bob arrived.*
(Jack was not there when Bob arrived.)

The phrases *by the time, by* (+ time phrase) are usually used in conjunction with the past perfect.

***By the time** we got there, the others **had left**.*
*He **had visited** over 20 countries **by the age of 20**.*

Use of articles (page 31)

1 The indefinite article *a* can only be used with singular, countable nouns. It can't be used with uncountable nouns, e.g.: *food, money, water, weather* or plural nouns, e.g.: *cats, dogs, trains*

We use *a*:
• when referring to something indefinite.

*He's got **a** good job.*
*Can I buy you **a** drink?*

• when referring to something for the first time.

*I met **a** nice couple on holiday.*

2 The definite article *the* can be used with singular, plural and uncountable nouns. We use it:
• to refer to known, familiar or unique items in the environment.

*I take **the** bus/train to work every day.*
***The** Prime Minister is abroad.*
*I'm reading **the** paper.*
***The** sun is shining.*

• when referring to something that has already been mentioned.

***The** couple I told you about were from Germany.*

• with countable singular nouns that refer to a whole class in general statements.

***The** computer is now part of everyday life.*
***The** dog is a social animal.*

Note: This is the only situation where *the* can be used for generic reference.

• with uncountable nouns which are defined – made definite or specific – by a following phrase/clause.

***The** society we live in today has become more violent.*
***The** life of a diver is a dangerous one.*

3 We don't use *the*
• with names of subjects.

I studied History/Economics/English at university.

• with uncountable nouns not modified by a following phrase/clause.

Society has become more violent.
Life can be dangerous.
Food and water are in short supply.
I like to relax and enjoy nature.

4 When talking about things in general, we use a plural or uncountable noun **without any article**.

***Dogs** are social animals.*
*Listening to **music** is my favourite method of relaxation.*

UNIT 3

Wish/If only (page 34)

Tense forms

Wish and *if only* are used to express a desire for things to be different from what they are. *If only* is more emphatic than *wish*. Both are followed by the same tense forms.
• When they refer to the **present** or **future**, they are followed by the **past** tense.

*I wish I **knew** the answer.* (but I don't)
*I wish I **didn't** have to get up so early tomorrow.* (but I have to get up early)

Note: The subjunctive form *I/he/she were* is used after *wish/if* only in more formal contexts.

*I wish I **were** rich.* (but I'm not)
*He wishes he **were** MD.* (but he isn't)

In spoken English, *was* is more usual, although the subjunctive is often retained in the fixed phrase *If I were you, ...*

- When they refer to the **past**, they are followed by the **past perfect** tense.

*I wish I **had asked** you earlier.* (but I didn't ask you)
*She wishes she **hadn't resigned**.* (but she did)

The use of a tense which is further back in the past helps to show that we are referring to something unreal, or imaginary.

wish + would

To refer to present and future actions which are **beyond our control**, we use *wish + would*.

*I wish the weather **would** improve.*
(but there is no sign of improvement)

*I wish you **wouldn't** smoke in the house.*
(but you do smoke)

*I wish he **would** try to be more punctual.*
(but he doesn't)

It is incorrect to say 'I wish **I** would ...'
*I wish I would have a bigger house.
You should say:
*I wish I **had** a bigger house.*
(This refers to something you don't have now.)

Regret

1 When the feeling of regret comes after the action, *regret* can be followed by:

- **the gerund (*-ing* form)**

*I regret **spending** my holiday in that place.*
(This means that I spent my holiday there first and regretted it afterwards.)

- **a noun or pronoun**

*I immediately regretted my **decision**.*
(I made the decision, then regretted it.)

- **a noun clause**

He regretted that he had left early.
They regretted what they had done.

2 Less frequently, *regret* is followed by the *to*-infinitive. This structure is usually used in written English.

*I regret **to inform** you that you have not been selected for interview.*

The action – *to inform* – comes **after** the feeling of regret.

Verbs which are used in this way are verbs of saying, e.g.:
announce, inform, tell, say.

Conditional sentences

The four main types of conditional sentences are:
- **zero conditional**

*You **lose** weight if you **exercise** regularly.*
This is something which is generally or always true.

- **first conditional**

*If they **buy** the house, they **won't** regret it.*
This is something which is likely to happen in the future.

- **second conditional**

*If he **worked** harder, he **would pass** his exams.*
This is something which is unlikely to happen in the future.

*If I **spoke** Chinese, I **would go** and live there.*
This is unreal or contrary to present fact – I don't speak Chinese.

- **third conditional**

*She **wouldn't have left** if she **had been promoted**.*
This is contrary to fact – she didn't get promoted. We use this conditional to speculate about what might have happened in the past.

Notes:

1 As well as *if*, conditional clauses can be introduced by:
as long as, unless (= if not), providing that.

*I won't come **unless** you pay my fare.*
***Providing that** you pay my fare, I will come.*

2 When the *if* clause is in second position, no comma is needed to separate the two clauses.

Mixed conditional sentences

In mixed conditional sentences, each clause refers to a different time.

*Sarah **would be** here (now) if she **had caught** the train on time.* (past)
*I **would have told** you (past) if I **knew** the answer.*
(I don't know now and I didn't before.)

Polite use of would/will

Would and *will* can occur in both clauses of a conditional sentence only when you wish to be polite or persuasive. It's correct to say:
*If you **would come** with me, I **would like to** introduce you to the President.*
*If you **will place** a large order, we **will give** you a generous discount.*

UNIT 4

be to + infinitive (page 48)

1 *be to* + infinitive is a kind of future tense and suggests that something is inevitable and fixed. It can refer to real future time.

*These men **are to be** transferred to another prison tomorrow.*

It can also be used to refer to future time in the past.

*Although I did not realise it at the time, I **was to regret** speaking those words.*

2 This structure can also be used to give orders or instructions.

*We **are to wait** for him at the gate before going in.* (He told us to wait.)

Gerunds and infinitives (pages 50–51)

Preposition + gerund

Any verb following a preposition is always in the *-ing* form (gerund). Note that *to* is a preposition in the following expressions: *be accustomed to, be/get used to, look forward to, stick to*

*I'm looking forward **to going** on holiday.*

Verb + gerund and/or infinitive

1 Certain verbs in English can only be followed by either a gerund (e.g. *enjoy*) or an infinitive (e.g. *agree*). Some verbs may be followed by both, but often with a difference in meaning. In general, the main difference between gerunds and infinitives is:

- the action in the **infinitive** often happens **after** the action of the main verb and looks forward.
- the action in the **gerund** happens **before** the action of the main verb.

Gerunds focus on the general idea of activity.

2 Some verbs are followed by the gerund and cannot be followed by an infinitive. These include:
admit, avoid, celebrate, consider, defer, deny, dislike, enjoy, finish, involve, keep (= continue), *mind* (= object to), *miss, practise, postpone, risk*

These verbs can also be followed by nouns and pronouns, so you can say:

*They enjoyed **playing tennis/a game of tennis/it.***
but you cannot say:
They **would enjoy **to play** tennis.*

3 Other expressions followed by the gerund include:
can't bear, can't stand, can't help (= prevent/avoid), *It's no good/use …, It's not worth …*

4 Some common verbs followed by a *to*-infinitive are:
afford, agree, decide, hope, intend, offer, plan, prepare, pretend, promise, refuse, want

Verb + gerund or infinitive

1 The verbs *begin, continue, hate, like, love, prefer, start* can be followed by the infinitive **or** gerund. But note that:

- the infinitive is more likely if the verb is in the conditional form.

*I **would like to meet** you tomorrow if that's possible.*

- the gerund is more likely when referring to something that has happened or is happening.

*He **hated getting up** early.*
*He **prefers walking** to work to catching the bus.*

2 There is a group of verbs where the use of the gerund or the infinitive changes the meaning completely. These include:
go on, regret, forget, remember, stop, try

- ***remember, forget, stop***
We use the gerund when something happened before the act of *remembering*, etc.

*He **remembered** (mental activity second) **meeting** the President (event first).*
*He **stopped** (second action) writing (first action) to **make** a phone call (third action).*

We use the infinitive when the act of *remembering*, etc., is first and the other verb second.

*He **remembered** (mental activity first) **to switch off** the light (action second).*
*He **stopped** (first – we don't know what he stopped) **to have** lunch (second action).*

(See *regret* **Unit 3, page 201**.)

- ***go on***
We use *go on* + gerund to show that an action continues.

*He'll **go on smoking**, despite the fact it's bad for his health.*

go on + infinitive means one activity has finished and another has started.

*After passing her exams, Susan **went on to study** English at Oxford.*

- ***try***
try + gerund means 'to make an experiment' or do something to see what will happen.

*He **tried using** every key he had but none of them would open the door.*

try + infinitive means 'to attempt to do something that is very difficult or impossible'.

*He **tried to lift** the box but it was too heavy.*

Gerund and infinitive nominals

1 Gerunds are often used as the subject of a sentence.

Going by bus will be cheaper than going by train.

Infinitives can also be used in this way, but it is more common to start the sentence with *It … .*

It is cheaper to go by bus than (to go) by train.

2 We can also use a nominal infinitive for things that might possibly happen in the future.

***To receive** a letter from you would be really wonderful.* (if you wrote one)

To refer to things that have actually happened we use a gerund.

Getting (rather than *To get*) *a phone-call from you yesterday was really nice.*

UNIT 5

Confusible structures (pages 63–64)

as/like, as if/as though

1 *As* can be used as a preposition before a noun, to describe a role or function.

*He found a job in the circus **as** a clown.* (not *like a clown*)

***As** your doctor, I advise you to do more exercise.* (not *Like your doctor*)

2 Both *as* and *like* can be used to introduce comparisons. Compare:

*He looks **like** his father.*
Like *your father, I think you should study harder.*
*She exercises regularly, **as** does her sister.*

In the first two examples, *like* is a preposition and can be followed by a noun or a pronoun.
In the third example, *as* is a conjunction, and introduces a clause of manner.

Note: In spoken English *like* is often used instead of *as*.

*She exercises regularly, **like** her sister.*

3 There is no difference in meaning between *as if/ as though*. Both are used to make a comparison and are followed by clauses of manner.

*He looks **as if** he's had a shock.*
*She talks **as though** she's an expert on art.*

Note: *as if/as though* is often replaced by *like* in colloquial spoken English.

*It seems **like** he's going to buy the painting.*

used to / be, get used to / use

1 *Used to* refers to repeated and regular activity in the past. It is followed by a *to*-infinitive. It has no present form. The equivalent present meaning of:

*He **used to** drive to work.* (past)
is:
*He **usually** drives to work.* (now)

Note: Question and negative forms drop the *-d*.
*Didn't he **use to** live in Oxford?*

2 *Be used to* means the same as *be accustomed to* and describes whether or not people feel comfortable and at ease. It can be used in any tense of the verb *be* but the past participle form, *used*, never changes. A gerund, noun or pronoun must be used after *to*.

3 When we say *get/become used to*, this emphasises a gradual process of change rather than a state.

*He is **getting used to** driving this car.*
(He feels more comfortable than he did to start with, but he isn't yet completely at ease.)

4 *Use* is a regular verb meaning 'employ, exploit or make use of', and is followed by an object.

*He **used** the tin opener to open the can.*

suppose / be supposed to

1 *to suppose* means 'to think/believe', so *I suppose so* is similar to *I think so*. It is usually followed by a noun clause.

I suppose (that) I'd better be going.

2 *be supposed to* means 'what is expected, what is right, what you are obliged to do', and is followed by an infinitive.

*He **is supposed to be** here now.*
(He should be here, but he isn't.)

Present participle clauses (page 67)

Participle clauses are a useful way of expressing yourself economically and avoiding repetition.

Present participle clauses can be used:
- to avoid repetition of the subject in a second clause with the same subject as the first.

She ignored him and she hoped he would go away.
She ignored him, hoping he would go away.

- in a similar way to adverbial clauses, indicating relationships of cause/reason, effect/result, time etc.

*It rained all day, **ruining our picnic**.* (result)
***Being a kind-hearted girl**, she was always ready to help.* (reason)
***Opening the window**, he looked down into the garden.* (time)

Note: The verbs *be, have, know, wish* can be used in the *-ing* form **only** in adverbial clauses, not in adjectival clauses. See below.

- after the following conjunctions and prepositions:
before, after, since, when, while, once
despite, in spite of, on

After leaving school, he did a succession of jobs.
On seeing him, she gave a little shriek.

- adjectivally, to give additional information about the nouns they relate to. They can replace both defining and non-defining relative clauses.

*The girl **who is playing** the piano is an excellent musician.*
*The girl **playing the piano** is an excellent musician.*
*They ignored Peter, **who was standing by himself** in a corner.*
*They ignored Peter, **standing by himself** in a corner.*

▶ For more information on participle clauses, see **Unit 13**, **page 211**.

UNIT 6

Grammatical cohesion

In extended speech or writing, we often need to refer again to things that have already been mentioned. This can be done in various ways without having to repeat the same words.

Reference (page 48)

We can use pronouns such as *he/she/it* etc., *this/that* etc. to **refer** to items mentioned.

*I met **the new manager** today. **He's** very impressive.*

Substitution (page 84)

We can **substitute** different words to stand in for a noun, verb or clause. The following words can be used as substitutes.

- *one/ones*
*'Do you like the red **sweater**?' 'I prefer the blue **one**.'*
(= sweater)

- *do*
*He promised to **come**, and he **did** (come).*
*'Could you **type this letter**?' 'I have **done**.'* (= typed the letter)

Sometimes *do so* is preferred as a substitute for non-finite verbs.

*He asked me to write and I promised to **(do so)**.*

- *so + auxiliary verb + subject*
*I live in London. **So does Peter**.* (= Peter lives in London too.)
*They've received a pay rise and **so have I**.* (= I have received a pay rise too.)

- *so + subject + verb*
*'There's a scratch on the car!' '**So there is!**'*

- *if so / if not*
*Do you want to come? **If so** (= if you want to come), let me know as soon as possible. **If not** (= if you don't want to come), it doesn't matter.*

- *the same*
*I thought the play was excellent and my friend thought **the same**.* (= thought that the play was excellent too)

Omission (ellipsis) (page 84)

We can omit words altogether. There are three types of ellipsis: omission of a noun or pronoun, a verb or a whole clause.

*Do you like the red **sweater**? I prefer the blue *.*
(omission of the noun *sweater*)
I moved to London and then * to Paris. (omission of subject and verb *I moved*)
We could go out but I'd prefer not to *. (omission of the verb *go out*)
'You must see that film.' 'I already have *.' (omission of the verb clause *seen that film*)

Making suggestions and recommendations (page 85)

1 The verb *suggest* can be followed by:

- **gerund**

*Sam **suggested going** to the theatre.*
This suggestion probably includes Sam and everybody in the group.

- **that clause**

*My brother **suggested (to Bob) (that)** he **(should)** apply for the job.*
The use of the prepositional phrase focuses the suggestion on one person. The words in brackets can be left out, either separately or all together.

My brother suggested Bob apply for the job.

Note:
The verb in the *that* clause is in the subjunctive form. This is the same as the base form, and doesn't change, so there is no third person -*s*.

- **noun/pronoun**
*Sally **suggested dinner**.*
*I like that idea. Who **suggested it**?*

Suggest **CANNOT** be followed by an object + *to*-infinitive.
* *He suggested us to go for a walk.*

2 Like *suggest*, *recommend* can be followed by a gerund, *that* clause, noun or pronoun.
However, we can also use *recommend* with an object + *to*-infinitive.

The teacher recommends students (to) buy a good dictionary.

Giving advice (page 85)

The verb *advise* can be followed by:
- **object + *to*-infinitive**

if you need to mention the person receiving the advice.

*I **advise you to wait** another week.*

- **gerund**

if you don't need to mention the person.
*I **advise waiting** another week.*

- **object + *that* clause or *wh-* clause**

*He **advised me that** I had a good chance of getting the job.* (= told me)
I can't advise you what you should do.

- ***against* + gerund**

*He **advised (me) against accepting** the offer.*

Notes:

1 *advise* is the verb and *some advice* or *a piece of advice* is the uncountable noun, so there is no plural noun form.

2 Other verbs and nouns with the same spelling difference are: *to practise/practice, to license/licence, to devise/device*. These do not necessarily have the same pronunciation and grammatical differences.

Giving warnings (page 86)

The verb *to warn* is always used to talk about negative things. It can be followed by:
- **object + (not) *to*-infinitive**

*He warned **me not to stay** there any longer.*

- **object + *that* clause**

*They warned us **that a storm was coming**.*

- ***against* + gerund**

*He warned (me) **against going** any further.*

- ***about/of* + noun/pronoun/gerund**

*He warned **(me) about/of the dangers**.*
*They warned us **about leaving** the door unlocked.*

Concession (page 86)

1 *even if/even though/although/though* are conjunctions and are followed by clauses containing a subject and a verb.

__Although her health was poor__, she completed her novel.
__Even though he was injured__, he continued to play.

2 We use *despite* and *in spite of* to combine opposing ideas or statements. They mean exactly the same and are followed by nouns, pronouns and gerunds.

__In spite of her poor health__, she completed her novel.
__Despite his injury__, he continued to play.

3 The phrase *despite/in spite of the fact that* already includes a noun – *the fact* – and can be directly substituted for *even though* or *although* without

making any further changes to the sentence.

__In spite of the fact that her health was poor__, she completed her novel.

4 The modal verb *may* suggests concession in certain contexts.

You may be right. (but I'm not convinced)

5 *Whatever, whoever, whichever, however, wherever* are conjunctions. The meaning is equivalent to 'It doesn't make any difference what/who etc.'

Whatever you say, I'm still going to be an actor.
Wherever you go, you should be careful.

However can be followed by an adjective or adverb and means the same as *even if/though*.

However successful you become, you should never forget your friends. (= even if you become very successful)
However much money he has, he wants more.

6 *No matter* is a conjunction. It is followed by *what/who/where/when/which/how/whose* + clause, and has a similar meaning to *whatever/whoever* etc.: what is being referred to won't make much difference.

I won't change my plans no matter what you say.

UNIT 7

Talking about the future (page 96)

We use the following tense forms to talk about the future.

1 Present simple:
for timetables, schedules, travel plans already fixed.

*The football match **begins** at 5.30 p.m.*
*When you **arrive** in London, **take** the underground train to Victoria station.*

2 Present continuous:
for planned meetings and definite arrangements (usually personal).

*Kathy's **meeting** John at the opera on Tuesday. She bought the tickets yesterday.*

3 *going to*:
- for intentions

*I'm **going to** finish painting the kitchen tonight.*

- for predictions based on evidence now (usually about something outside your control).

*Look out! That car's **going to** crash!*

4 Future simple:
- for spontaneous decisions

'We're going for a walk.' 'I'll come with you.'

- for predictions ('pure' future)

*In the next century, people **will live** a lot longer.*

5 Future continuous:

for planned events in progress in the future.

This time next week, we'll be sitting on a beach in Hawaii.

6 Future perfect:

to refer to the time something will finish/be completed.

By the year 2020 the new complex will have been completed.

Other expressions used to talk about the future

1 be about to:

for things which will happen very soon and so are quite certain.

The parachutist is about to jump.

2 be bound to:

for things which are certain to happen.

They're 3–0 down. The England team are bound to lose.

3 Modal verbs can also have future meaning.

We should arrive soon. (= this is probable)
By the year 2050, people could be holidaying on the moon. (= possible/probable)
They may/might win. (= possible)

4 be to + infinitive
See **Unit 4, page 202**.

Future time in subordinate clauses

(page 97)

1 In subordinate clauses which begin with conjunctions of time, such as *once, when, until, after, before, as soon as* and *while*, the present or perfect tense is used. The future simple occurs only in the main clause.

*As soon as he arrives (**not** will arrive), I will come down and greet him.*

The main verb of the sentence (*I will come down*) clearly refers to future time. It's therefore unnecessary for the verb in the subordinate clause (*he arrives*) to be in the future.

2 The present perfect is used to show that the action in the subordinate clause is completed **before** the action in the main clause.

*I won't make a decision until **I have heard from you.***

3 Subordinate clauses introduced by *if, whether, on condition that*, and question words also use the present tense.

*If he **comes**, I will be very pleased.*
*I'll accept the job on condition that I **get** a company car.*

UNIT 8

Nominal clauses (pages 106–107)

1 Verbs denoting mental processes may be followed by a nominal clause introduced by *that* or a *wh-* question word.

*She hadn't realised **that her husband was a criminal**. She didn't know **what she was going to do**.*

Common verbs that can introduce nominal clauses include:

accept, agree, believe, decide, demand, explain, feel, forget, hear, hope, imagine, know, mean, predict, notice, prefer, promise, recommend, regret, remember, reply, say, suggest, teach, think, understand, warn, wish, wonder

Notes:

1 In informal English *that* is often omitted.

He noticed (that) she was worried.

2 A nominal clause introduced by a question word doesn't require a question mark.

2 Nominal clauses may also be used:
- after nouns related to verbs of thinking or speaking.

*She didn't share his **belief that** everything would be all right.*
*They broke into the house in the certain **knowledge that** the owners would be out.*

- after adjectives describing reactions and opinions, e.g. *(un)certain, (un)sure.*

*She was **certain that** she had locked the door.*

Indirect speech (page 107)

1 Changes that take place after past tense reporting verbs are:
- sequence of tenses

Present simple > Past simple
'I live in London,' he said.

*He said that he **lived** in London.*

Present continuous > Past continuous
'Where is Jack going?' he asked us.

*He asked us where Jack **was going**.*

Present perfect > Past perfect
'What has happened to my car?'

*He asked what **had happened** to his car.*

Past simple > Past perfect
'What did you say to Tom?' Sally asked me.

*Sally asked me what I **had said** to Tom.*

Past continuous > Past perfect continuous
'What was everyone talking about?' she asked.

*She asked what everyone **had been talking** about.*

will > *would*

'I will be here on Tuesday,' Mary told me.

Mary told me she **would** *be there on Tuesday.*

Notes:

1 The 'sequence of tenses' rule only applies after a past tense reporting verb (e.g. *said, asked*). If the reporting verbs are in the present, present perfect or future, tenses usually remain unchanged.

She **says** *(that) it's all your fault.*

I'll **tell** *him (that) the match has been cancelled.*

2 Past tenses don't always change to past perfect, if the sequence of events is clear.

3 Past perfect verbs don't change.

4 Modal verbs don't normally change, except that *must* can change to *had to*, and *can* can change to *could*.

- **time and place words**

These change if the time and place really have changed.

today	> *on that day*
yesterday	> *the day before/the previous day*
tomorrow	> *the day after/the next day/the following day*
now	> *right away/straightaway*
last week	> *the week before*
this	> *that*
here	> *there*

2 In indirect questions, the subject usually comes before the verb, and the auxiliary *do* is not used.

'Where does he live?'

She asked me **where he lived**.

3 'Yes/No' questions are reported with *if*.

'Are you going to be on time?'

He asked me **if I was going to be on time**.

Other reporting verbs (page 107)

1 A variety of reporting verbs can be used to introduce indirect speech. These reporting verbs are followed by different structures. Common patterns are:

- **verb + *that* clause:**

e.g. *admit, agree, argue, boast, complain*

- **verb + *that* clause + *should*:**

e.g. *advise, demand, insist, suggest, recommend, request*

- **verb + *to*-infinitive:**

e.g. *agree, offer, promise, refuse, threaten*

Note: The infinitive can only be used if the subject of the infinitive clause is the same as the main clause. Compare:

He promised to telephone me.

He promised that his secretary would telephone me.

- **verb + object + *to*-infinitive:**

e.g. *advise, ask, beg, forbid, order, persuade, tell, urge, warn*

- **verb + gerund:**

e.g. *admit, deny, mention, suggest*

- **verb + preposition + gerund:**

e.g. *apologise for, insist on, object to*

Note: The verbs *insist on* and *object to* may be followed by an object or a genitive, e.g.:

Tom **insisted on my** *attending the meeting.*

They **objected to us/our** *taking part.*

2 We often avoid indirect speech tense changes by using reporting verbs that paraphrase what was said. For example, 'I'll be there on time. You can depend on it.' is a promise and can be reported as:

He **promised** *to be there on time.*

'Why don't we go to the cinema?' is a suggestion and can be reported as:

Sally **suggested** *going to the cinema.*

Verbs with two objects (page 112)

Verb + indirect object + direct object

Common verbs that can be followed by two objects in this pattern include:

buy, bring, get, give, hand, offer, pay, send, teach, write

as well as many reporting verbs (where the direct object can be a *that* clause), e.g.:

inform, persuade, promise, remind, tell

Verb + direct object + *to/for* + indirect object

Some verbs with two objects can take this alternative pattern, with a preposition. The prepositions *to* and *for* are not usually interchangeable, but depend on the meaning of the verb:

+ *to*: *lend, write* sth to sb

+ *for*: *buy, get, save, spare* sth for sb

+ *to* or *for* depending on meaning: *give*

- The preposition *to* is used when there is a recipient (someone who receives something).

She wrote **to** *all her friends.* (They received letters.)

I lent my book to John.

- *for* is used to indicate a beneficiary (someone who benefits from the action).

She bought a present **for** *her friend.*

We're getting new curtains **for** *the living room.*

I can spare some time **for** *a meeting.*

I've saved some of the pie **for** *you.*

Compare:

He gave all his money to a charity. (The charity received money.)

They gave a party **for** *Andrew.* (Andrew is the beneficiary.)

- The verbs *save* and *spare* cannot be followed by *to* or *for* in this way.

He spared/saved me the trouble of writing by telephoning me.

- The verbs *cost* and *cause* cannot be used with a preposition at all.

It cost me a great deal of money.
He caused us a lot of problems.

UNIT 9

Writing complex sentences (page 123)

Independent clauses

Two sentences/clauses can be connected by means of
- **a co-ordinating conjunction:**

and (addition), *but* (contrast), *so* (result)

These conjunctions form a compound sentence in which both clauses are grammatically independent. A comma is not normally needed before a co-ordinating conjunction, unless both parts of the sentence are long.

- **a connector or link word:**

moreover, in addition
therefore, as a result
however, nevertheless

When they are used in an independent clause, connectors can appear in different positions, e.g.

I was very tired when I got home.
***However**, I managed to do a further two hours' work.*
*I managed, **however**, to do a further two hours' work.*
*I managed to do a further two hours' work **however**.*

They are usually separated from the rest of the clause by commas when in initial or middle position.

When they are used in compound sentences, a semi-colon (;) is used before these connectors. They may be followed by commas.

I was very tired when I got home; however, I managed to do a further two hours' work.

▶ For more information on how present participles can be used to replace *and* in co-ordinate clauses, see **Unit 5, page 203**.

▶ For information about sentence relative clauses, see **Unit 2, page 199**.

Dependent clauses

Sentences or clauses may be connected by means of a subordinating conjunction. The clause introduced by the subordinating conjunction cannot stand alone, but is dependent for meaning on the main clause.

***Although it was hot**, she shivered.* (contrast)
*I like him **because he's funny**.* (reason)

Subordinate clauses in initial position are followed by a comma.

List of subordinating conjunctions and link words

- **Addition**

in addition, moreover, furthermore, what's more, besides, also

*The holiday was awful. **What's more**, we were burgled while we were away!*

- **Time sequence**

as soon as, when, immediately, the moment/minute, just as, by the time

***By the time** he arrived, the party was over.*

- **Condition**

if, unless, as long as, in case, even if, provided, on condition that

*I'll cook **as long as** you wash up.*
*Take an umbrella **in case** it rains.*

- **Cause and effect/result**

because, as, since, so that, with the result that, as a result, therefore, consequently, for this reason

Since she'd inherited some money (cause), *Jackie decided to buy a new house* (result).

- **Contrast**

although, even though, whereas, while, on the other hand, however, nevertheless, despite/in spite of (this), in contrast, on the contrary

***Even though** he'd worked all night, Sam wasn't tired.*
*I was very worried about what had happened, **whereas/while** the others weren't bothered at all.*

▶ For more information on in *spite of, in spite of the fact that, even if/though,* see **Unit 6, page 205**.

- **Example/illustration**

For example/instance, in other words, that is, namely, to illustrate this

UNIT 10

The Passive (page 130)

1 We form the passive with the verb *to be* in the appropriate tense or form and the past participle of the main verb.

- **modal (present)** + *be* + **pp**
*You **should be promoted** soon.*

- **modal (past)** + *have been* + **pp**
*He **could have been killed**.*

- **verb with infinitive** + *to be* + **pp**
*He **wants to be made** Head of Department.*

- **verb with gerund** + *being* + **pp**
*I **enjoy being pampered**.*

- **verb + adjective** + *to be* **(present)/*have been* (past)** + **pp**
*They **were pleased to have been awarded** the prize.*

2 To change an active sentence to a passive one, the object of the active sentence must be made the subject of the passive sentence. The subject of the active sentence becomes the agent or can be dropped.

The police arrested **the suspect.**
The suspect was arrested **(by the police)**.

Note: The passive cannot be used with intransitive verbs. In the following example the active sentence has no object, so there is no subject for the passive sentence.

We arrived in Paris at midday.

3 Sometimes *get* can be used to form the passive instead of the verb *to be*. This use is more colloquial, and tends to suggest something more accidental.

Be careful! You could have got run over.

▶ For more information on the uses of *get*, see **Unit 13, page 211**.

4 We use the passive:
- to focus on the action when the agent is either not important, unknown or obvious.

*The criminal **was sentenced** to life imprisonment.*

- to focus on the agent (when it is new information) by placing it at the end of the sentence.

*The new art gallery will be opened **by the Prince of Wales**.*

- to focus on new information by making it the topic of the sentence.

Three basic types of stalker have been identified.

- to make a statement more impersonal and formal by avoiding the use of personal pronouns or vague words such as *people*.

It is generally recognised that smoking is bad for your health.

make, see and *let* (page 130)

Most verbs have the same pattern in the passive as they do in the active. If they are followed by a gerund or infinitive in an active sentence, then they will be followed by a gerund or infinitive in a passive sentence. Exceptions include:

- *make*
In the active form it is followed by an infinitive without *to*.

*They **made us pay** £10 for each ticket.*

But in the passive form we need a *to*-infinitive.

*We **were made to pay** £10 for each ticket.*

- *see*
Compare:

*The police **saw** the burglar **enter** the house.*
*The burglar **was seen to enter** the house by the police.*

- *let*
This is followed by an infinitive without *to* in the active.

*They **let** the prisoner **go** free.*

However, it cannot be used at all in the passive. We have to use another verb with a similar meaning.

*The prisoner **was allowed/permitted** to go free.*

Impersonal constructions

After verbs referring to mental processes, or reporting verbs, the passive can be formed in two ways.
- **It** + **passive verb** + *that* + **subject**

It is rumoured that the President is unwell.

- **subject** + **passive verb** + **present/perfect infinitive**

The President is rumoured to be unwell.

This construction is generally used in written English. It is often used in newspaper reports to avoid mentioning the source of the information.

Reduced relative clauses (page 131)

In relative clauses containing a passive verb, the auxiliary *be* can be omitted together with the relative pronoun. Such clauses can be defining e.g.:

*The man (**who was**) arrested on Friday has been released.*
or non-defining, e.g.:

*They returned to the village, (**which had been**) evacuated during the floods.*

▶ For more information on past participle clauses, see **Unit 13, page 211**.

UNIT 11

Cleft sentences (pages 147–148)

Cleft (or 'divided') sentence constructions can be used to emphasise important information in a sentence. They are more common in spoken English, but can also be used to signal emphasis in writing, where it cannot be indicated by intonation. There are two types of cleft construction.

Wh- + be

This structure – a relative clause introduced by a *wh*-word – focuses attention on the subject, object or complement of a sentence by making it the subject or complement of the verb *be*.

My shoulder causes me pain. (subject of *cause*)
*My shoulder **is what** causes me pain.* (subject of *be*)
***What** causes me pain **is** my shoulder.* (complement of *be*)
I really miss swimming in the sea. (object of *miss*)
***What** I really miss **is** swimming in the sea.* (complement of *be*)
*Swimming in the sea **is what** I really miss.* (subject of *be*)

This structure can also focus on the verb, by using the auxiliary verb *do/does* or *did* as a substitute in the *wh*-clause.

They haven't sent us a cheque for the money.
***What** they've haven't **done is** (to) send us a cheque ...*

The cleft structure often implies a contrast with something else.

*I **like** the work – **what** I **don't like is** the low pay!*

Note: The *wh*- structure can sometimes focus on an adverbial or prepositional clause, usually with the addition of expressions such as *the place where, the time when* etc.

Paul and Jane met in a cafe in New York.
***The place where** Paul and Jane met **was** a cafe in New York.*
They got married in June.
***The month when** they got married **was** June.*

It + be

This type of cleft structure can be used to emphasise almost any part of a sentence other than the verb by making it the complement of *It + be*. Like the *wh*-type, this structure implies a contrast with a previous statement.

Peter decorated the living room last month.
*It was **Peter** who decorated the living room.* (not someone else)
*It was the **living room** that Peter decorated.* (not another room)
*It was **last month** that/when Peter decorated the living room.* (not the month before)

UNIT 12

Uses of *get* (page 160)

Get is a very common verb in English and has many meanings. It's mostly used in informal English, and rarely appears in very formal language. The meaning is dependent on the word or structure which follows it.

- ***get** + direct object (noun/pronoun)*
*I **got the food** from the local shop.* (= obtain)
*She **got a lot of presents**.* (= receive)

- ***get** + adjective, adverb or preposition*
*You'll **get better** soon.* (= become)
*Things have **got better**.* (= improve)
*We **got there** after midnight.* (= arrive)
*He finally **got to** the top of the hill.* (= reach)

- ***get** + past participle*
to describe what we do to ourselves: *He **got lost** on the way to the station.*
passive sense: *He **got wounded** in the attack.*

- ***get** + object + past participle*
manage with difficulty: *We **got the work finished** eventually.*
experience something, usually unpleasant: *I **got my wallet stolen**, unfortunately.*
cause something to happen or be done: *I've got to **get my bike repaired** soon.*
*We're going to **get an extension built**.*

- ***get** + infinitive*
have the opportunity: *We **got to see** the film.*

- ***get** + object + infinitive*
persuade someone to do something: *I think I can **get John to agree**.*

- ***get** + object + present participle*
to arrange: *We've **got some people coming round** for dinner.* (= Some people are coming round for dinner.)

Note: There are various common, fixed phrases with *get*:
get engaged/married/divorced, get old, get dressed etc.

Inversion (page 165)

Subject/verb inversion

The normal order for English sentences is:
subject + verb + object
However, it is possible to invert the verb and the subject after an introductory adverbial of place, time or movement in order to make the sentence sound dramatic.

The boxer had trained hard for the fight. **Then came the big day** *and he was knocked out in the first minute.* (Instead of: *Then the big day came and he was ...*)

Inversion of the verb and complement is also possible for emphasis.

Not to be forgotten *is the issue of money.*

In order to use this pattern, we must first set the scene. This pattern cannot introduce a new topic.

Inversion after negative adverbials/conjunctions

The following negative adverbials and conjunctions can be placed first in a sentence for emphasis. The subject and verb must then be inverted. If there is no auxiliary verb in the sentence, the appropriate form of the auxiliary *do* is used as a substitute.

Never, seldom, rarely, at no time, on no account, nowhere (else)
Only (then/later/when ...)
Not until
Not only .. . but (also)
Hardly ... when
No sooner ... than

Examples:
Never had he seen *such a wonderful sight.*
Nowhere else will you see *such a wonderful collection of paintings.*
Only *when he saw the photographs* **did he** *realise what had happened.*
Not only do I have to *start early,* **but I also** *have to finish late.*
I didn't know the answer and **neither/nor did he**.

Inversion in conditional sentences

This occurs only in very formal English. *If* is omitted and an auxiliary verb (*had, were* or *should*) is placed before the subject.

• First conditional sentences can invert after *should*.

If you **should** *get lost, contact us on the following number ...*
Should you get lost, *contact us on the following number ...*

• Second conditional sentences can invert after *were*.

If our team **were** *to win, there would be a big celebration.*
Were our team to win, *there would be a big celebration.*

• Third conditional sentences can invert after *had*.

If I **had** *known, I would have informed you earlier.*
Had I known, *I would have informed you earlier.*

UNIT 13

Present and perfect participle clauses
(page 176–177)

▶ See also **Unit 5, page 203**.

1 Present participle clauses can be used without a time conjunction to show that one action took place immediately after another.

Picking up his bag, he got off the train. (After he picked up his bag, he got off the train.)

Perfect participle clauses suggest a bigger time gap.

Having done badly at school, Churchill was not expected to have a brilliant career.

2 Stative verbs such as *be, have, believe, know, live* can be used in adverbial participle clauses, and suggest a reason or cause.

Being a careful man, he decided not to risk the climb. (Because he was ...)

3 If the subject of the participle clause is not stated, it is assumed to be the same as that of the main clause.

Shining through the curtains, **the sun** *woke me up.* (The subject of the participle clause must be 'the sun'.)

The following sentence is incorrect, because *I* (the subject of the main clause) can't be shining through the curtains.

* *Shining* **through** *the curtains, I was woken by the sun.*

If the subject of the participle clause is stated, it can be different from the subject of the main clause.

The club *being closed,* **we** *looked for another one.*

Past participle clauses (page 177)

1 Like present participle clauses, past participle clauses can be adjectival (see **Unit 10, page 209**) or adverbial. They have a passive meaning. Adverbial participle clauses can be used to indicate cause/reason conditions.

Terrified by the noise, the horse bolted. (cause)
Produced by Steven Spielberg, the film is bound to be a box office hit. (reason)

2 As with present participles, if a past participle begins a sentence, it is assumed that it refers to the **first** noun or pronoun in the main clause.

Marooned *on the island,* **he** *had to hunt for food.*
Compare:
* *Damaged in the storm, he couldn't leave the island by boat.*
This should be:
His boat having been damaged in the storm, he couldn't leave the island.

Punctuation Rules

1 Capital letters: at the beginning of a sentence and for names of people and places

2 Full stops: at the end of a sentence

3 Commas

3.1 after introductory elements:
Introductory elements may be
- **adverbial phrases:**

Finally, I managed to pass the exam.
As a result, we lost the match.
- **adverbial clauses:**

When we got there, they had already left.
If you know the answer, please tell me.

Note: Adverbial phrases and clauses don't require commas when in final position.
- **participle clauses:**

Being a kind man, he agreed to help.
Too frightened to move, they clung to the ledge.

Note: This type of clause **must** be separated off by a comma in final position.

3.2 around inserted elements:
Inserted elements may be:
- **adverbial:**

I decided, **nevertheless**, to continue with the tour.
My friends, **although they had never visited Spain before**, had no problems getting around.
- **adjectival:**

The boy, **tired after his long journey**, fell into a deep sleep.

3.3 in a series:
Items in a list of three or more are separated by commas. There is no comma before the final *and*.

I like golf, tennis, swimming and basketball.

4 Commas and quotation marks in direct speech
Quotation marks are used around direct speech. A comma is used to separate quotations from the reporting verb.

'Please hurry up,' he said.
They shouted to us, 'Why don't you join us?'.

5 Apostrophes
Apostrophes are used:
- to indicate possession

Mary's bag
- to indicate omission

It's mine. (= It is mine.)

Note: An apostrophe is **not** used for the possessive pronoun *its*.
*The animal was close by. **Its** breathing could be heard clearly.*

Not * *It's breathing* ...

6 Dashes
A dash is often used to set off a phrase or clause for dramatic effect in less formal writing.

Mr Bradley was no help at all – he never even got out of his car!
A trip around the world is a wonderful opportunity – I really envy you!

Spelling Rules

-ie- and -ei- words

The -ie- spelling is used when the sound is /iː/ as in *belief, chief, niece, piece.*

Exceptions:
after the letter *c*: *deceit, receive*

The -ei- spelling is used when the sound of the letters is other than /iː/, as in e.g. *neighbour, reins, their*

Exception: *friend*

Adding syllables

1 Doubling final consonants

If a word ends in a consonant preceded by a **single** vowel, and the last syllable is stressed, the final consonant is doubled before an added syllable.

One-syllable words:
slim – slimming/slimmed
drop – dropping/dropped
hot – hotter/hottest

Two-syllable words:
forget – forgetting
omit – omitting/omitted
occur – occurring/occurred/occurrence
prefer – preferring/preferred

Compare:
open – opening/opened
happen – happening/happened
prefer – preference

Here, the stress is on the **first**, not the **final** syllable, so the consonant is not doubled.

Note: In British English, words ending in -*l* or -*p* normally double the consonant regardless of stress.
travel – traveller, kidnap – kidnapper

2 Words ending in -e and -ie

• **consonant + silent -e**

Silent -*e* after a consonant is dropped before a vowel.
make – making, take – taking,
arrive – arrival, remove – removable

Exceptions: *likeable, mileage, sizeable*

Note: The rule doesn't apply when syllables beginning with *a, o* or *u* are added to words that end in -*ce* or -*ge*, e.g. *noticeable, changeable, singeing.* Otherwise the pronunciation would be affected.

Silent -*e* is kept before a consonant.
advertise – advertisement, judge – judgement, care – careful

• **words ending in -ie**

When an ending beginning with -*i* is added, -*ie* changes to -*y*.
die – dying, lie – lying

When an ending beginning with -*e* is added, e.g. -*ed*, one -*e* is dropped.
die – died, lie – lied

• **words ending in -ee**

These words do not add a third -*e* when an ending beginning with -*e* is added.
agree – agreed, free – freer

The two -*e*'s are retained when other endings are added.
agree – agreeable, see – seeing

3 Words ending in -y

• **final consonant + -y**

-*y* following a consonant changes to -*ie* when adding -*s*.
variety – varieties, city – cities, cry – cries

-*y* doesn't change before -*i*. Verbs ending in a consonant + -*y* just add -*ing* to the base form.
pay – paying, study – studying

-*y* changes to -*i* before other consonants or vowels.
happy – happiness, lonely – loneliness
pretty – prettier, glory – glorious

• **final vowel + -y**

-*y* following a vowel doesn't change.
monkey – monkeys, journey – journeys
pay – pays – paying, say – says – saying

Exceptions:
Verbs ending in a vowel + -*y* form the past participle by changing -*y* to -*i* and adding -*d*, not -*ed*.
pay – paid, say – said, lay – laid

The adjectives *gay* and *day* change -*y* to -*i* when -*ly* is added: *gaily, daily*

Checklist for Writing

The task

✓ Have you answered the whole question?
✓ Is all the necessary information present?
✓ Is there any irrelevant information you should delete?

▶ Tick off the key points you highlighted in the question to check you haven't forgotten anything.

Purpose and target audience

✓ Have you put your message across clearly and effectively?
✓ Is the register and tone appropriate for your readers?

▶ Put yourself in the reader's position. Would you understand what the writer wants to say? Would you feel put off or offended by the tone?

Layout and organisation

✓ Is the layout appropriate for the task type?
✓ Is the information organised into coherent paragraphs?
✓ Does each paragraph begin with a clear statement of the topic and deal with one main idea?
✓ Is the sequence of ideas from one paragraph to the next logical and easy to follow?
✓ Are linking expressions and paragraph transitions used to tie sentences and paragraphs together?

Variety

✓ Is there a range of vocabulary? Have you used precise and interesting words rather than vague, dull ones?
✓ Have you used a variety of sentence patterns and not just a series of short, simple sentences?
✓ Have you avoided unnecessarily complicated sentences?

Accuracy

✓ Is the grammar correct? Check for correct use of
• articles and determiners
• subject and verb agreement
• verb forms and tenses
• prepositions and particles
• pronouns and pronoun reference
• structures after verbs (gerunds, infinitives, noun clauses)

✓ Is the punctuation correct? Check for correct use of
• capital letters and full stops
• commas
• apostrophes
• quotation marks

✓ Is the spelling correct? Check for typical errors.

Addison Wesley Longman Limited

Edinburgh Gate, Harlow,
Essex CM20 2JE, England
and Associated Companies throughout the World.

© Alan Stanton, Susan Morris 1999

First published 1999

Set in ITC Slimbach 10/12.5pt

Printed in Spain by Gráficas Estella

ISBN 0582 32340 1

Publishers' acknowledgements

The publishers would like to express thanks and appreciation to the following reporters: Nigel Bell, Argentina; Catherine Bravidis, Greece; Irena Brewis, Poland; Jain Cook, Greece; Sylvie Donna, Greece; Sarah Hellawell, Spain; Phil Hopkins, Greece; Elspeth McConnell, Greece; Catherine Mitchell, Brazil; Jacky Newbrook, UK; Helen O'Neill, UK; Annette Obee, Greece; Anne Robinson, Spain; Jayne West, UK; Clare West, UK; Russell Whitehead UK; Simon Williams, UK; Kevin Windell, Greece.

Acknowledgements

We are grateful to the following for permission to reproduce copyright material:

Andromeda Oxford Ltd for an extract from 'Raising a smile' from *EYE TO EYE: How People Interact* by PM (1988); H Bauer for an extract from the article 'The Woman who dare not show her face' by Jane Cameron in *TV QUICK* Magazine, Issue 32, 14 - 20.8.93; BBC Worldwide Publishing for an adapted extract from 'He changed the face of music in Britain' by Nicholas Kenyon in *BBC MUSIC MAGAZINE* Oct 1997; Deidre S. Channing, Editor of *The Stamford Advocate* for an extract from her article 'Is the high road just the middle ground?' in *THE STAMFORD ADVOCATE*, Stamford, Connecticut 1998; Solo Syndication for an adapted extract from the article 'In the eye of the storm' by Michael Nicholson in *THE DAILY MAIL* 3.3.97; the Editor, *The Daily Yomiuri* for an adapted extract from the article 'Virtuoso craftsman laments decline in Japanese skills' by Nobuko Matsushita (staff writer) in *THE DAILY YOMIURI* 11.8.94; Trevor York on behalf of the author for an extract from the article 'Do men and women speak the same language?' by Anne de Courcy; EMAP Publications Ltd for adapted extracts from review of 'Tin cup' by Mark Salisbury in *EMPIRE MAGAZINE* Nov 96; The Financial Times Ltd for adapted extracts from the articles 'And the miller told his tale ...' by Clive Fewins in *THE FINANCIAL TIMES* 13.8.94, 'Macho managers under fire' by Lucy Kellaway *THE FINANCIAL TIMES* 3.7.93 & 'The art of running a gallery' by Heather Farmbrough in *THE FINANCIAL TIMES WEEKEND* 10-11.7.93;

the Editor, Focus Magazine for adapted extracts from the articles 'How to survive the cold' by Ed Douglas in *FOCUS* Feb '96 & 'Your neighbours are animals' by Trevor Lawson in *FOCUS* Dec '95; Guardian Newspapers Ltd for adapted extracts from the articles 'Teenage TV addicts prone to crime and drugs' by Stuart Millar in *THE GUARDIAN* 3.9.96, 'The difference a day made' by Annie Taylor in *THE GUARDIAN* 28.11.96, 'Sports myth scotched' by Chris Milhill in *THE GUARDIAN* 12.12.96, 'Putting on the smile' by Geoffrey Beattie in *THE GUARDIAN* 12.1.89, 'The uses and abuses of people' by Dorothy Rowe in *Home Front* column in *THE WEEKEND GUARDIAN* 20.5.95, 'Earthbound' by Ed Douglas in *THE WEEKEND GUARDIAN* 1-2.8.92, extracts from articles 'The au pair's tale' in *THE GUARDIAN* 23.10.97, 'Forked tongue toaster trauma' in *THE GUARDIAN* 14.8.92, 'Innocents abroad' by Elaine Jacobs from the Women section in *THE GUARDIAN* 21.7.93, 'Welfare wagon-train west' by Maggie O'Kane in *THE GUARDIAN* 2.7.94, 'Noise annoys' from *Private Lives* column in *THE GUARDIAN* 5.9.96, 'Set on the sporting courses' by John Crace and Emily Moore in *THE GUARDIAN* 26.8.97, 'Cycling furiously', by Nick Varley in *THE GUARDIAN* 23.9.97, 'Growing pains' by Libby Brooks in *THE GUARDIAN* 26.3.97, 'The fire next time' by Bill McGuire in *THE WEEKEND GUARDIAN* 11.12.93. extracts from articles, 'The war against crime begins at home' by Charles Leadbetter in *THE OBSERVER* 8.5.94; the author, Phil Healey for text and illustrations to 'The dockyard thief', 'Call me mother' & 'Totally Fobbed Off' by Healey & Glanville from *URBAN MYTHS* published by Virgin; Newspaper Publishing plc for adapted extracts from the articles 'Role-playing with attitude' by Lesley Gerard in *THE INDEPENDENT* 1.12.94, 'A rich man in his garden' by James Woodall in *THE INDEPENDENT MAGAZINE* 27.11.93, extracts from the articles 'What price more time with the children?' by Tim Kahn in *THE INDEPENDENT* 20.10.93, 'Downhill all the way - to casualty' by Jeremy Hart in *THE INDEPENDENT* 25.9.94, 'Restaurant shells out for oyster surfeit' by Phil Reeves in *THE INDEPENDENT* 12.10.93, 'My daughter's a militant veggie' by Virginia Ironside from *Dilemmas* column in *THE INDEPENDENT* 28.11.96, 'Still cleaning after all these years' by Geraldine Bedell from *Real Life* column & various quotes including Peter Stringfellow & Steve White from *Opinions* column in *THE INDEPENDENT ON SUNDAY* 16.8.92; Loch Lomand Resort Ownership Group for an extract from time share advert in a *CAMERON HOUSE* brochure; the author, Jonathan Margolis for an adapted extract from his article 'Husband who logged out of his marriage' in *THE SUNDAY TIMES* 21.3.93; the author, Ian Parker for an adapted extract from his article 'Diary of a Nobody' from *THE SUNDAY TELEGRAPH* 21.7.96; Reader's Digest Association Ltd for adapted extracts from the articles 'In Quest of the Ideal Image', 'Making Creativity a Matter of Method', 'How We Choose Our Friends', 'How do you choose the right job?' and 'What factors influence a person's choice of a first job?' from *Marvels and Mysteries of the Human Mind* in *READER'S DIGEST* 1992; Reuters Editorial Reference Unit for the article 'Zoo to auction paintings done by elephant' (Alberta, Calgary) 28.8.94; Richmond and Twickenham Informer for an adapted extract from the article 'It stops their kids getting boa'd!' by Paul Smith in *THE RICHMOND AND TWICKENHAM INFORMER* 18.8.95; Catherine Scharnberger for an adapted extract from 'Basile' in *BARFLY MONTHLY*, July 1995 (taken from Barfly Internet); Ewan Macnaughton Associates Ltd for an extract from the article 'Alms for the rich but not for the poor' by Adam Nicholson in *THE SUNDAY TELEGRAPH* 25.9.94; Times Newspapers Ltd for adapted information from the article 'Flamboyant life and death of a wild man' by Margarette Driscoll in *THE SUNDAY TIMES* 21.3.93, extracts from the articles 'Can laws stop the obsessed?' by René Riley-Adams in *THE TIMES* 22.2.93, 'Liz McColgan Dundee' by Alastair Riley in *THE TIMES MAGAZINE* 20.4.96. © Times Newspapers Limited 1993, 1993 & 1996; Tunbridge Wells Borough Council for an extract from the leaflet *'Royal Tunbridge Wells'* supplied by *The Marketing & Tourism Development Service* 1997; the editor, TV Times for an extract from the article 'Wild Thing!' by Pamela Townsend in *TV TIMES*; The Washington Post for an extract from the article 'What do people most regret? The paths they failed to take' by Sally Squires. © 1994, The Washington Post; the Editor, What's on TV for adapted extracts from the articles 'I'll never be able to forget' by Julie Powell in *WHAT'S ON TV* 12.4.97, 'We were sold a dream' by Tessa Cunningham in *WHAT'S ON TV* April 1997, 'The Good Old Days' by Andrew McKenna in *WHAT'S ON TV* (Real Life).

We have been unable to trace the copyright holders of the articles 'Does correct spelling matter?' by Bernard Richards & 'Shakespeare had a word for it', and would appreciate any information which would enable us to do so.

Illustrated by Philip Bannister, Jeremy Banx, Phil Healey, David Hitch, Tim Sanders and Katherine Walker.

Photo acknowledgements

Commissioned photography by Gareth Boden
Picture Research and photo direction Rebecca Watson

We are grateful to the following for permission to reproduce copyright photographs:

Arcaid/Richard Bryant for page:95t;Australian Tourist Commission for page:74m;AWL/Gareth Boden for page:11,82b;AWL/Hodder&Stoughton educational:101br;BBC /John Rosetti for page:149;Bruce Coleman ltd/William Paton for page:170;Colorific for page:142tl;Corbis UK Ltd for pages:58,95b;Environmental Images for page:142, 185b

Financial Times/Colin Beere for page: 115b;Financial times/Ashley Ashwood for page:116t;Hulton Getty for pages:32br,32ml, 89l,143;Lebrecht Collection /Wladimir Polak for page: 67;Mike Watson for page: 103;Network/Mike Abrahams for page: 61;Pictor International for pages: 8mr,43,53,101bl,116;Planet X/Phil Healey for page: 183; Rebecca Watson for page: 89r;Rex Features for pages:20bl,

32bl,134,154br;Superstock for pages:8b,65bm;Christies images/Superstock for page: 65br;Musee des Beaux-Arts Tournai, Belgium/Giraudon Paris/Superstock for page 65bl;The Guardian/David Sillitoe for page:24;The Guardian /Hugo Gendinning for page: 64; Image bank for pages: 46,53br,79t,113bl,113m,113br,142t,169tl;The Independent/Edward Webb for page:77;The Oldie for page:44;The Ronald Grant Archive for page:108,136;Tate Gallery,London 1998 for page 65tl;Telegraph Colour Library for pages:74r,79b,101m,115t, 126tl, 126bl, 169c,180; Tony Stone Images for pages: 8cl,8t,20t,20m,20br,23,53t,32t,

53bl,74 ,101t,113t,126r, 142b, 144 ,154, 167,164,169,172,185t,186;

Tunbridge Wells borough council for page: 152/153